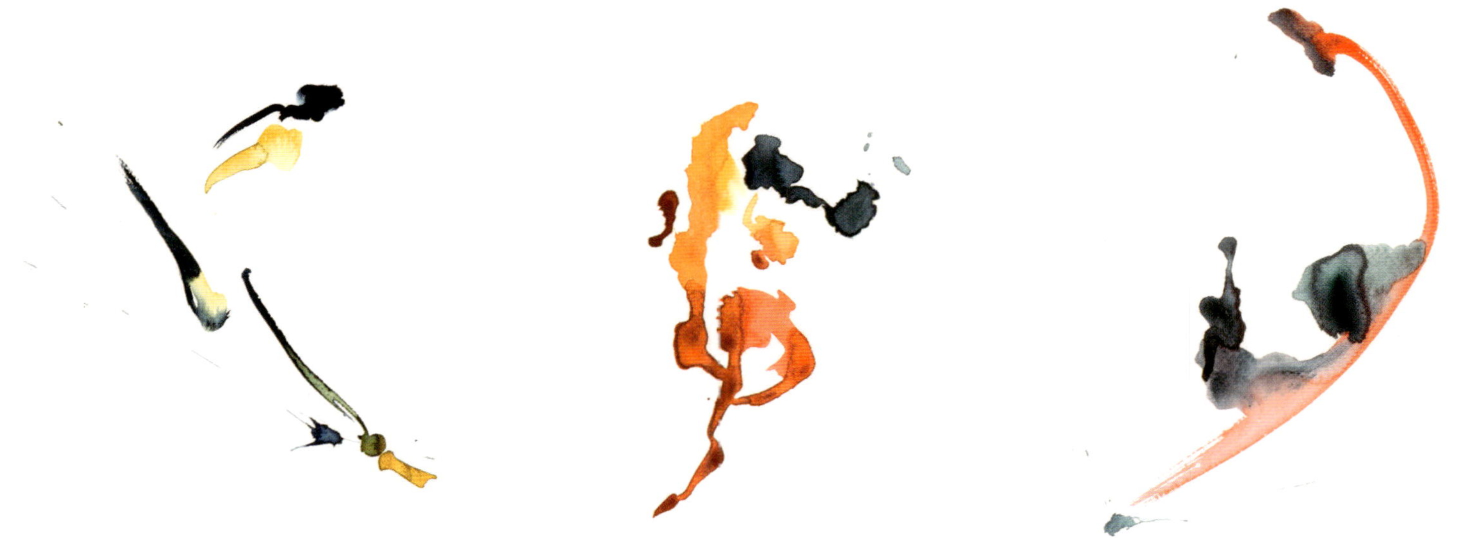

Contemporary Figures in Watercolour

Leo Crane

with Roy Joseph Butler

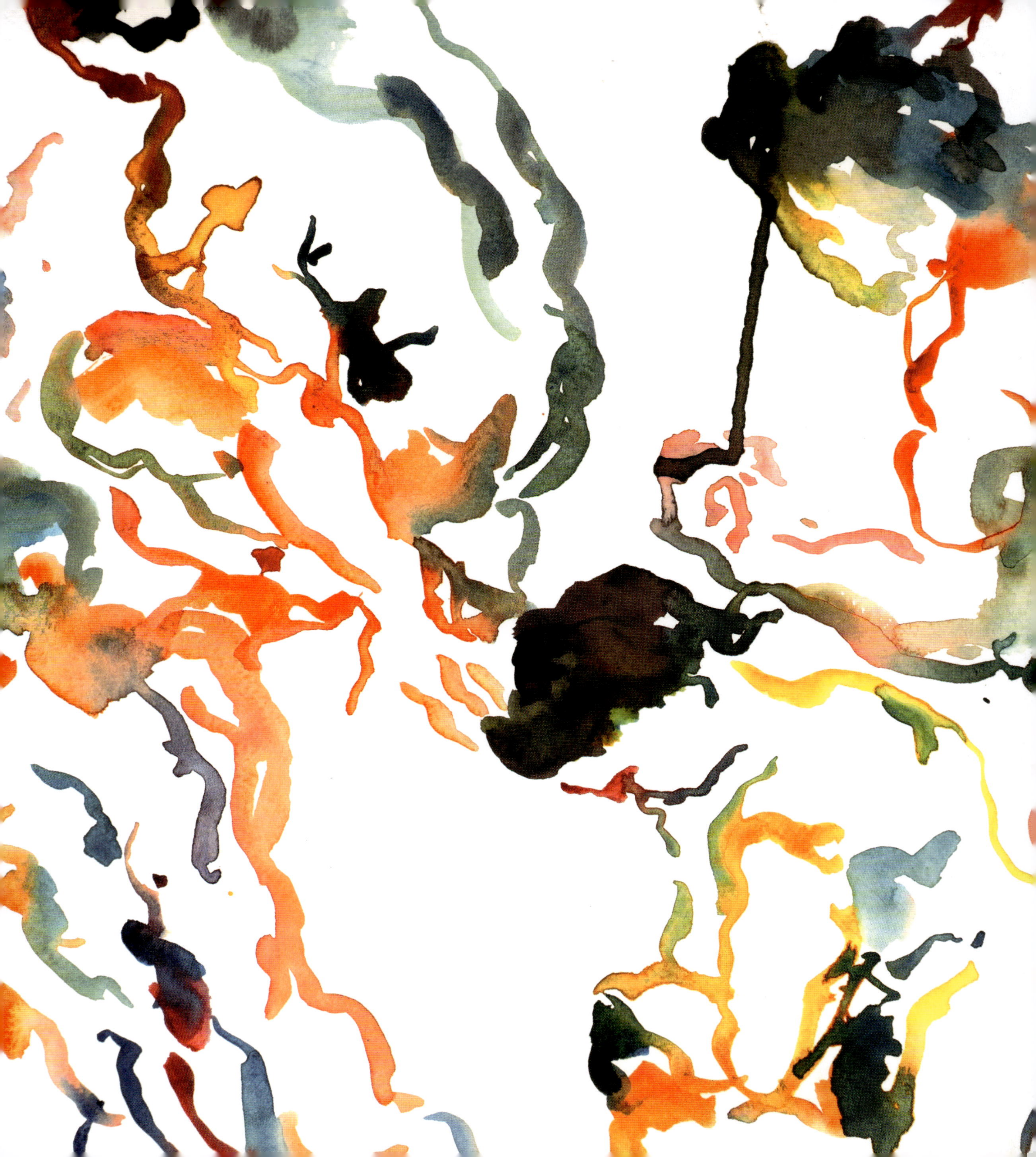

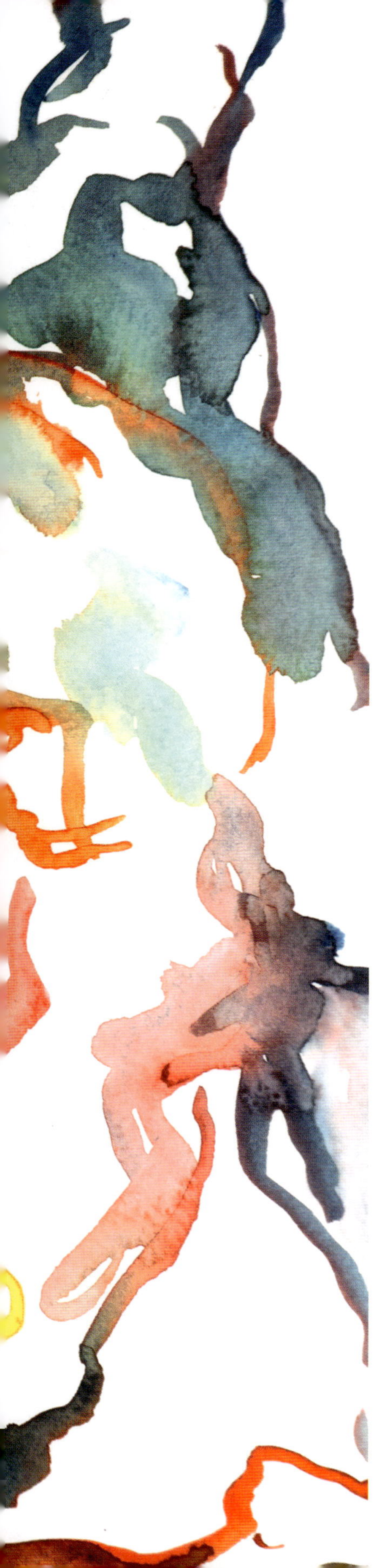

Contemporary Figures in Watercolour

Leo Crane

with Roy Joseph Butler

BATSFORD

Dedication

I dedicate this book to the life models whose creativity and generosity are the foundations for my artistic practice. Boundless gratitude goes to Roy Joseph Butler, who introduced me to this world and has been my constant inspiration ever since.

A special thank you to Maggi Hambling CBE for challenging me to be fearlessly creative every day.

First published in the United Kingdom in 2021 by
Batsford
43 Great Ormond Street
London WC1N 3HZ
An imprint of Pavilion Books Company Ltd

ISBN: 9781849946681

A CIP catalogue record for this book is available from the British Library.

30 29 28 27 26 25 24 23 22 21
10 9 8 7 6 5 4 3 2 1

Reproduction by Rival Colour Ltd, UK
Printed by 1010 Printing International Ltd, China

This book can be ordered direct from the publisher at the website www.pavilionbooks.com, or try your local bookshop.

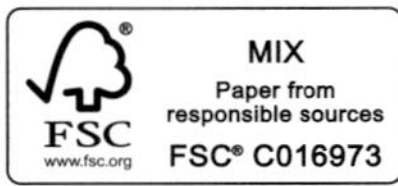

PAGE 1: *Lidia Energy Paintings*
These energy paintings represent Lidia's gesture and are explored on pages 66–67.

PREVIOUS PAGE: *Many Kams*
Layering up your paintings makes unexpected connections between the figures (see pages 52–53).

> *Matthew Standing* Study paintings help you explore the unique ways that watercolour can express a pose, as in these three paintings of Matthew.

Contents

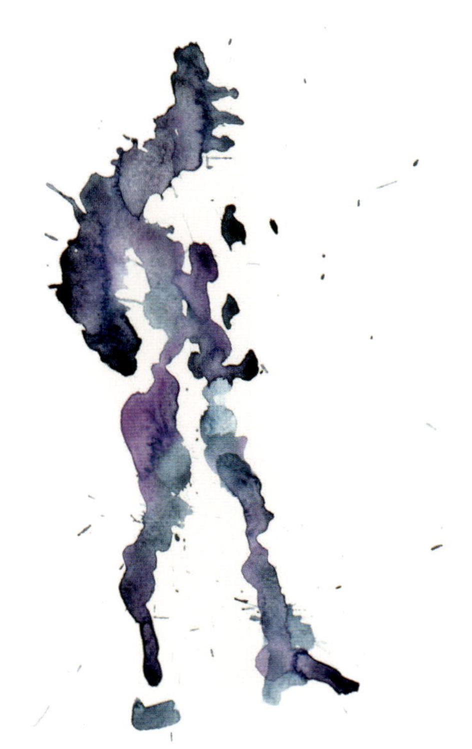

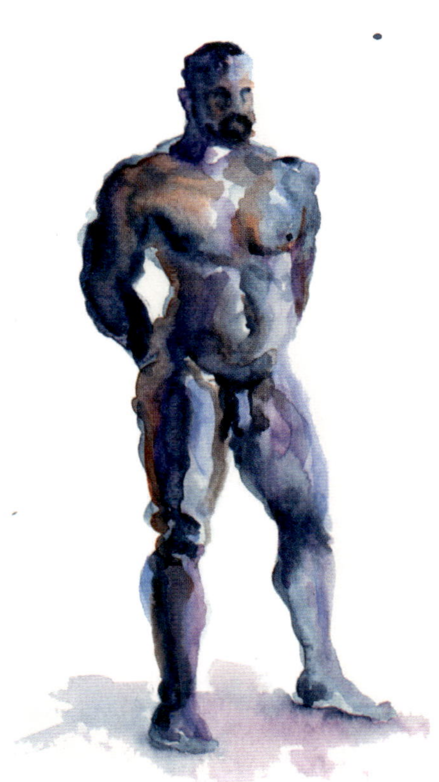

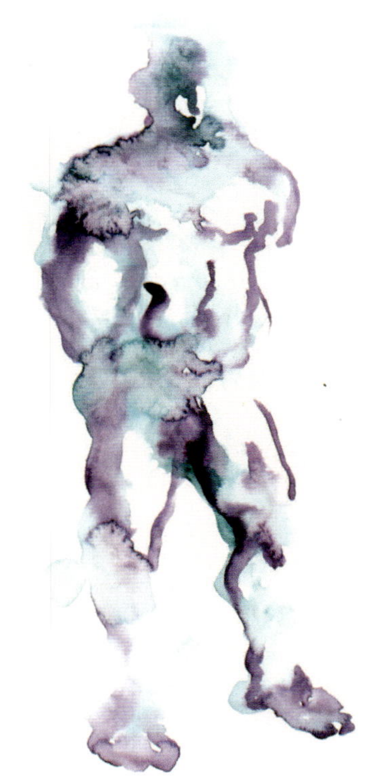

Foreword

Roy Joseph Butler

The life room is an exceptional place, unlike any other creative space I've ever confronted. In fact, the idea of 'confronting' was a part of my experience of the life room only once: the first time. I stepped across the threshold into an amphitheatre of young artists, their collective attention split between their painting and drawing materials, and an assortment of boxes and plinths arranged just so for an already-sitting model. I was up next, just twenty years old and taking my clothes off for the first time in the name of art. Did I need to perform? Was there a trick to it, a special secret I would magically acquire in the pressure of the moment? Would the artists make me perfect on paper or scramble roughly over my own and their own intrinsic imperfections? From the moment the timer started I realized that what made the life room so exceptional, so special, was its reliance on one thing that underpinned all of my reservations and eventual joys: the model–artist relationship.

Contemporary Figures in Watercolour starts with that foundational relationship between the painter and the subject, something writer (and painter and animator) Leo Crane puts at the centre of his creative practice. Some would say that this isn't really how it goes, that the artist is there to interpret what's in front of them, bringing their skills to bear to create a work all their own thanks to the physical presence of a professional subject. But as a model, I've always known that that same work of art is created as much from what I bring as from the artist's technique and vision. And the outcome? A tangible product of the unspoken (and sometimes spoken) dialogue between us. It's constantly fluid, like air, like water.

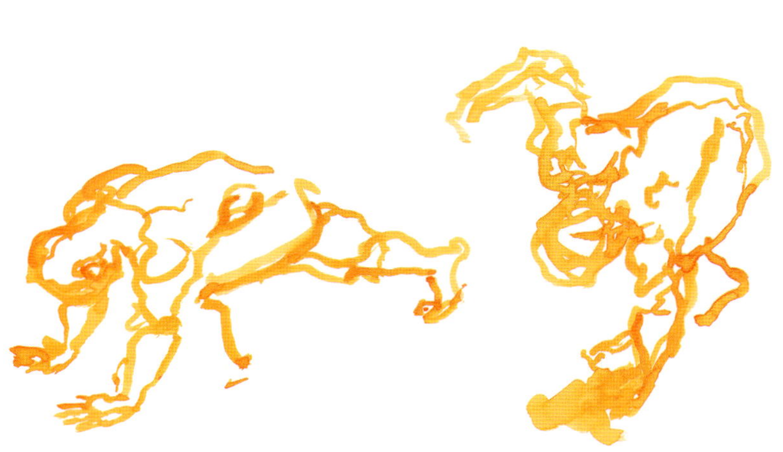
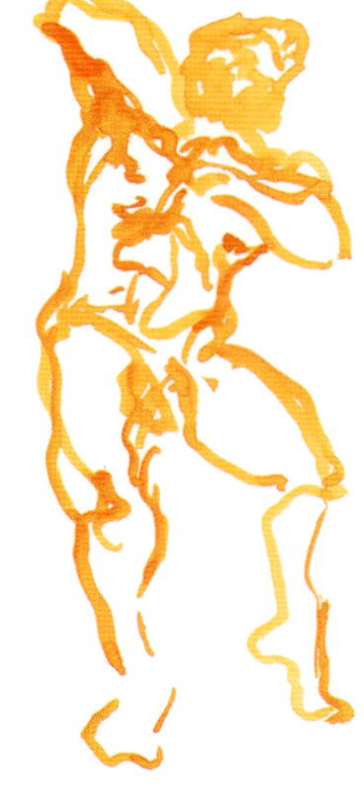

I've known Leo since 2013, having met him in a life-drawing class in which I was modelling. Since then, we've collaborated on a number of projects in both digital and fine-art mediums, culminating in the founding of our creative studio Figuration in late 2016. Our first joint film, *Nude Triumphant* (2020), took audiences into the animated watercolour world of a first-time life model. It was (and is) a performative commentary on how the fusion between the artist's creation and the model's inspiration complement each other instead of existing in mechanical confrontation. And it's hard to find a better medium than watercolour to illustrate that relationship, or indeed to highlight its power to accentuate and elevate art and life – the way it flows into itself, naturally, unbounded, forcing one to see something new and stunningly unpredictable in it.

From a chance encounter in the life room, I never expected to be so much a part of Leo's work over the years. *Contemporary Figures in Watercolour* is a real testament to the fruits of our work, but more than that it highlights just how far anyone can go in exploring their own potential in the life room ... and in life.

What I love about this book is its unapologetic approach to chance, experimentation and creative prerogative in the artistic process. Whether you're relatively new to watercolour painting or consider yourself well-versed, *Contemporary Figures in Watercolour* holds something you're bound to integrate into your own practice. And whatever that may be, I hope you embrace it, never confront it, and allow it all the freedom in the world to develop your art and yourself.

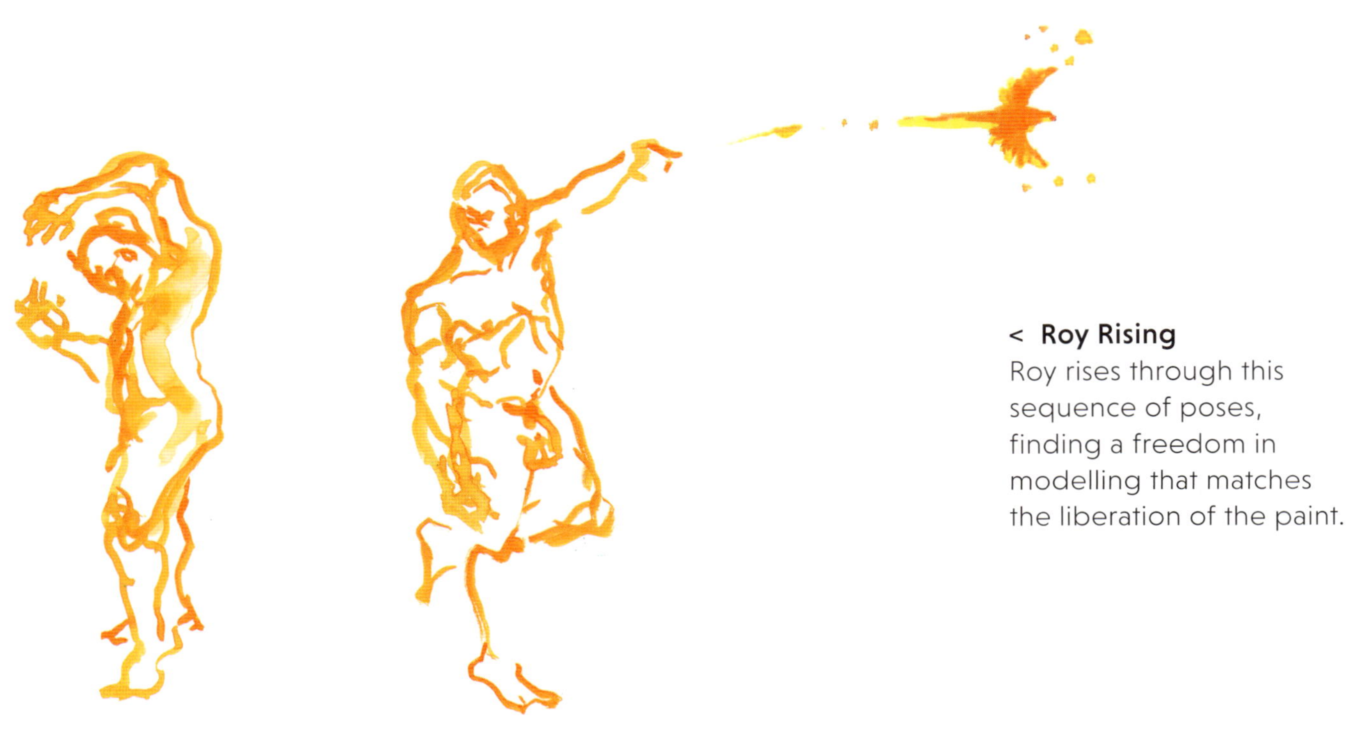

< Roy Rising
Roy rises through this sequence of poses, finding a freedom in modelling that matches the liberation of the paint.

Introduction

My journey into figure painting has been an unplanned and joyful path through art history, animation, performance and, finally, the art studio. Throughout, I have followed an unbreakable thread of physical expression: what do we say with our bodies and how do we read and respond to the bodies of others?

This book continues that thread, celebrating the connection between painter, model and medium. As a painter, I look to the model for the initial spark that fires up our creative exchange. I communicate this through watercolour, whose lively unpredictability ensures I am never quite in control, giving the painting a life of its own.

In the following pages, I introduce the figure as subject and watercolour as a means of communication. I then share examples of my process in four sections. The first, Speed, unlocks the joy of dynamic poses and the freedom of fearless mark making. The second, Gesture, explores the emotion of the human form and the flow of its energy. The third, Story, considers how composition can draw the viewer into a narrative. I then look Beyond the Figure to show how these same principles can be applied to any painting, from landscapes and still life to imagined realities.

Alongside the text are my paintings, demonstrating how I understand the human form through direct observation: the rich colours of flesh, the distribution of weight, the mechanics of movement. Through sustained practice, this observation has become second nature, with instinct pulling me towards the idiosyncrasies that give a particular model or pose their unique personality.

This book has evolved out of my ongoing collaboration with Roy Joseph Butler, co-founder of our creative studio Figuration. Roy's experience and research are the foundations for my text. As part of his research, Roy interviewed three fellow life models, Lidia Lidia, Kam Wan and Leonora Smith. Their insights into the painter-model dynamic are shared in this book, giving a fresh perspective to my painting process.

As well as Roy, Lidia, Kam and Leonora, the book features Matthew Oghene, Maya Williams, Valentina Rock and a number of other models who are named when their image is used. My relationships with them have been built over many months or years, leading not only to paintings, but also workshops, performances, exhibitions, films and animation. I am grateful to all of them for their part in our shared creative process.

I have chosen to guide you on a path of self-discovery. I encourage you to develop your figure-painting skills by jumping straight in. Experiment and surprise yourself with the results. Most of all, indulge in the process and enjoy the collaboration with your subject as you paint the figure in watercolour.

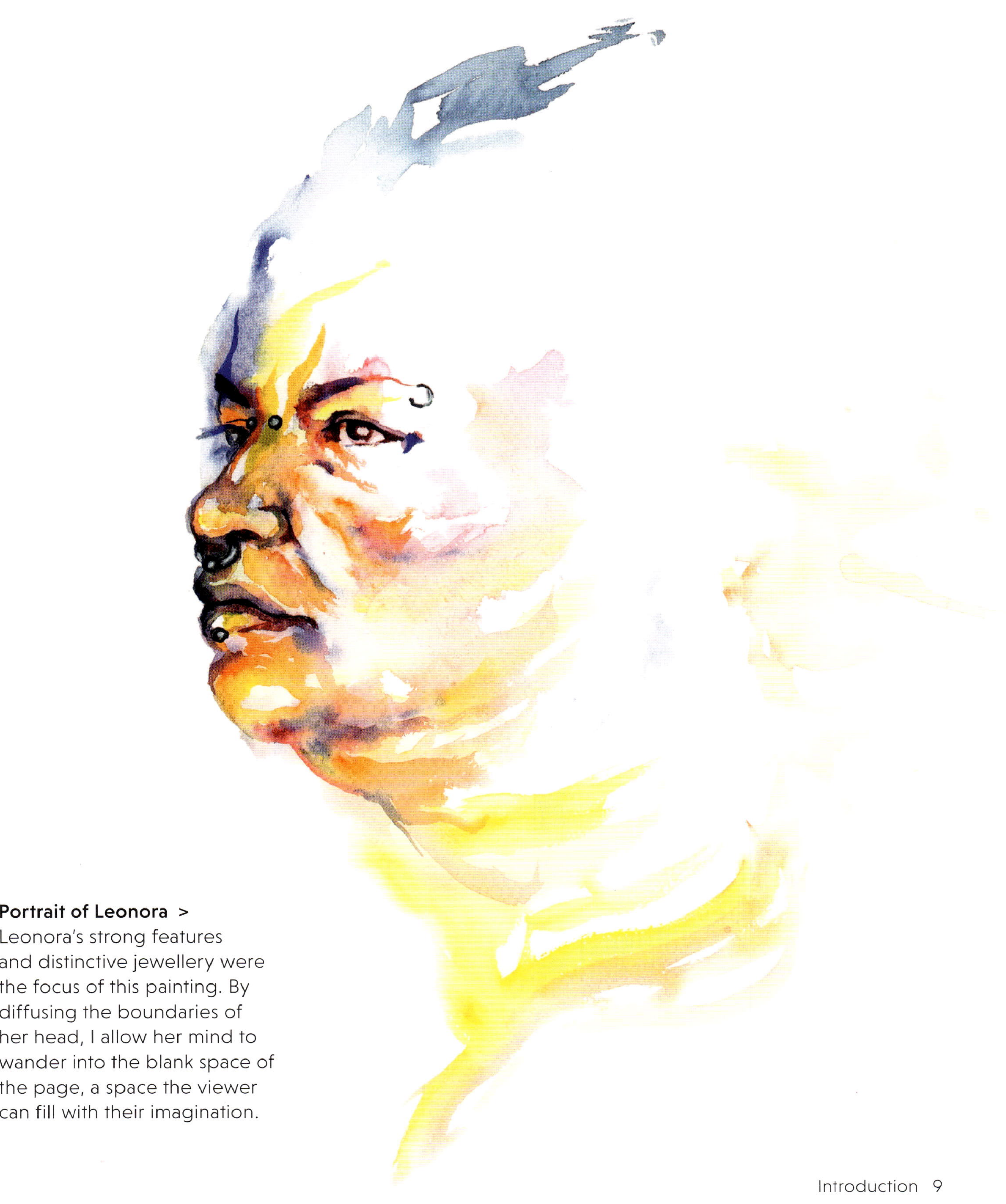

Portrait of Leonora >
Leonora's strong features
and distinctive jewellery were
the focus of this painting. By
diffusing the boundaries of
her head, I allow her mind to
wander into the blank space of
the page, a space the viewer
can fill with their imagination.

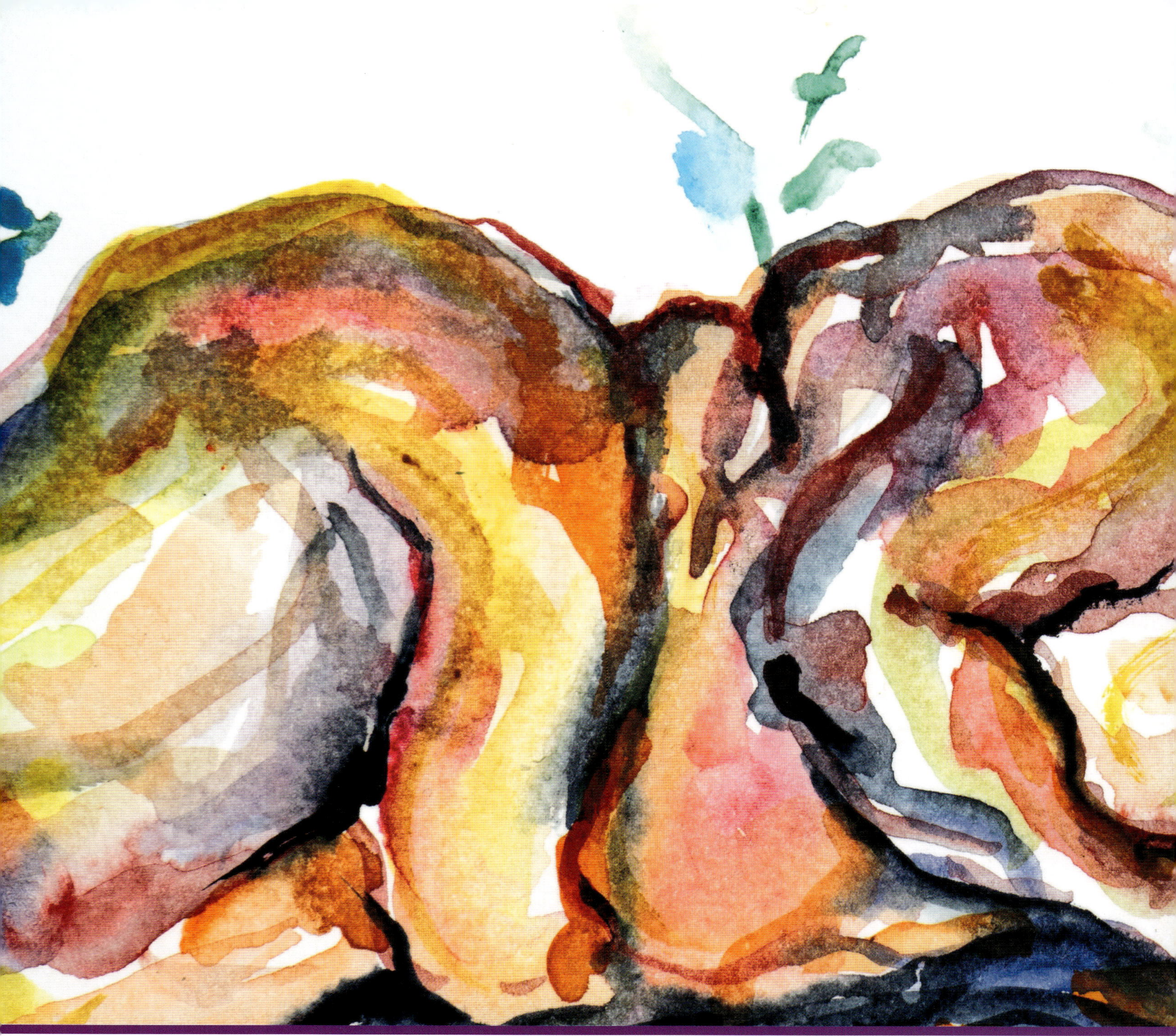

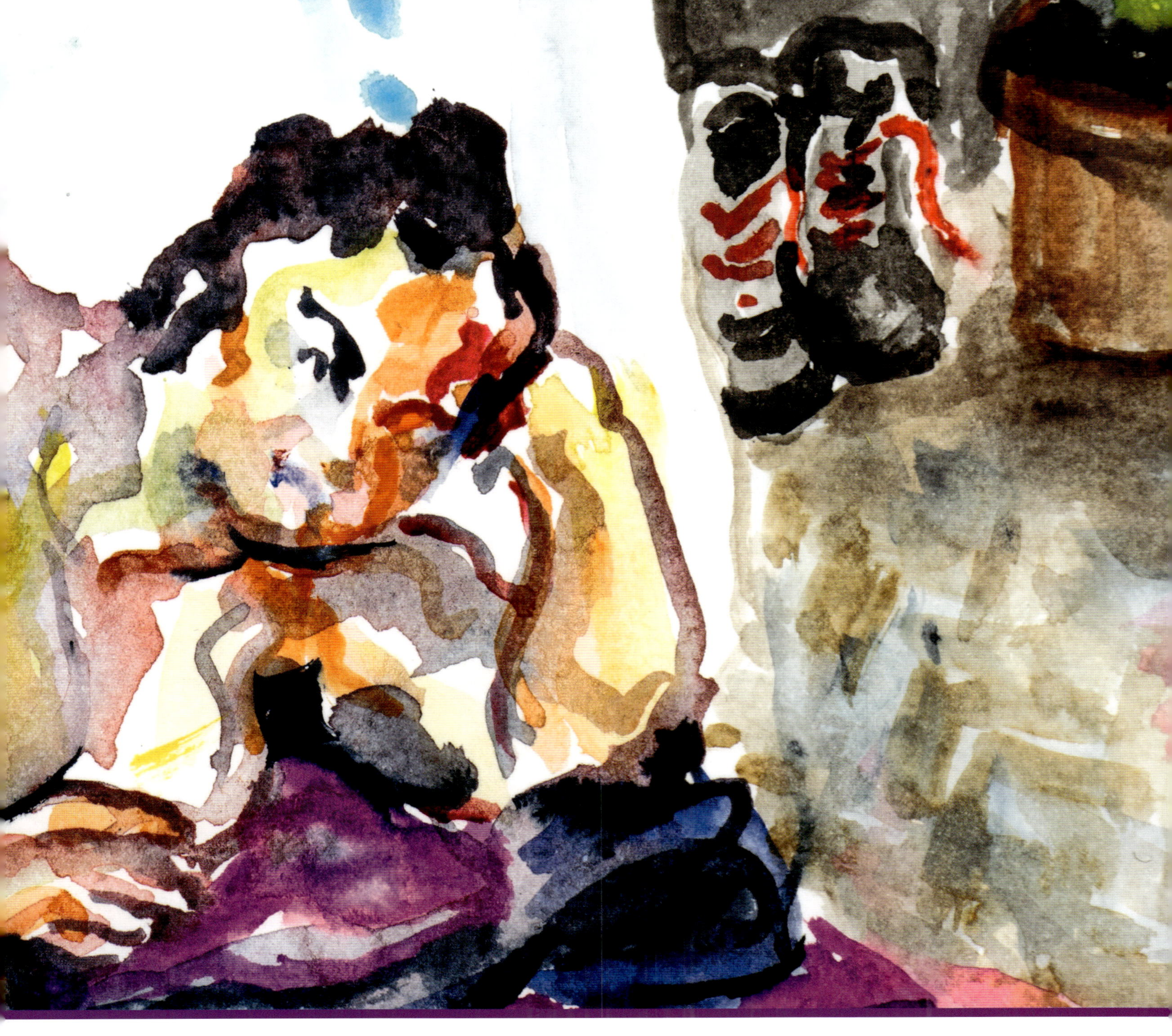

The Figure

Our most fundamental form of expression is through our bodies. Instinctively, we use our physicality to communicate and connect with others. By observing, reading, interpreting and responding, we forge a shared human experience.

The life room is a laboratory to experiment with this exchange. The model strips back to their essential self and opens a dialogue with a pose. The painter explores the figure, feels the space, and finds a personal connection to enable a response. The dialogue continues back and forth: the air circulates, the light changes, sounds come and go as the model poses and the painter interprets with marks, colours and composition.

In this first section, I begin by considering the life model and the language of paint. I then share some tips on getting the most out of the painter-model relationship.

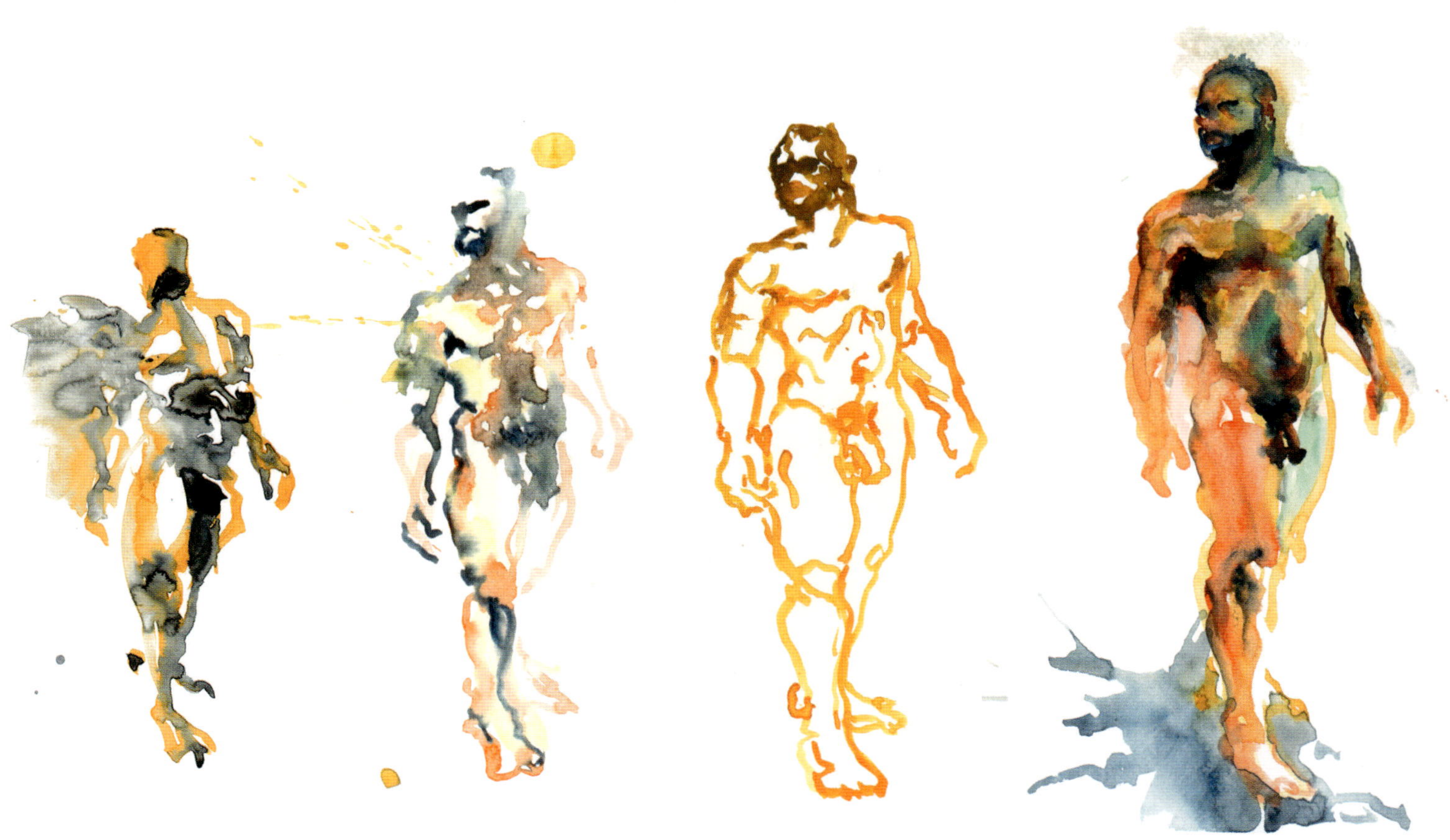

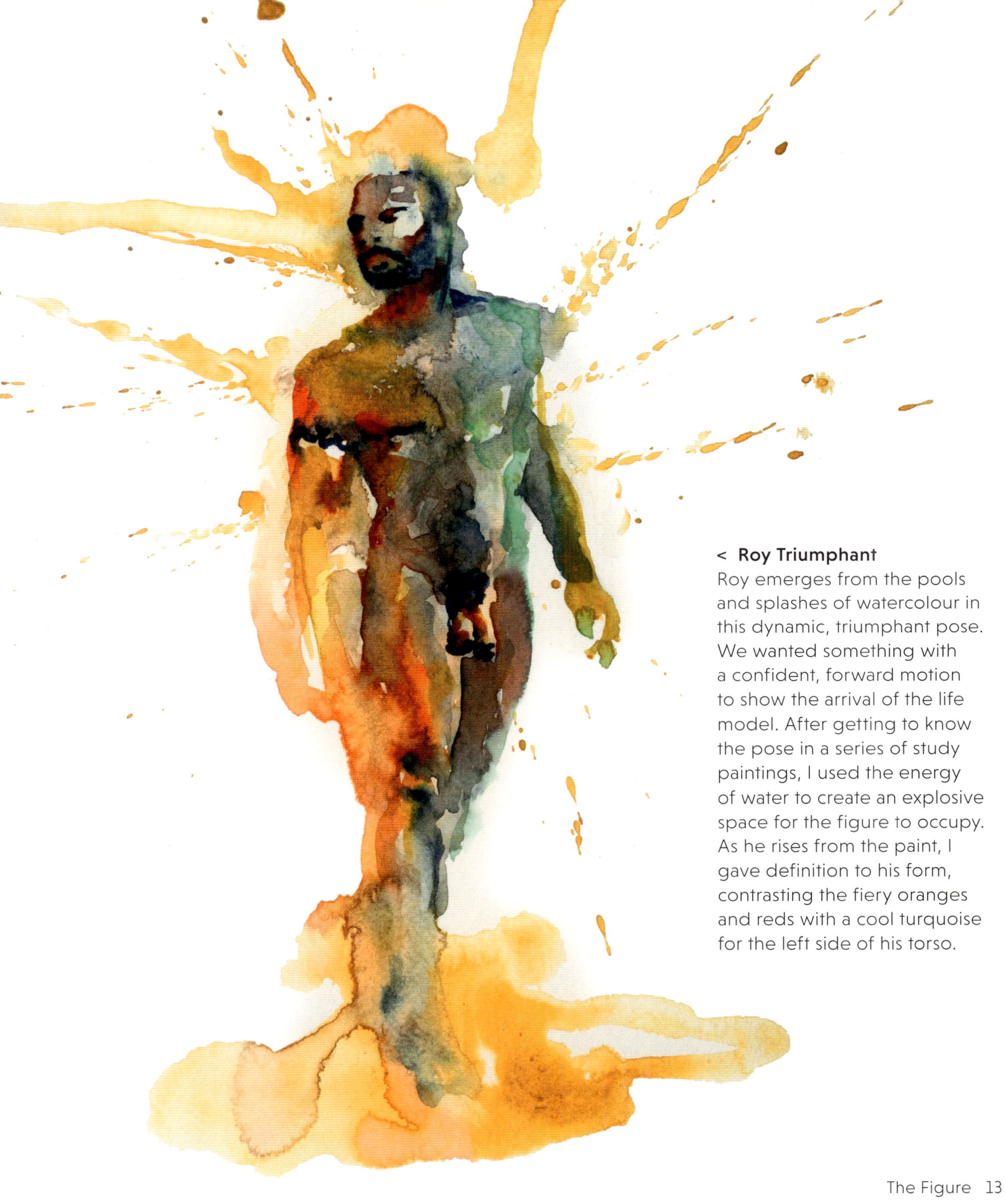

< Roy Triumphant

Roy emerges from the pools and splashes of watercolour in this dynamic, triumphant pose. We wanted something with a confident, forward motion to show the arrival of the life model. After getting to know the pose in a series of study paintings, I used the energy of water to create an explosive space for the figure to occupy. As he rises from the paint, I gave definition to his form, contrasting the fiery oranges and reds with a cool turquoise for the left side of his torso.

Visual Language

As a figure painter, you are communicating a human connection in an image. You may choose to document the external appearance of a model; or you may describe the tension of held movement, the subtle shifts in pose, their breath, heat, and imagined inner thoughts. You may be telling a story, interpreting and embellishing your experience; you may want to share a feeling or emotion through the physical act of mark making. You may be doing all of these and more.

The way you paint is as personal as your handwriting or your voice. Some painters develop a distinct and unwavering visual language; others enjoy the freedom of sustained experimentation and accidental discoveries. Some prioritize self-expression over representation; others indulge a technical virtuosity to show a mastery of their medium. The more you paint, the more nuanced your language will become, representing you as much as your subject.

However much (or little!) you enjoy my paintings, I hope they will spur you on to develop your own distinct form of expression, full of the unique personality that makes you, you.

Self-Portrait, Caithness >
After an intense and difficult few months, I was recuperating on the wild coast of northern Scotland. With a degree of confidence returning, I was ready to take a long hard look at myself and share what I saw in a self-portrait. I worked quickly, building up the painting in wet-on-wet layers, discovering the figure through the flow of paint across the surface. There was no drawing or preparatory work, allowing the form to emerge as the paint dripped and pooled and bloomed.

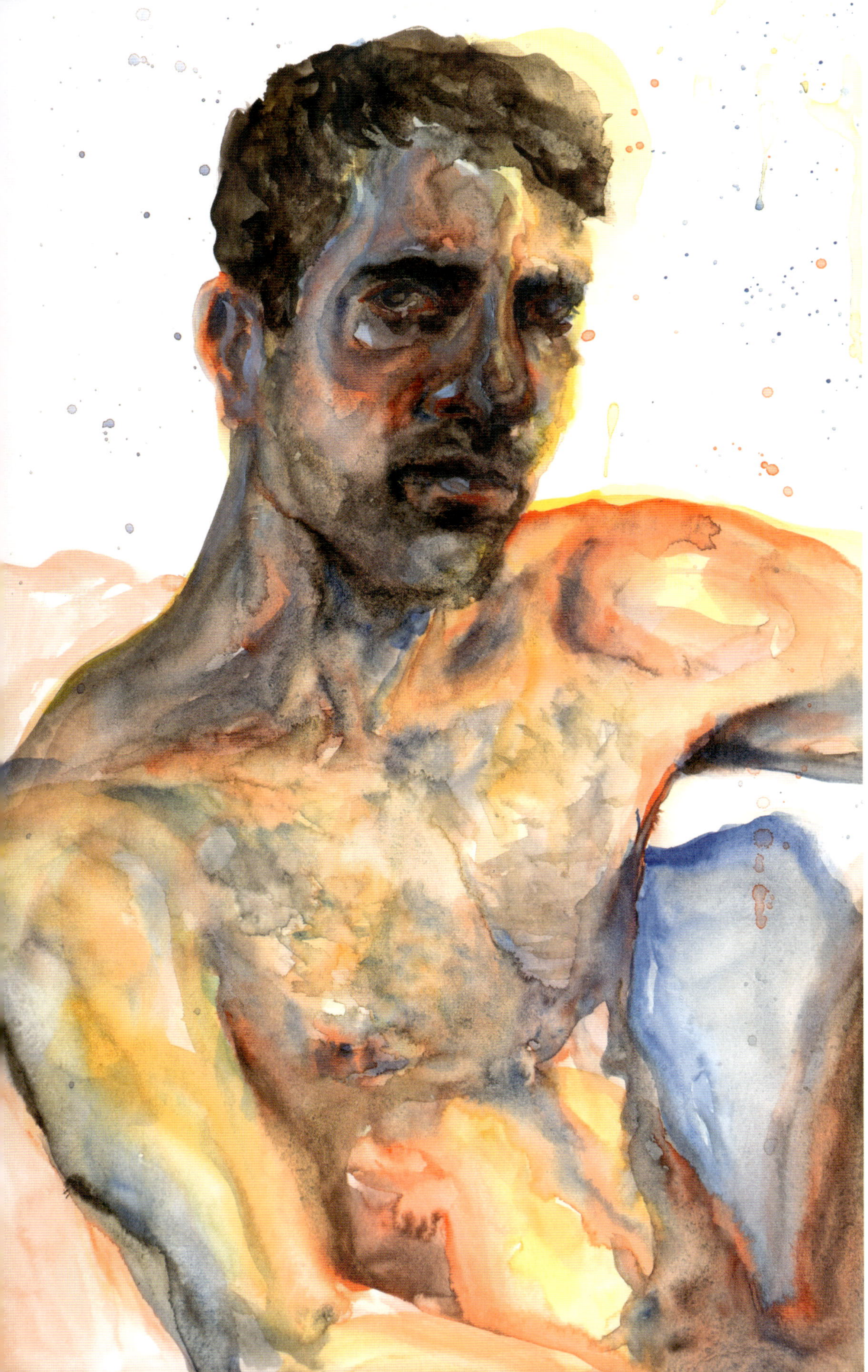

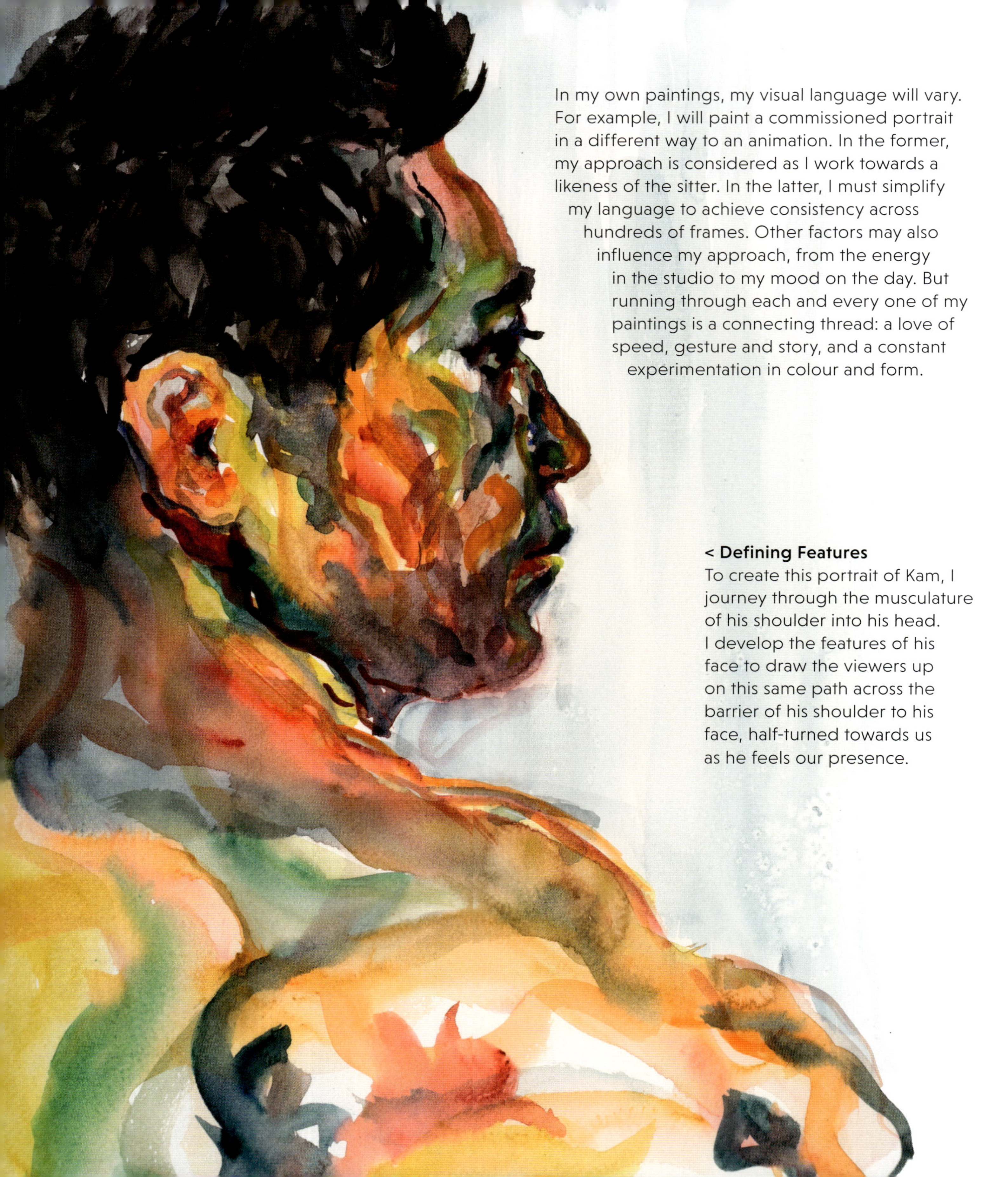

In my own paintings, my visual language will vary. For example, I will paint a commissioned portrait in a different way to an animation. In the former, my approach is considered as I work towards a likeness of the sitter. In the latter, I must simplify my language to achieve consistency across hundreds of frames. Other factors may also influence my approach, from the energy in the studio to my mood on the day. But running through each and every one of my paintings is a connecting thread: a love of speed, gesture and story, and a constant experimentation in colour and form.

< Defining Features
To create this portrait of Kam, I journey through the musculature of his shoulder into his head. I develop the features of his face to draw the viewers up on this same path across the barrier of his shoulder to his face, half-turned towards us as he feels our presence.

˅ Simplified Form

Maya collaborated as poet and model for the animated film *Nude Triumphant*. We developed a distinctive style for their character, with a dominant green and a linear description of form. This suited the animation technique and complemented the other characters in the narrative.

˅ Abstracting the Figure

Lidia was brimming with her famous energy and this time I was ready to match it. She gave me a series of thirty-second poses, so dynamic that the human form seemed almost redundant. This painting shows her energy flow, rooting her body to the floor and shooting upwards where it explodes into the space. Abstracting the figure can play with concept, memory or the very notion of what is human.

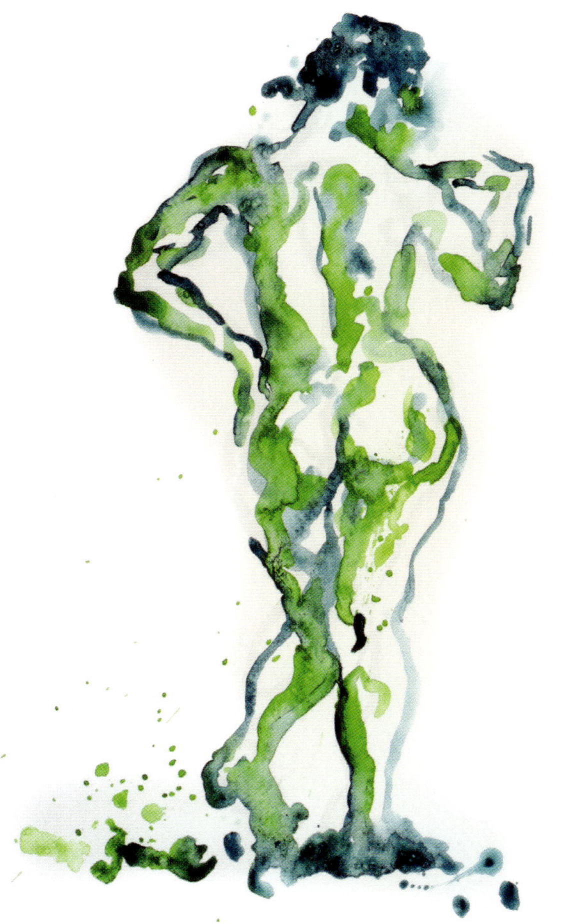

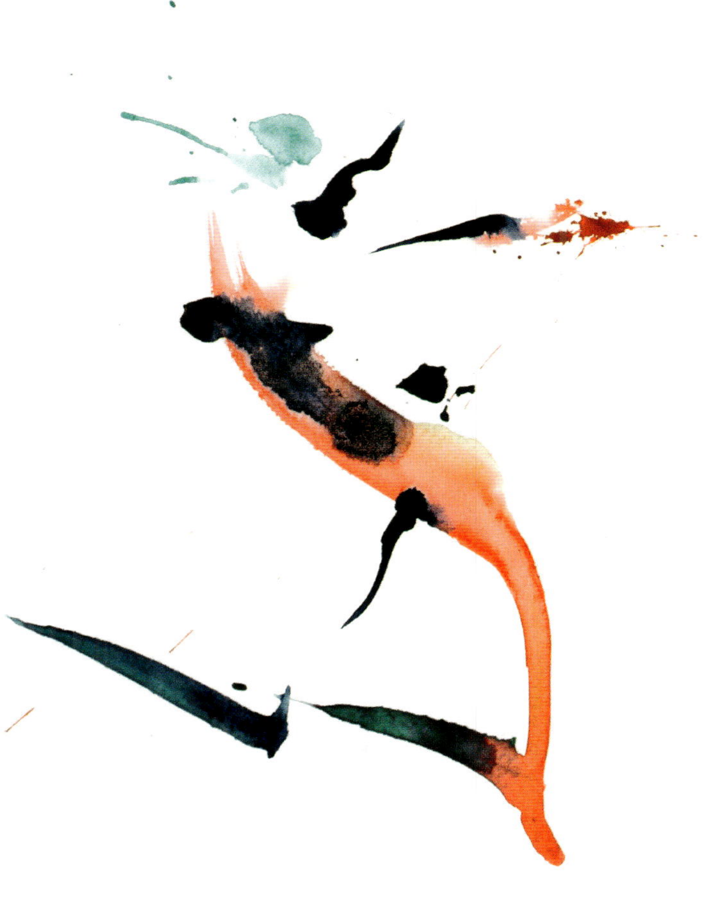

It Takes Two

Whatever visual language you choose, you will need to find a connection with your subject. In this book, the subject is the human figure: the life model.

A great painter-model relationship is often described as 'Artist and Muse', one in a bubble of creative genius while the other inspires with their mere presence. In reality, it's a hard-working collaboration, each partner bringing a craft honed through professional practice. Get it right, and you'll have a painting that expresses the dynamic between two creative people at that very moment in that very space.

Even in a single session, you can feel the personality of the model by observing how they interact with you and the group, how they occupy the space, and the gestures they choose for their poses. The more you work together, the more you will understand each other's motivations. This can give you a valuable insight into your subject and act as a catalyst for your creativity.

'Painting is not just about technical skills or the medium that you use, but a way to see life. At the start, I was very ignorant. I didn't understand that everyone paints in a unique way. Everyone has their different marks that express their personality. Now, when I see the works in a class or a private session, I see the way people see me – and the world as well. It's like being inside them. It is an incredible honour to get involved in something so intimate.'

Lidia

'We're exploring this notion of bodies: body positivity, queer bodies, the exposed body, the performative body, the sexualized body. I'm entering into life modelling at a time when issues around body image and attitudes towards our bodies are really opening up. And it comes hand in hand with a resurgence in painting from life, which has never been more popular or more accessible.'

Kam

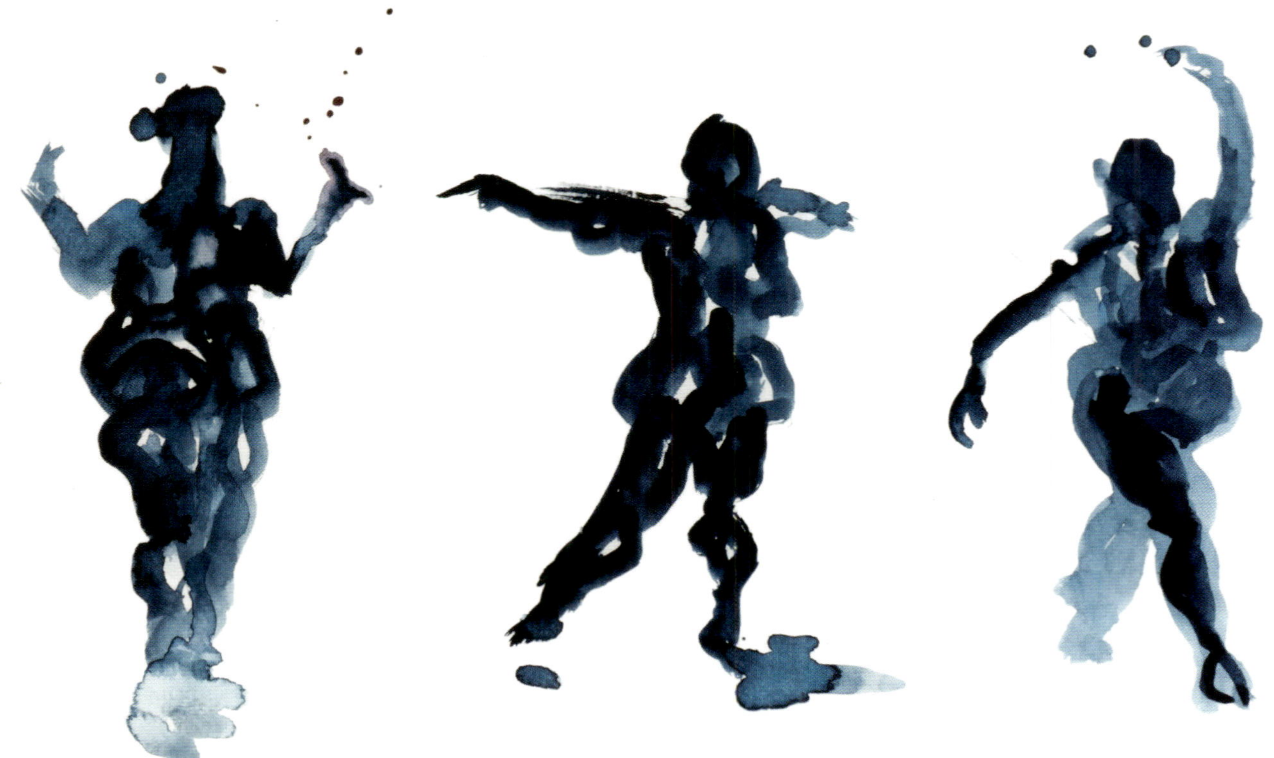

'One of the things I really enjoy is there aren't many women models of my size, which makes me a little bit niche. I haven't encountered as much fat-phobia as I had expected and people are definitely glad for the variety. It also gives me an opportunity to represent that what I am is okay to younger women who perhaps haven't got that message yet.'

Leonora

^ Dynamic Leonora
Leonora's silhouettes show her strength and versatility of poses. There is a dynamism in the way she uses her limbs, which the paint follows in drips and pools.

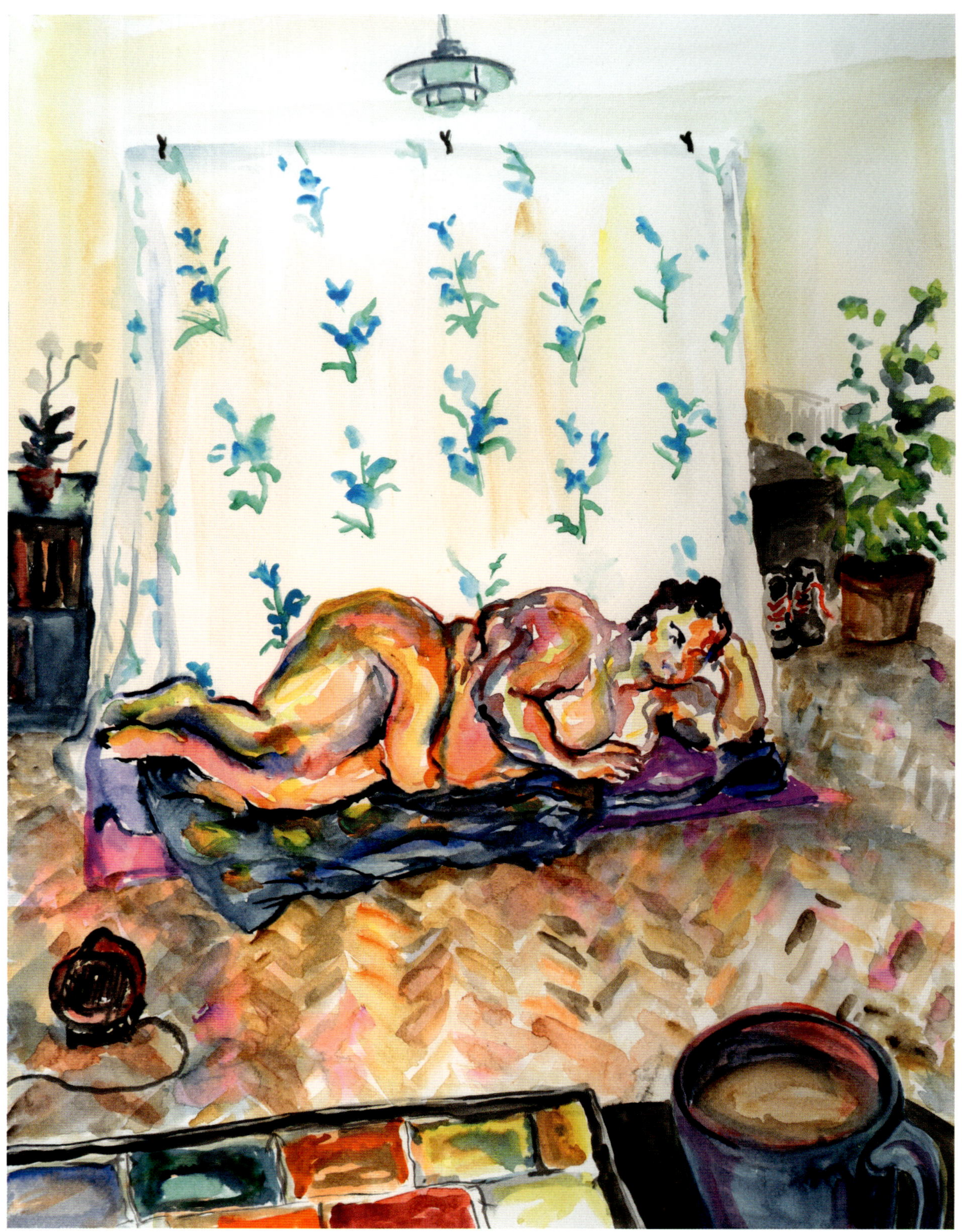

Space to Create

For many, painting the figure begins as a group experience. You may have been lucky enough to have had access to a model at school; or you may have chosen to take a short course at an adult education college or drop into an informal session in a room above a pub. Or perhaps you are accessing one of the many online spaces for life drawing.

My own experience began through short courses and developed through community groups. From the pure nude to the fabulous and theatrical, I have found an inexhaustible supply of inspiration.

I have also witnessed a wide range of working environments, some more conducive than others to a positive painter–model relationship.

The best relationships come with the understanding that the model is not only a fellow artist, but also a professional colleague. Here are some things I find helpful to consider:

- Communicate with the model beforehand. Agree a fee in writing, which should include paid breaks.

- Discuss any specific intentions for the work you will create together, including whether or not photographs may be taken during the session.

- Provide a suitable working environment, large enough for at least 2m (6½ft) between you and the model, and a separate area for the model to change. Cover windows so that the model is not visible to the outside world.

- Bring a heater, yoga mat, a couple of cushions and perhaps a chair or stool.

- Agree the timing for each pose. Use a timer with an alarm.

- Trust that your model knows their craft. If you are trying to capture a specific pose, work with the model to ensure it's physically possible and that rest breaks are clear.

- If working online, protect the model's privacy by ensuring no unauthorized recordings or screenshots are taken. It may be appropriate to increase their fee to acknowledge the extra work in setting up and managing their space.

< Working from Home
I invited Leonora to a painting session at my home. I hooked up a printed cloth to serve as a backdrop, with yoga mats, cushions and a heater for her to use as she liked while posing. She used the area behind the screen to change, while I kept us both supplied with plenty of cups of tea.

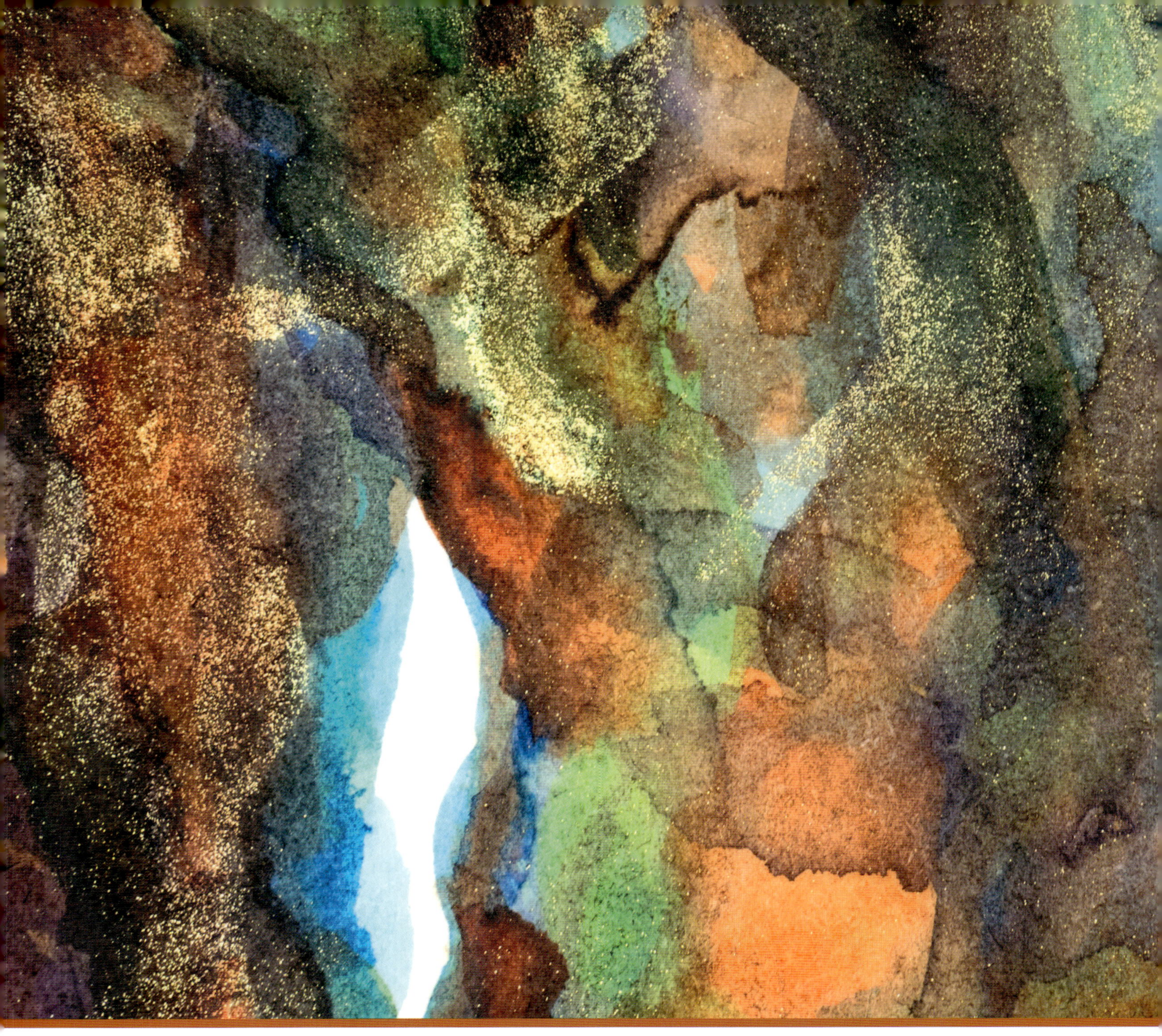

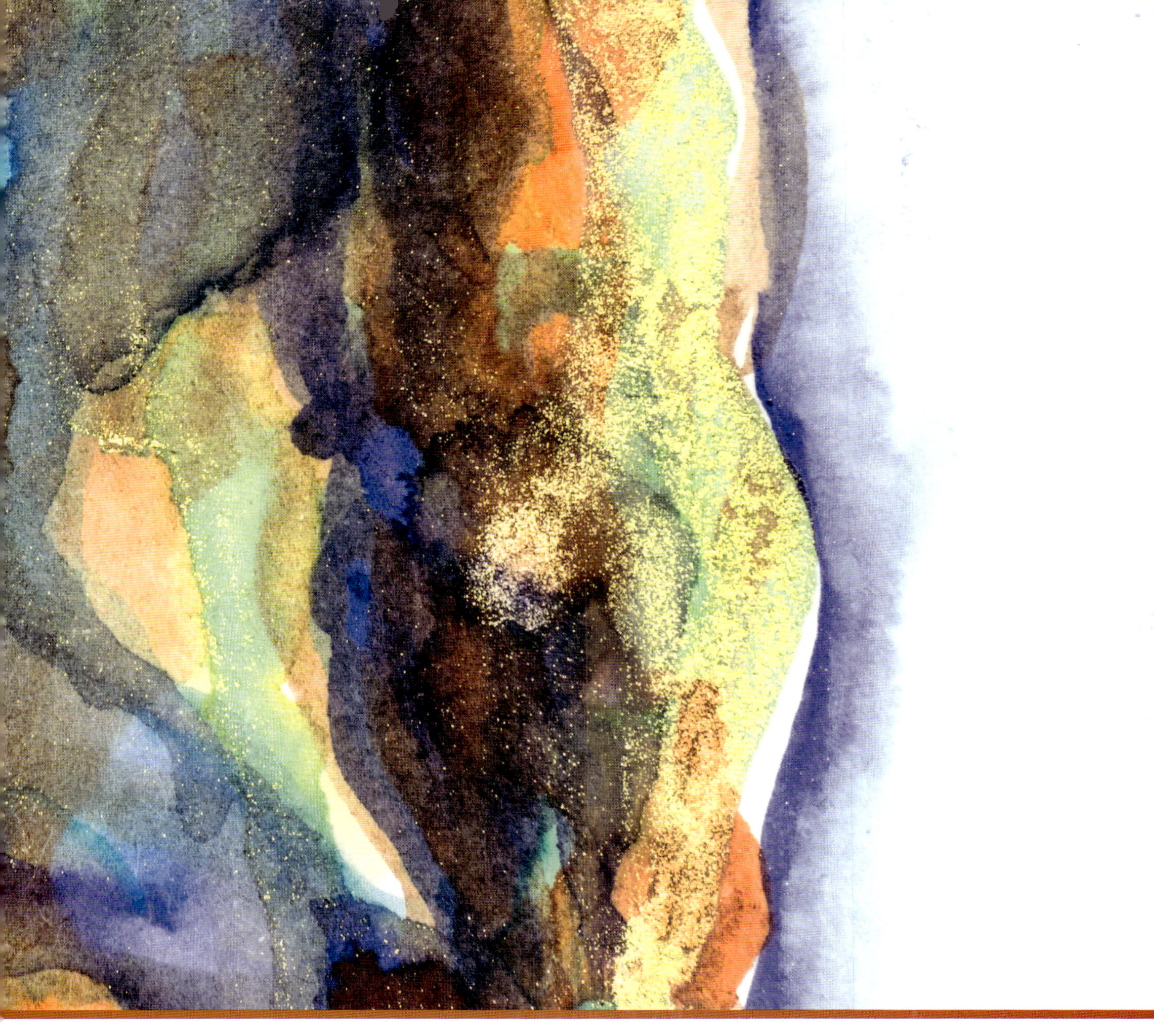

Watercolour

Temperamental, wilfully disobedient and utterly magical: I can't deny I am under the spell of watercolour. Although it has not been an easy relationship to navigate, I find its unpredictable personality to be the perfect match for a living subject.

In this section, I share my experience of working with this lively medium. After an introduction to materials, I describe techniques for unlocking its unique water-based properties. I then move on to the expressive potential of its vibrant colour.

Reaching for the Stars >
Roy originally conceived this pose as the last in a sequence that rose from a grounded crouch to a sweeping upwards reach. I wanted to work further on this final gesture of triumph, emphasizing its thrust upwards and confident stride forwards. I started with splashes and flicks, tilting the page to encourage an upwards flow. I then layered in a fiery palette of colours, emphasized with contrasting blues. Throughout, I celebrated the fluidity and vibrancy of this unique medium.

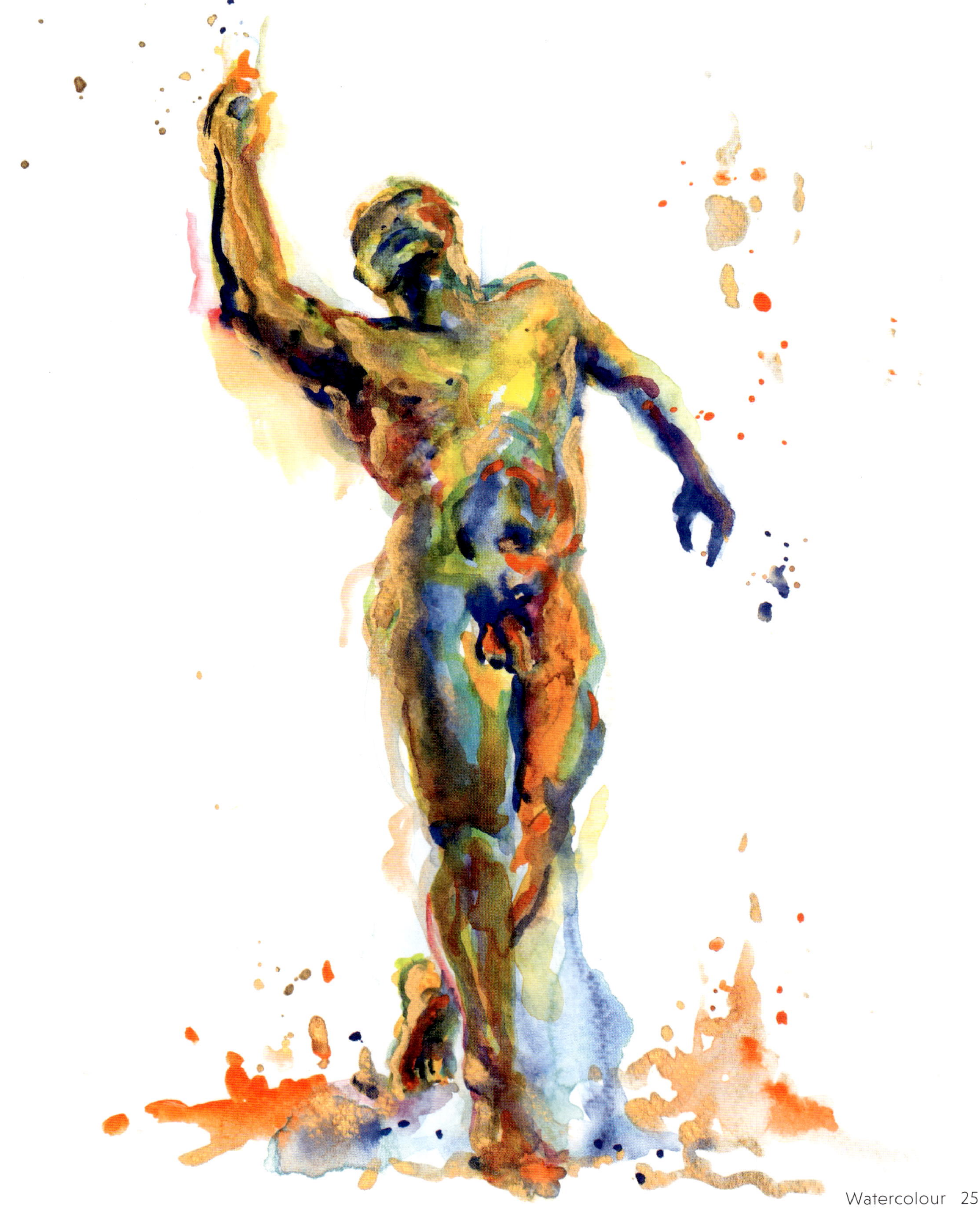

The Art of Letting Go

In the act of painting, I'm reconnecting with the present moment. It's an act of mindfulness, when the senses awaken and instinct takes over. I'm concentrating, but not thinking; observing critically, but without judgement. Everything I see and feel is valid.

It starts with the ritual of setting up: opening my paint box, lining up my favourite brushes, laying out paper, two pots of water and my rags. The model poses, the timer starts, a hush descends. I receive what I see, let it flow through my body into the brush and onto the paper, where the painting reveals itself.

I always start directly with paint. There is no drawing to conflict with the fluid marks of brush on paper. If I need to plan or explore, I make a series of study paintings first.

The hardest part is not caring about the result. If I think it's going well, the spell is broken. If I decide it's 'wrong' and try to correct it, I lose the power of spontaneous mark making. But if I can give myself over to the act of painting, I can discover an image that just seems to have happened on the page, full of a life of its own.

I try not to work from photographs, videos or live streams, because I relish the energy that flows between two living beings sharing the same space at the same moment. However, I know that for many, a life-drawing group may be difficult to access or too public a setting in which to lose yourself in paint. If you are working in the privacy of your own home, use this as the safest possible place for experimentation. Push yourself into your own world of interpretive mark making, rather than replicating what is in front of you.

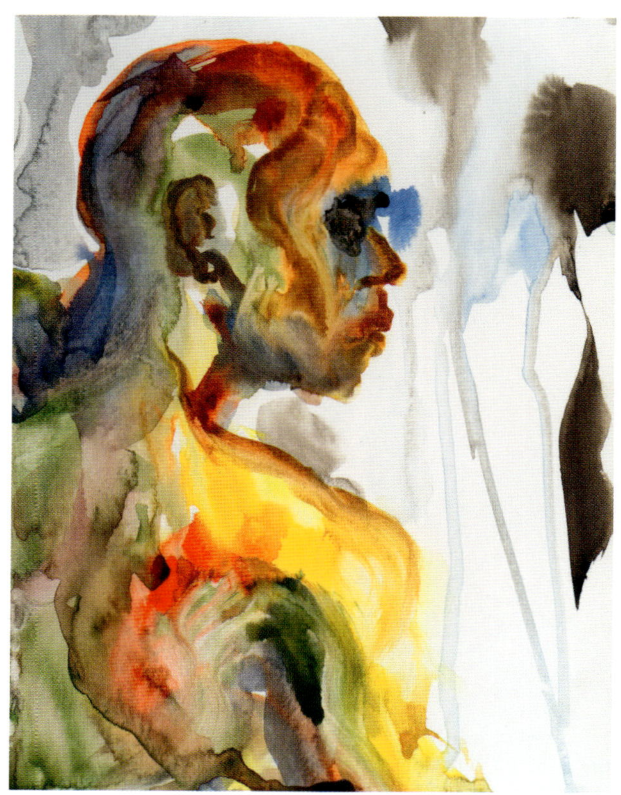

^ Fluid Roy
This painting was my last in a two-hour drop-in workshop with Roy. Having started by describing the form with crisp, linear brushstrokes, I pushed myself away from drawing and into the wateriness of the paint. Working on a gently angled board, the pigments seeped into each other, pulled downwards by gravity through the water.

Scott Online >
Painting via video link has a dynamic all of its own. Apart from the difference in colour, perspective and scale, the model and painter do not share the same space. In this session with Scott, I noticed the strange effect of heightened contrast and distorted perspective. As he settled into a fifteen-minute pose, I used this to emphasize the barrier between us, made stronger by the distracting clutter of a computer desktop (see also page 49).

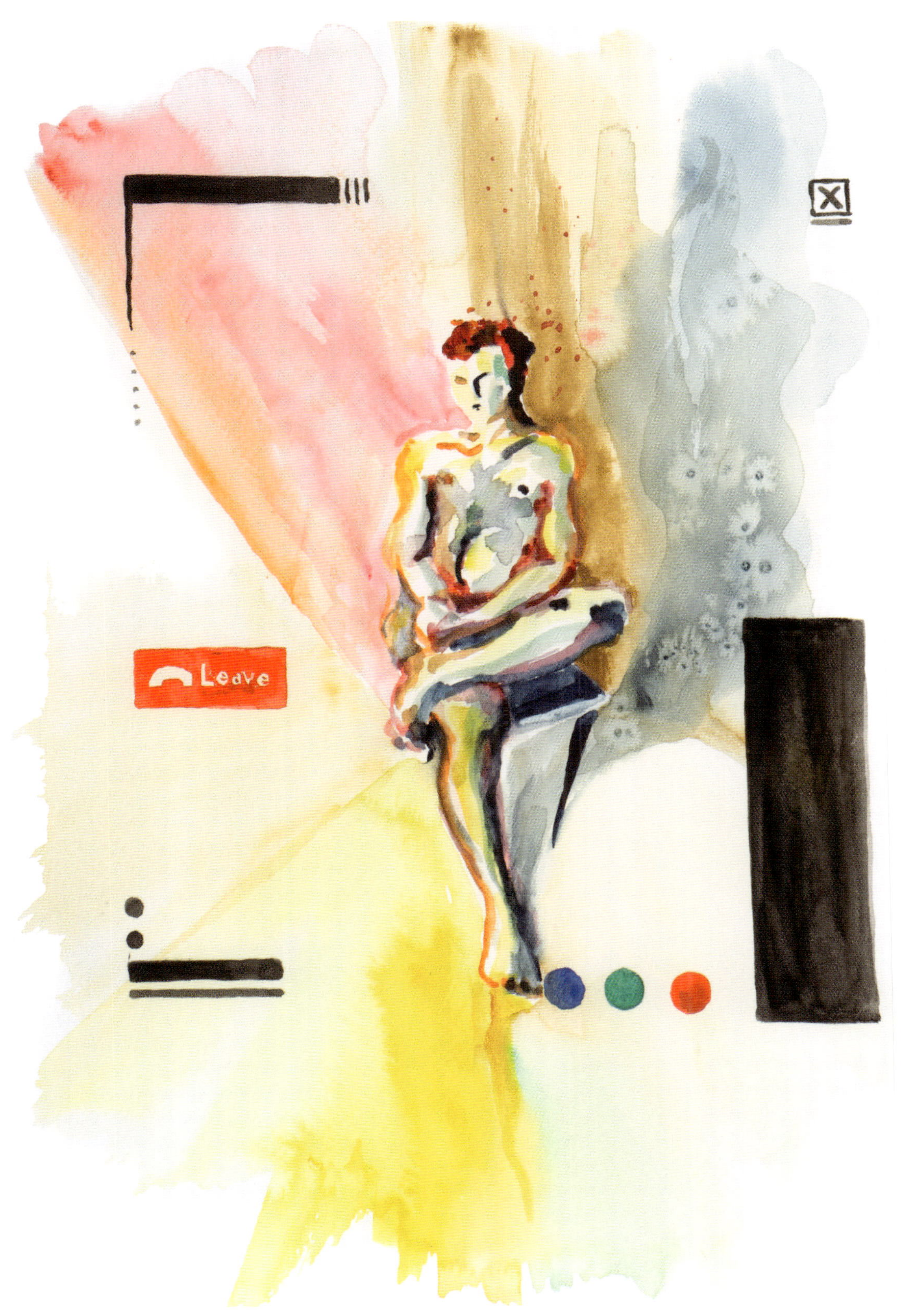
Leave

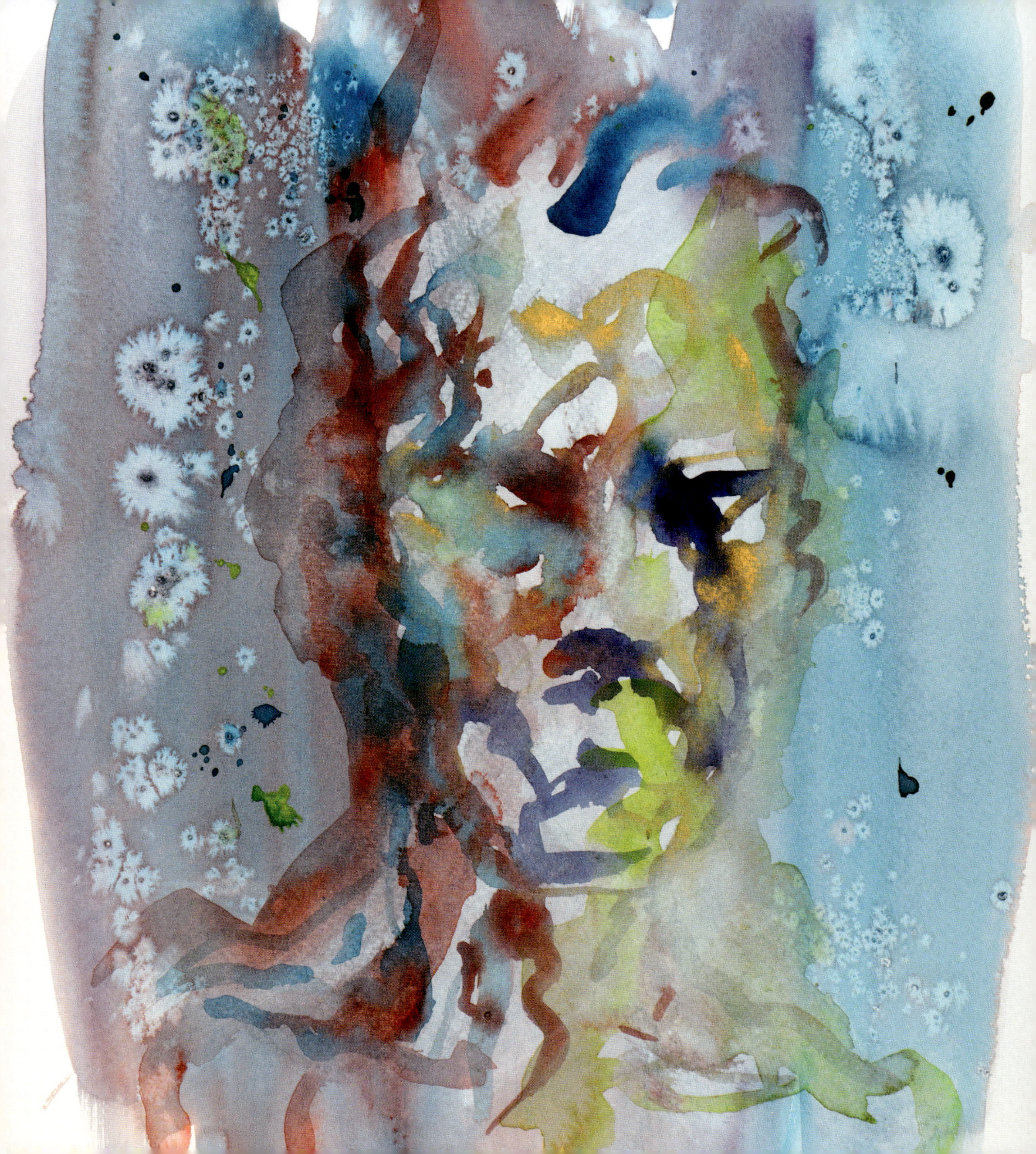

Watercolours don't need much to release their personality, making them a popular choice for painters on the go. Whether you're in a luxurious studio or balancing a drawing board on your knees in a busy community space, they're ready at a moment's notice.

Once released, watercolours challenge the painter to be instinctive and experimental. If oil paints are like a dinner guest, at times sparkling with conversation, at others deep in existential thought, then watercolour is the spontaneous friend who drags you onto the dancefloor to throw caution to the wind.

Will it get on with the paper? Will it decide to run off with the water or just plonk itself in a little puddle? Maybe it will soak up the heat or maybe (if it's humid) it will just lounge around a little longer than you would wish.

As a painter, you can take many different approaches to forge the relationship that suits you. Some choose to lead, plotting a path and guiding with a firm hand. Others follow, daring watercolour to propel them in an unexpected direction.

< Watery Self-Portrait
This painting was one of several versions of an experimental self-portrait. I put it aside unfinished as I felt other versions were working better. On clearing up, I noticed this painting had continued to develop as the pigment moved through the drying water. Crystal patterns had appeared where I had used salt, yellows and blues had formed new greens, and a half-formed figure was emerging from a dreamy, underwater world.

Paints

Watercolour paints are made of a dry pigment held together with a binder and activated with water. The denser the pigment, the more vivid the colour. Some pigments are opaque, while others have a natural luminosity, which becomes transparent with water. Products may note the transparency of individual colours on the packaging or on the website of the manufacturer.

Paints come in tubes (liquid) or pans (solid). With tubes, you will need a water-resistant palette (typically plastic or ceramic). Here you can squeeze out what you need and mix colours before applying them. Pans are more practical when you have limited time and space to set up. Some painters like to spray pans with water before starting so they are activated and ready to go.

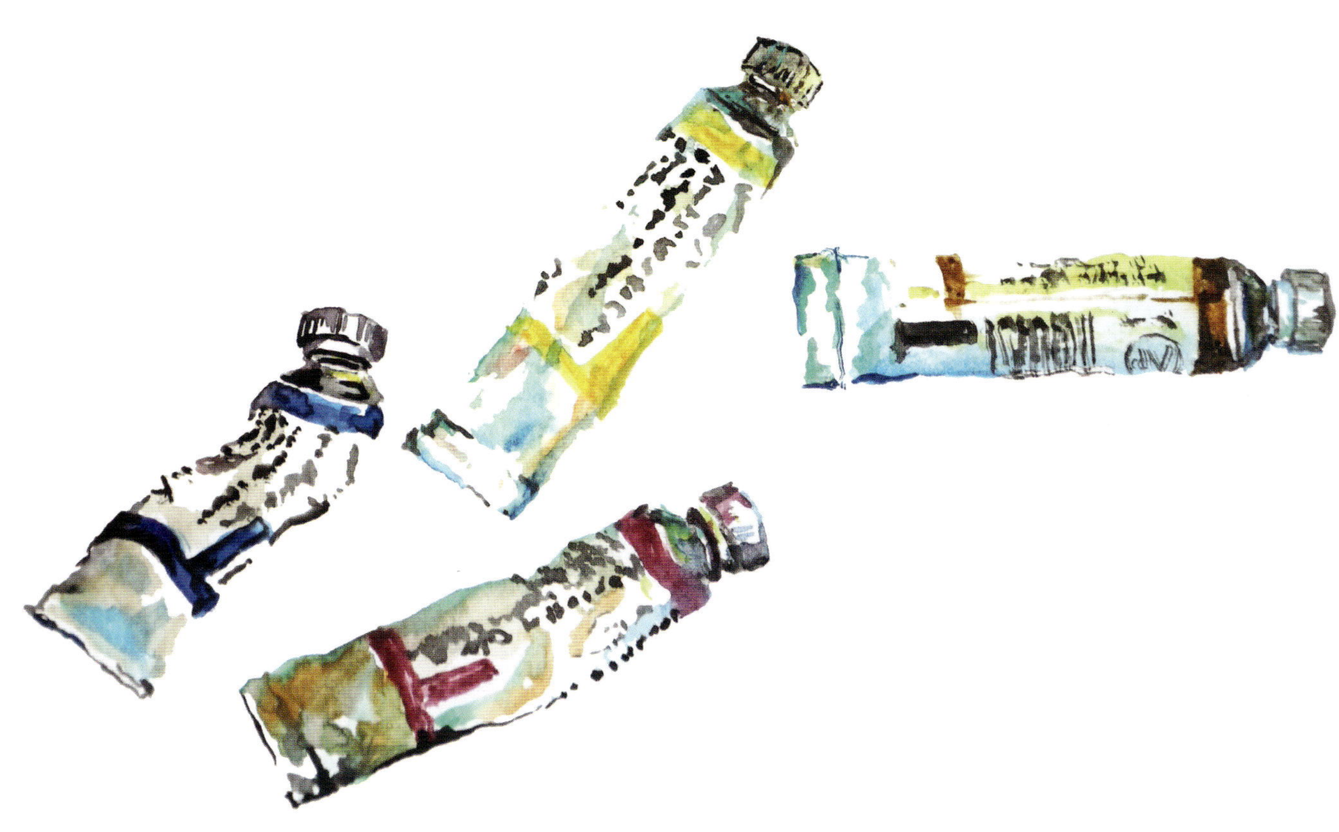

Brushes

Look in any art shop and you'll see a vast array of brush shapes, sizes and materials. Natural sable brushes respond well to subtle shifts in pressure to release paint at different intensities, but they are considerably more expensive than their synthetic counterparts. My go-to brush has a medium round head. I have a large flat brush for washes and a small round head for finer details. I also keep a couple of Japanese ink brushes handy, which I use for more experimental mark making, as well as an old toothbrush for spattering.

Water

I have two tubs of water: one for cleaning my brush and one for mixing with paint. I change the water regularly. Next to it, I have an absorbent rag or kitchen towel to dab off excess water from the brush. I keep another clean rag in case I need to dab water off the paper without leaving any dirty smudges.

Sometimes you won't have access to running water or you'll be in a busy group where your tub may be knocked over. Reservoir brushes are handy tools for these situations: the plastic handle is a refillable container, which releases water through the bristles when squeezed.

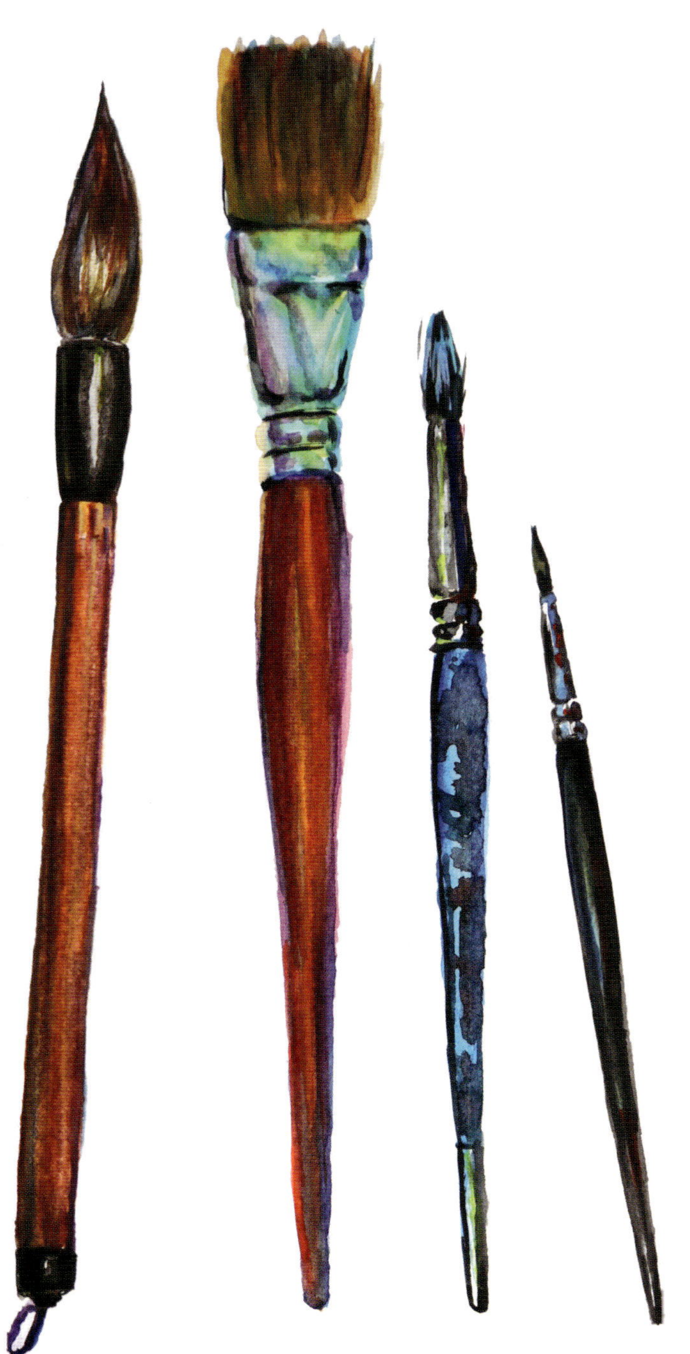

Paper

When it comes to watercolour painting, it helps to understand how the texture and weight of paper transforms the way it absorbs water. Paper designed specifically for watercolour is less likely to buckle, absorb paint unevenly or tear as you paint.

Texture

Watercolour paper is prepared in one of three ways. The most common has been pressed through cold metal rollers. This cold-pressed paper (also called Not) has a tooth to its surface. These little dimples help absorb water and leave a subtle texture. Hot-pressed paper has a smoother finish, so the paint is less likely to bleed. This is great for fast paintings, wet-on-dry techniques and finely detailed illustrations. Rough paper is pressed between felt and has a noticeable texture. This can exacerbate the unpredictability of watercolour and bring out its expressive potential.

Hot-pressed paper (HP)

Cold-pressed paper (Not)

Weight

The weight of paper is expressed as grams per square metre (gsm) or pounds (lb). Heavier paper absorbs more water, holds its shape and tends to be more expensive. 300gsm (140lb) is a good place to start. To minimize the risk of buckling (especially when working with lots of water), you can stretch your paper by wetting it, taping it to a board and letting it dry flat. Alternatively, you can buy a paper block, which is glued on all four sides and supported by a hard backing. You'll need a craft knife to separate the finished painting from the block when dry.

Other materials

In addition to the essentials mentioned above, I prepare a small pot of coarse- and fine-ground salt. This can be sprinkled onto wet paint to soak up pigment, leaving crystalline marks. Some artists mix their watercolours with a specialist medium: aqua pasto, for example, adds the kind of body you get in acrylics or oils; others add gloss, improve transparency or flow, or add a pearlescent effect. Finally, you can use masking fluid or wax to ensure designated parts of the paper stay untouched by paint.

Rough paper

< Paper Textures

I painted the same pigment on three different types of paper. You can see how smoothly it glides across the hot-pressed surface. On the cold-pressed, it starts to catch a little on the tooth of the paper. On the rough, you can see the pigment collecting in the larger dimples, highlighting the texture.

Techniques

∧ Wet Wash
Wet a wide brush in clean water, load it with paint and stroke it across the full width of the paper in the same direction, slightly overlapping the previous stroke each time.

∧ Graded Wash
Paint a square with clean water. Then paint a strip of colour at one edge. It will be drawn into the wet shape.

∧ Dry Scumble
Dab your brush dry and load it with paint. See how it catches unevenly on the dry surface of the paper.

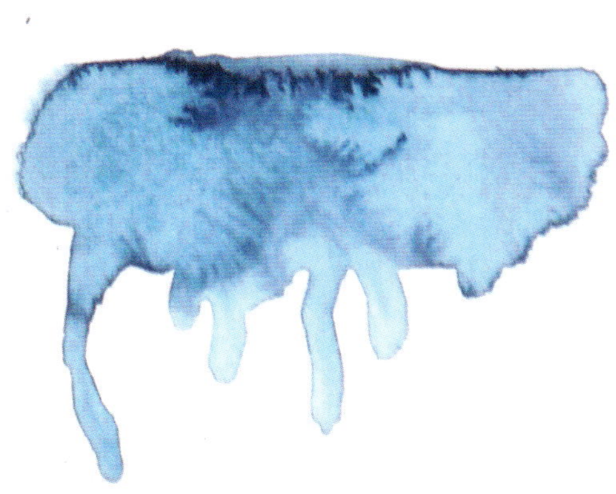

∧ Drips
Load a wet brush with paint and make a mark on dry paper. Tilt the paper so the paint runs in drips.

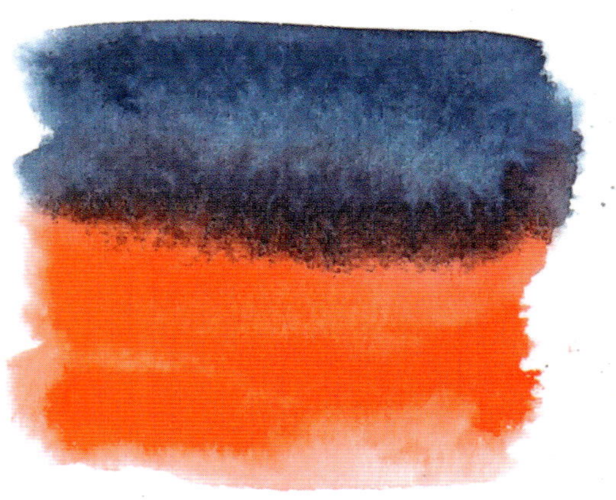

∧ Variegated Wash
Paint a square with clean water. Paint one colour above and another below. Watch them seep into each other.

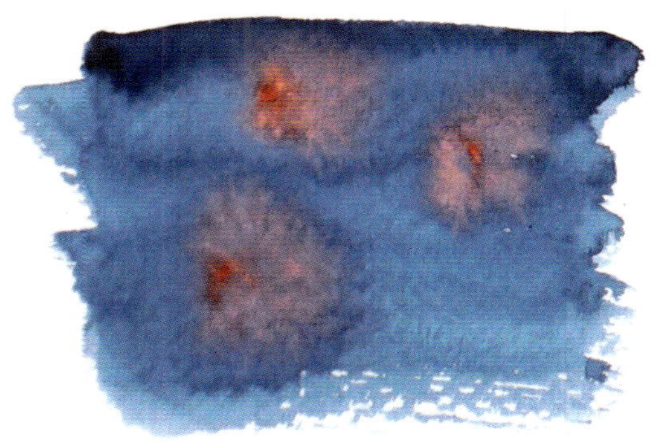

∧ Wet on Wet
Dab, drip or spatter a second colour into a wet or damp wash. The wetter the wash, the more the colour will bleed out.

∧ Spattering
Load your brush (or an old toothbrush) with paint and flick the bristles with your finger. Notice the difference when it lands on wet or dry paper.

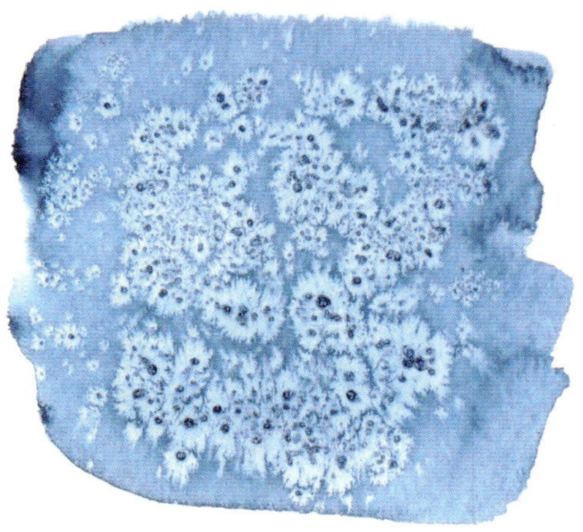

∧ Salt
Drop salt crystals into wet paint. The salt will soak up the pigment leaving crystalline patterns. Rub the salt off when dry.

Blooms

The love affair between pigment and water is like a romantic comedy. The pigment is constantly running away from the water, but can never bring itself to break free entirely. In the end, they find an equilibrium, creating a distinctive mark on their world that neither could have achieved alone.

The hallmark of this is a bloom, or backrun. Once dry, pigment is more or less locked into the paper. But if you add liquid to a wash while it is still damp, you'll see the pigment run away, gathering in a saturated border around the wet area. As the newly added liquid dries, it pulls the pigment back, and you get a bloom.

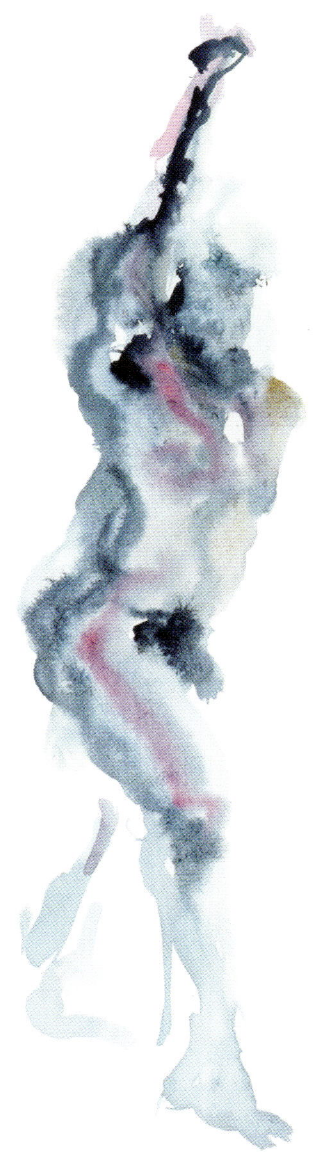

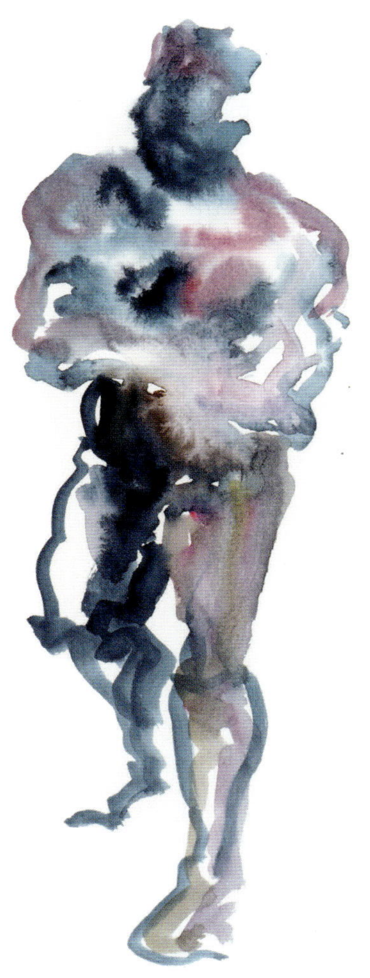

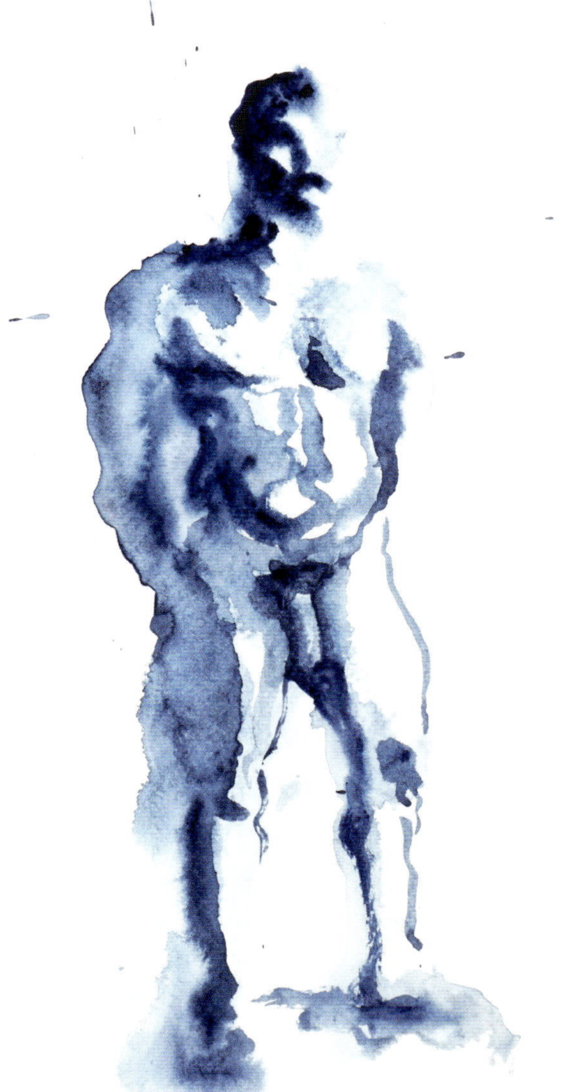

The extent of the bloom will depend on many factors: how wet the paper is when you apply more liquid; how much liquid you apply; the absorbency of the paper; even the temperature and humidity of the air. Its unpredictability makes it a gift for experimental painting and a complete liability for precision detail.

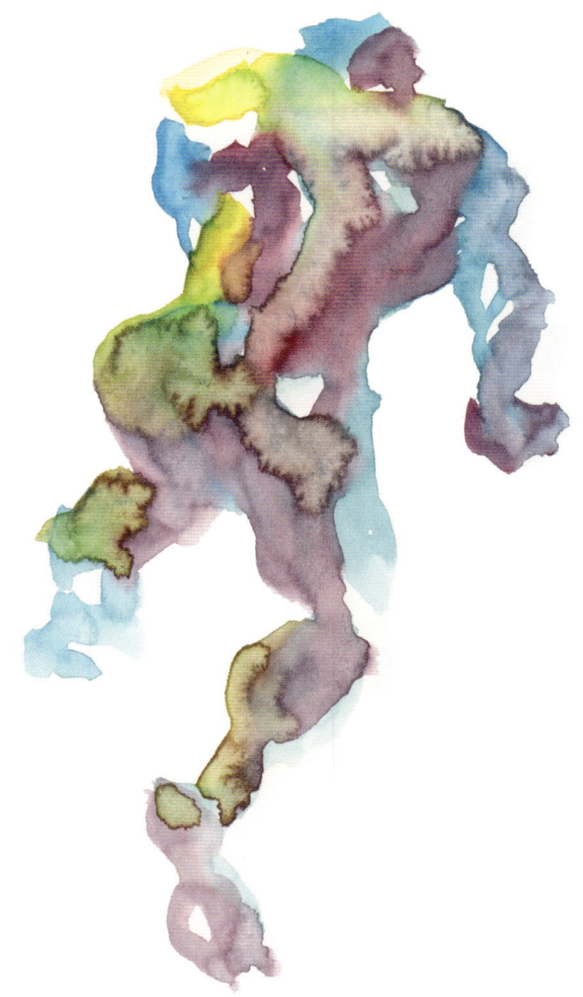

< > Matthew in Bloom

For these two-minute paintings of Matthew, I worked with a lot of water, adding pigment to the wet shapes instinctively. When I put one painting aside to work on the next, the pigments continued to move as the water dried. I only saw the finished result when we stopped for a break later. The blooms accentuate the form, contrasting with the definition of the wet-on-dry strokes.

Colour Theory

As well as its unique water-based properties, watercolour is defined by its vibrant colours. Some paintings have an intensity that makes you forget about pigment on paper. The image seems to glow with energy: a crash of golden light, a deep blue you could dive into, a green you can almost taste.

We see colour in relation to the colours that surround it. Colour theory is understanding the fundamentals of these relationships. If you've played with colour paints, you will have noticed that you can mix new colours from the three primary colours of red, blue and yellow. Secondary colours are mixes of two primaries:

orange, green and purple. Laying these out on a colour wheel is the easiest way to see their relationships (see opposite).

Complementary colours sit opposite each other on the wheel. Placing a colour and its complement next to each other in a painting will strengthen their intensity: to make a red appear redder, put it next to a green. Analogous colours are neighbours on the wheel, a useful relationship to lift a monochromatic palette. A pleasing harmony comes from a careful balancing of either complementary or analogous colours, whereas upsetting this balance has the power to grab the attention and unsettle the viewer.

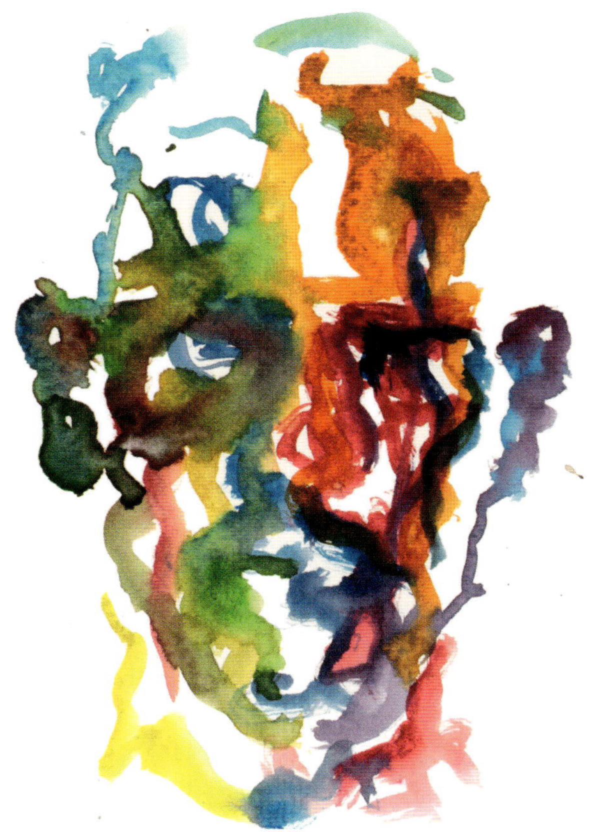

< Rainbow Selfie
This tiny self-portrait was painted for Pride, using the colours of the rainbow flag in solidarity with diversity and equality. You can see how this spectrum of colour correlates with a colour wheel.

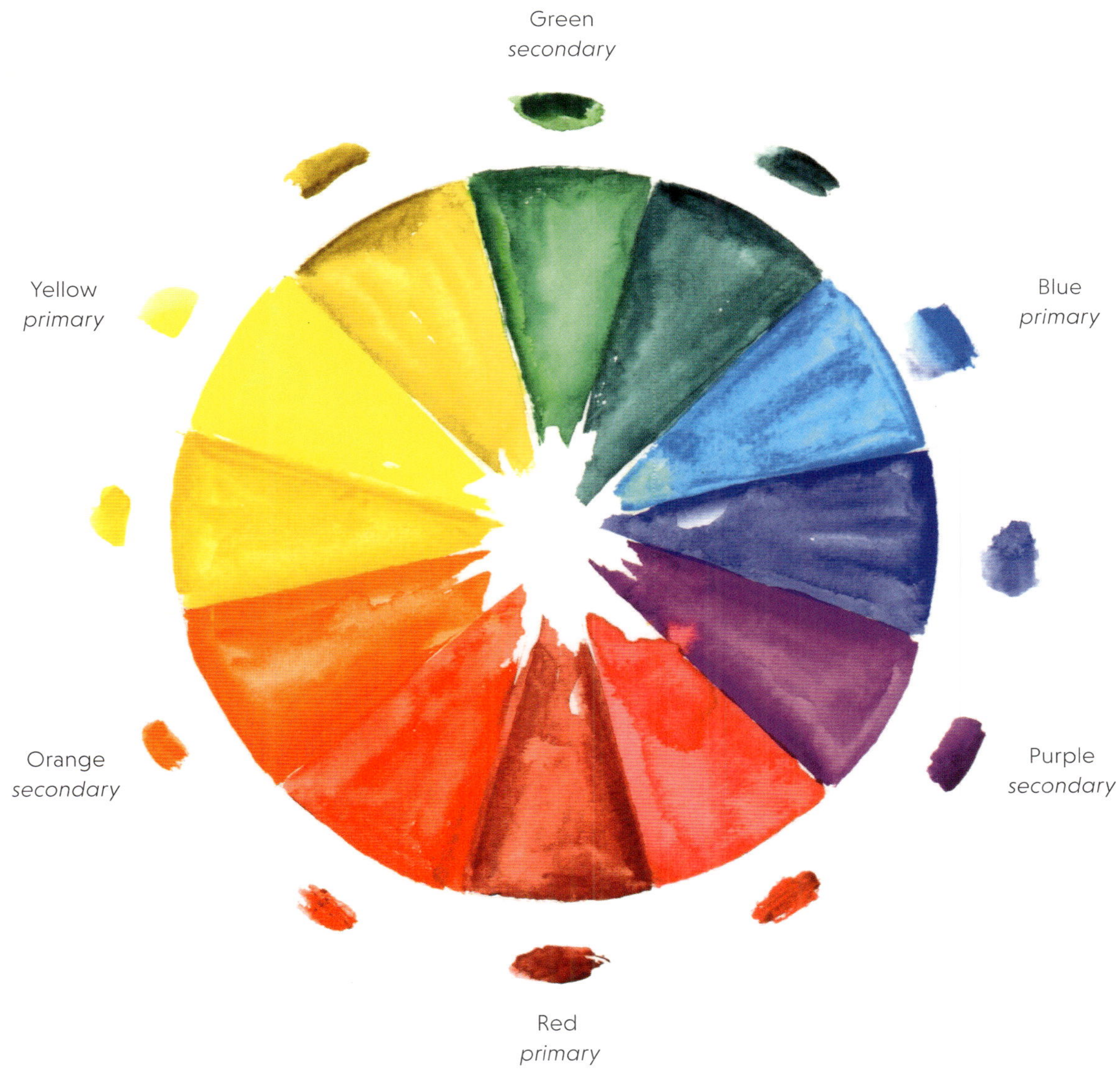

∧ Colour Wheel

The colour you see in a pan will change when water is added and change again as it dries on the page. Painting a colour wheel helps you get to know your palette. In this wheel, I subdivided a circle to test twelve unmixed colours. I orderec them from reds through orange to yellow, through green to blue, and through purple back to red.

Colour Temperature

A burst of hot colour is likely to rouse the viewer while a cool monochrome may soothe. You can feel the power of a dominant red or the calm of a blue. You may also have noticed that some blues can feel energetic and some reds calming: this is to do with the relative value of colour temperature.

If you look again at the colour wheel, you can see that red is cooler when it tends towards blue, while when a blue tends towards red, it gets a bit warmer.

v Relative Temperature
A purple square next to orange will feel warmer than the same purple next to green.

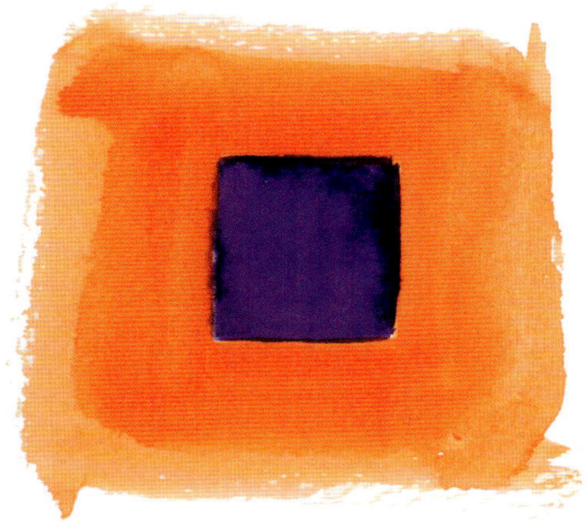

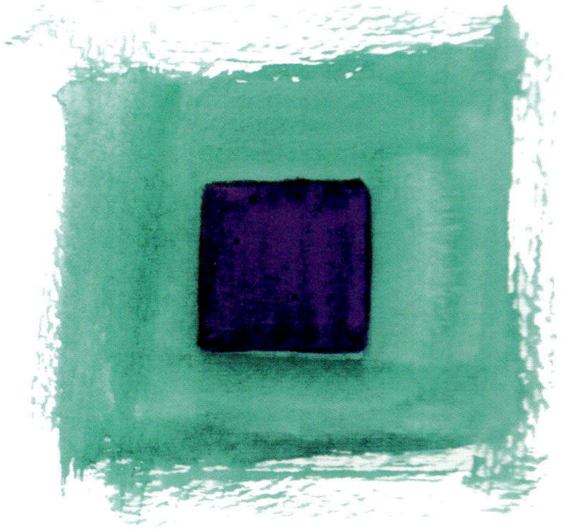

You can use this understanding of colour temperature to drive the emotion in your painting: a cooler colour palette commands an emotional range from soothing calm to sadness; whereas warm colours can suggest anything from cosy warmth to exciting drama.

Temperature can also be used to help create depth by using strong warm colours in the foreground and muted cool colours for the far distance. You can see this in my painting of 'Roy on Caithness Beach' on page 85.

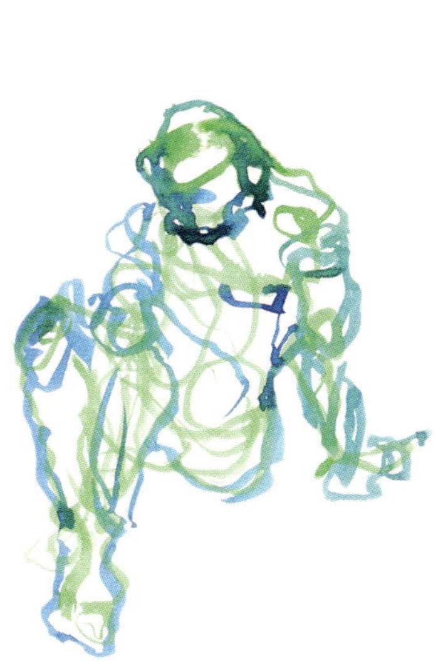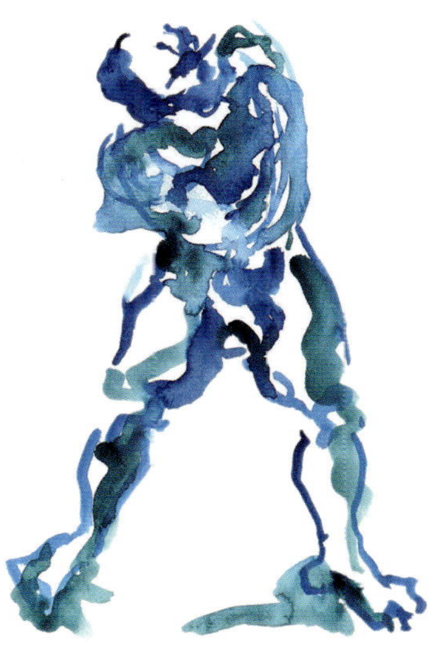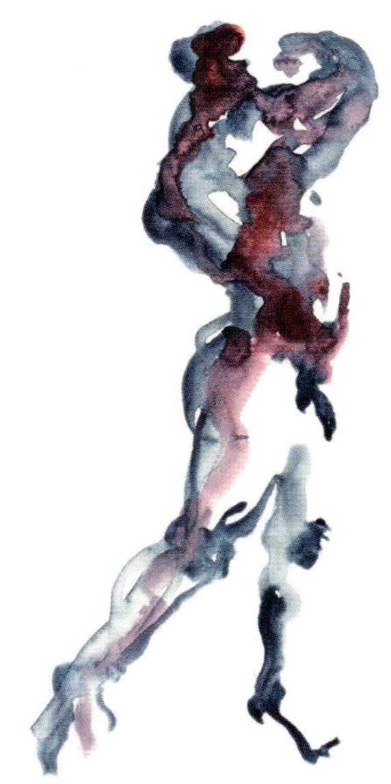

∧ ∨ Cool Roy and Hot Valentina
Roy is cool in green and blue, warming up a little as
I introduce a crimson. Valentina is at her most fiery in
shades of orange, cooling off as she tends towards pink.

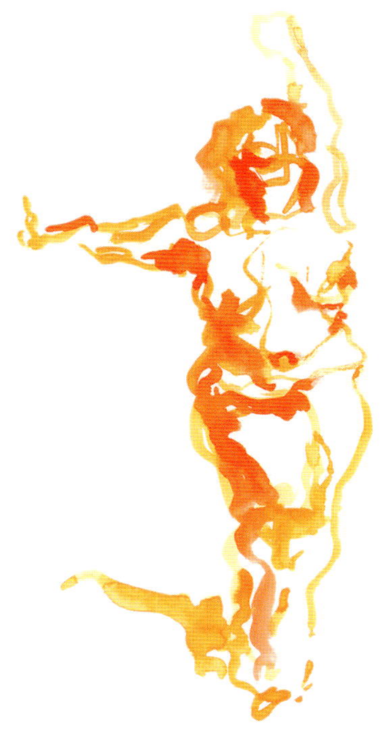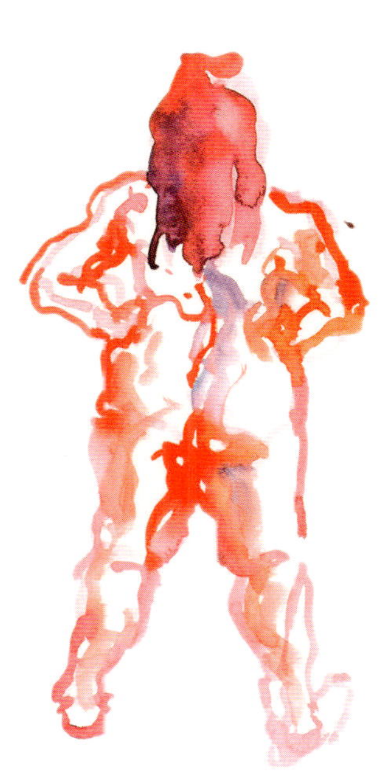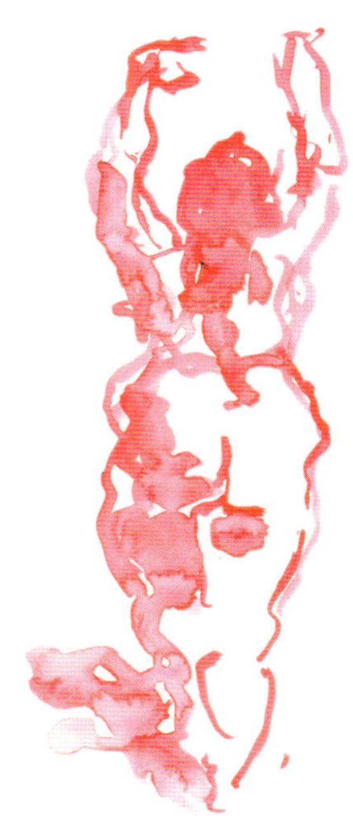

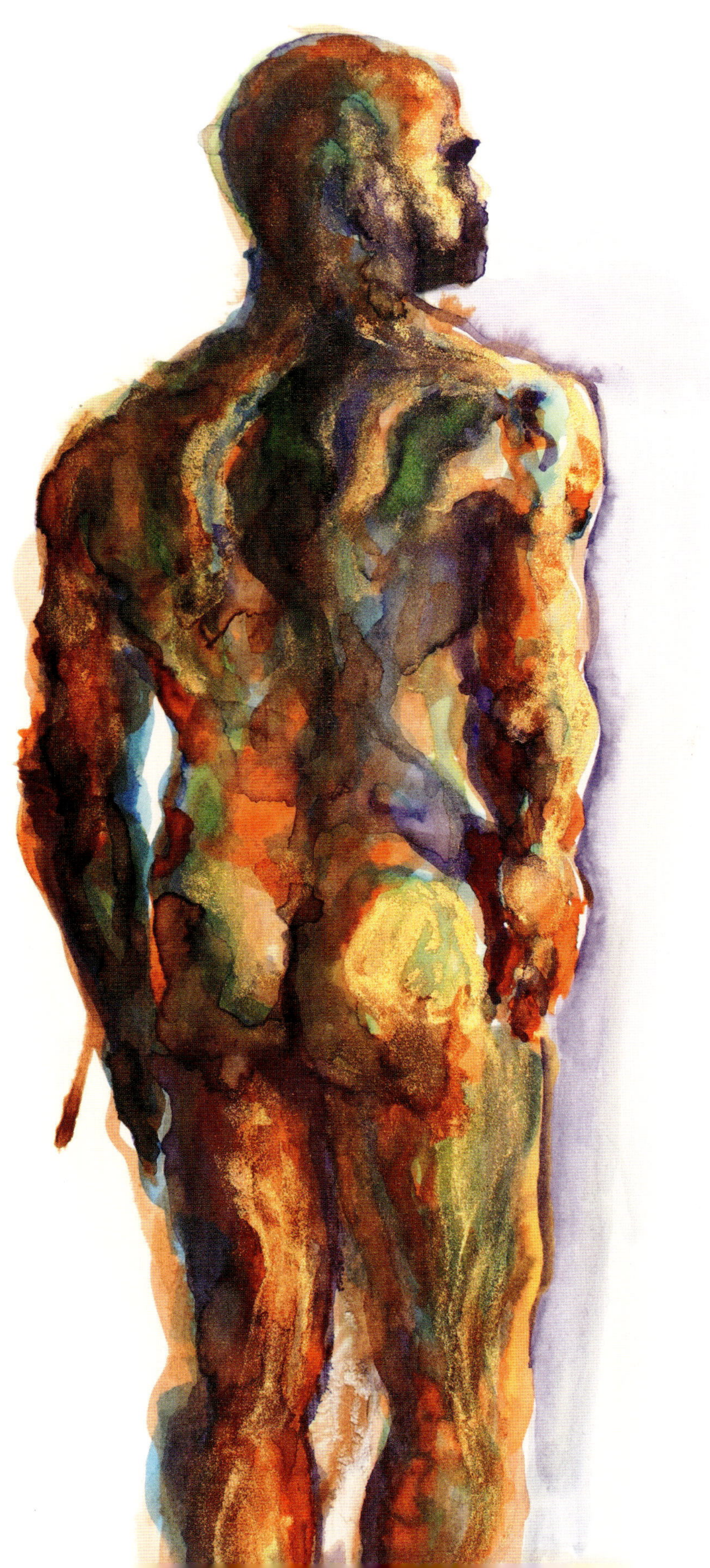

Colours of the Flesh

As light hits a surface, some of it is absorbed, some reflected.
This reflected light determines the visible colour that hits your eyes.
The more that is reflected, the closer to white the surface appears,
bleaching out colour. In watercolour, these are the areas you want
the paper to shine through. It is therefore the darker areas to which
we must devote our greatest attention. When painting the figure,
it is these shadows of the flesh that hold the richest colours.

In my journey to see colour, I have had to banish two things.
The first is the idea of 'skin tone'. I am not painting the colour of
skin, but the shadows that fall upon it. I leave aside soft pinks and
browns – as well as black and white – in favour of blues, purples,
greens, deep reds, oranges and bright yellows.

The second – controversially – is tone, also known as colour value.
For many painters, tone is an essential tool for modelling the figure
and a direct extension of monochrome drawing. In my practice, I
have learned to keep drawing and painting as separate disciplines.
In paint, I start by applying colour to the surface and let the
'drawing' happen where one colour meets another. As I build
up my painting, I strengthen deep areas of shadow, but only
after the colour is firmly established.

< Roy's Back
In this study of Roy, I was
particularly struck by the way
a golden light crashed onto
the flesh, creating rich, warm
shadows across the landscape
of his back. I layered up
transparent washes of purple,
green and blue before moving
in with warm orange and red,
finishing off with an opaque
flourish of gold.

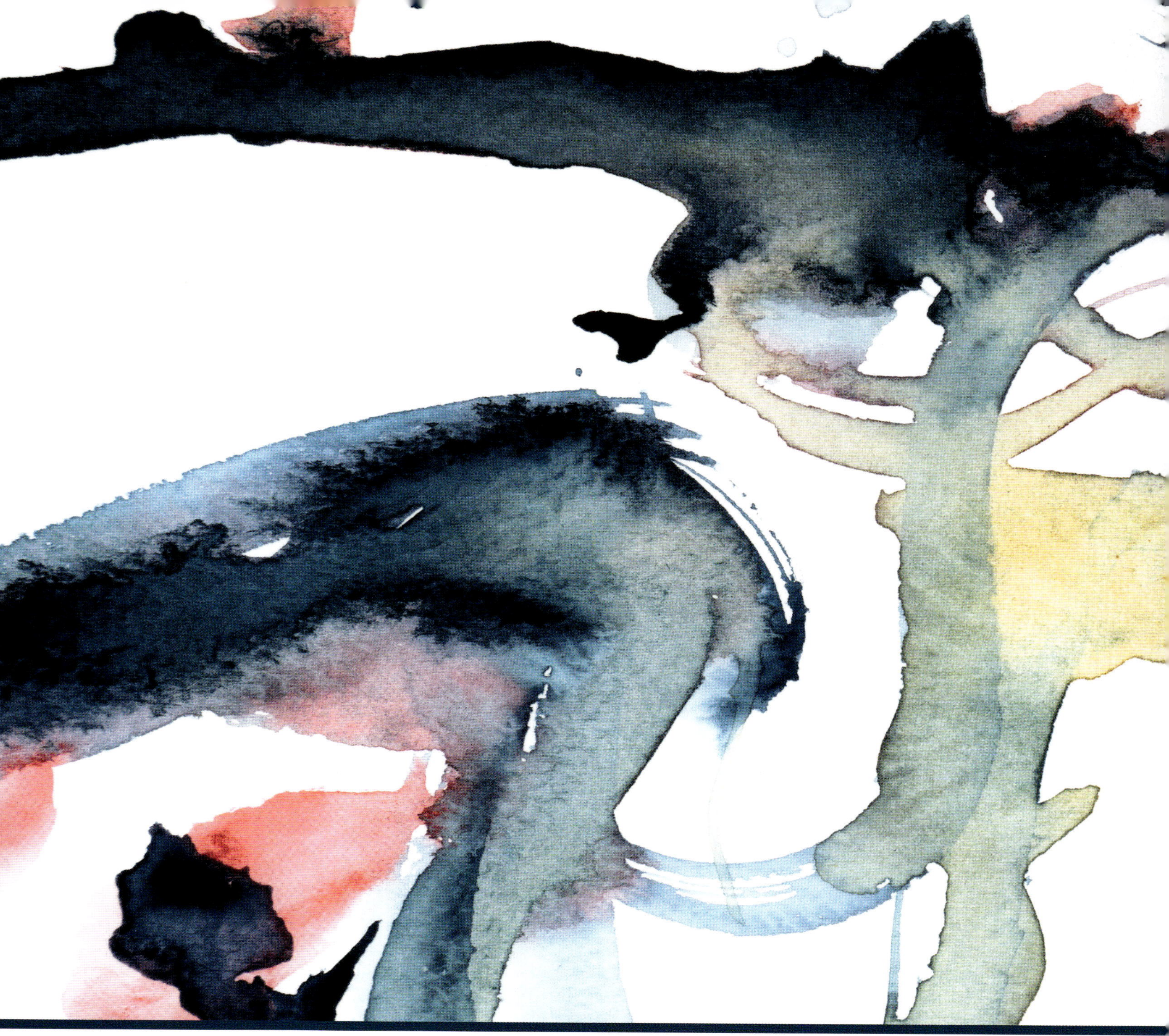

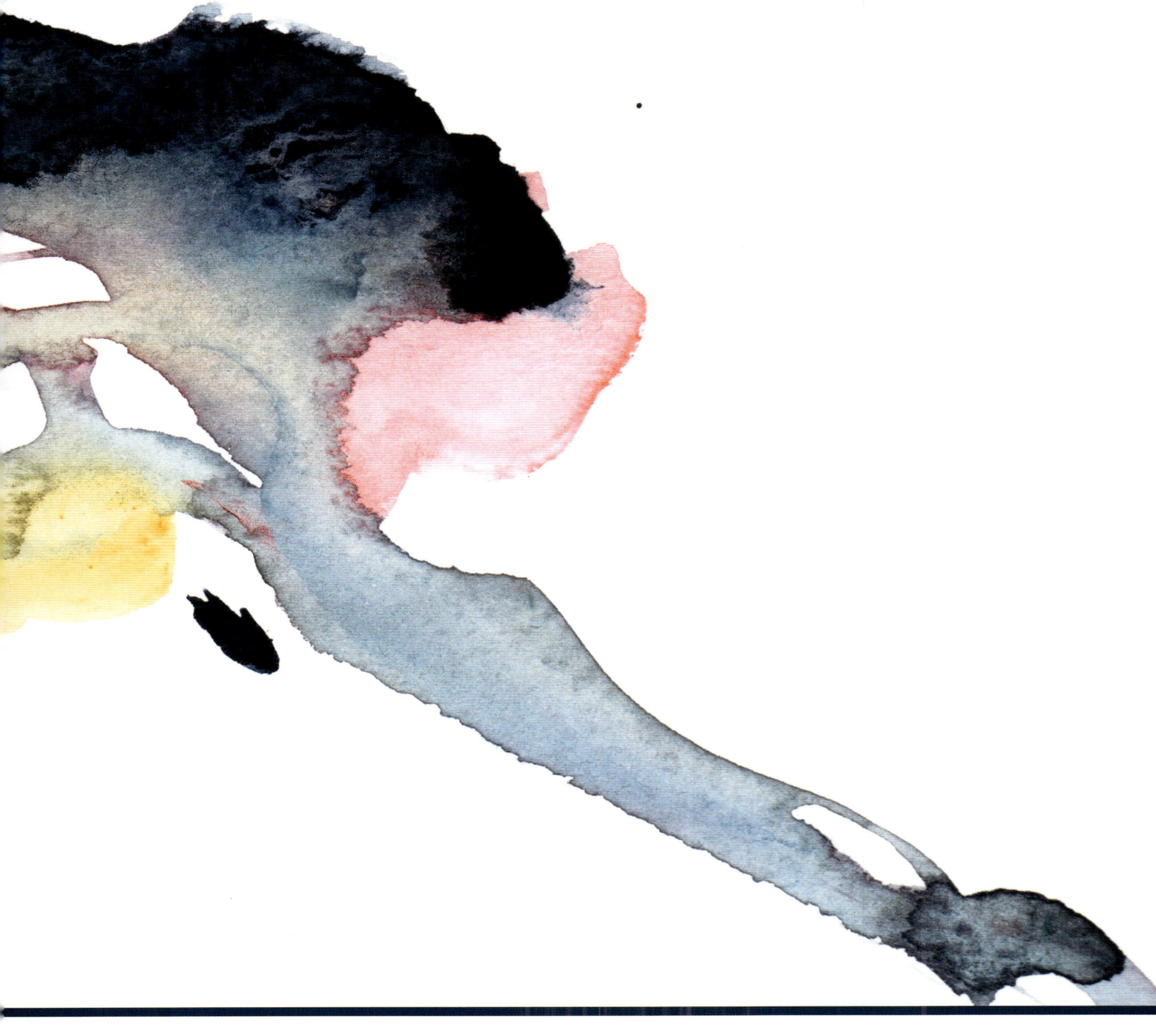

Speed

Painting from life is full of movement. The model breathes and tenses, holding a pose against the clock; the painter channels this energy, making expressive movements with the brush to apply paint to paper; the pigment itself seeps into the page, moving through water until it is dry.

I use speed to connect instinctively to the energy of this movement. The journey from the model to my eye, down my arm, through the brush and onto the paper is short-circuited, and that's where the sparks really fly. I'm forced to give myself over to the paint and let it surprise me. And if it all goes wrong, I know the next opportunity is just a few seconds away.

In this section, I share the foundation of my practice: painting at speed.

Lidia at Speed >
These two-minute paintings capture Lidia's ability to contort her body into any number of extraordinary poses. I loaded a brush with ink and allowed it to trail and drip across the paper, barely taking my eyes off the model.

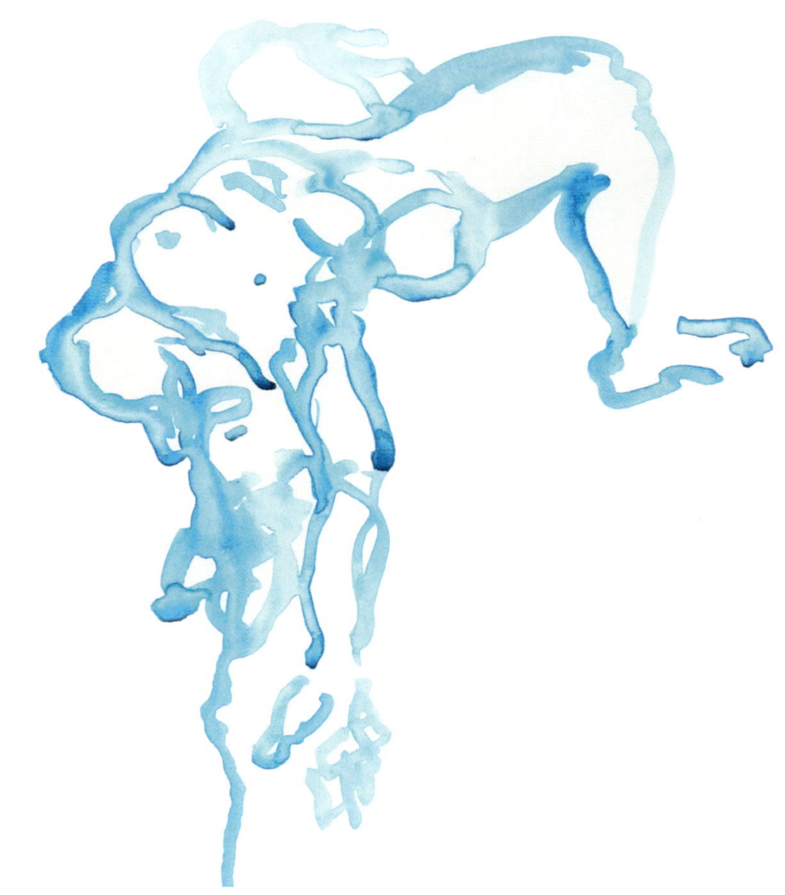

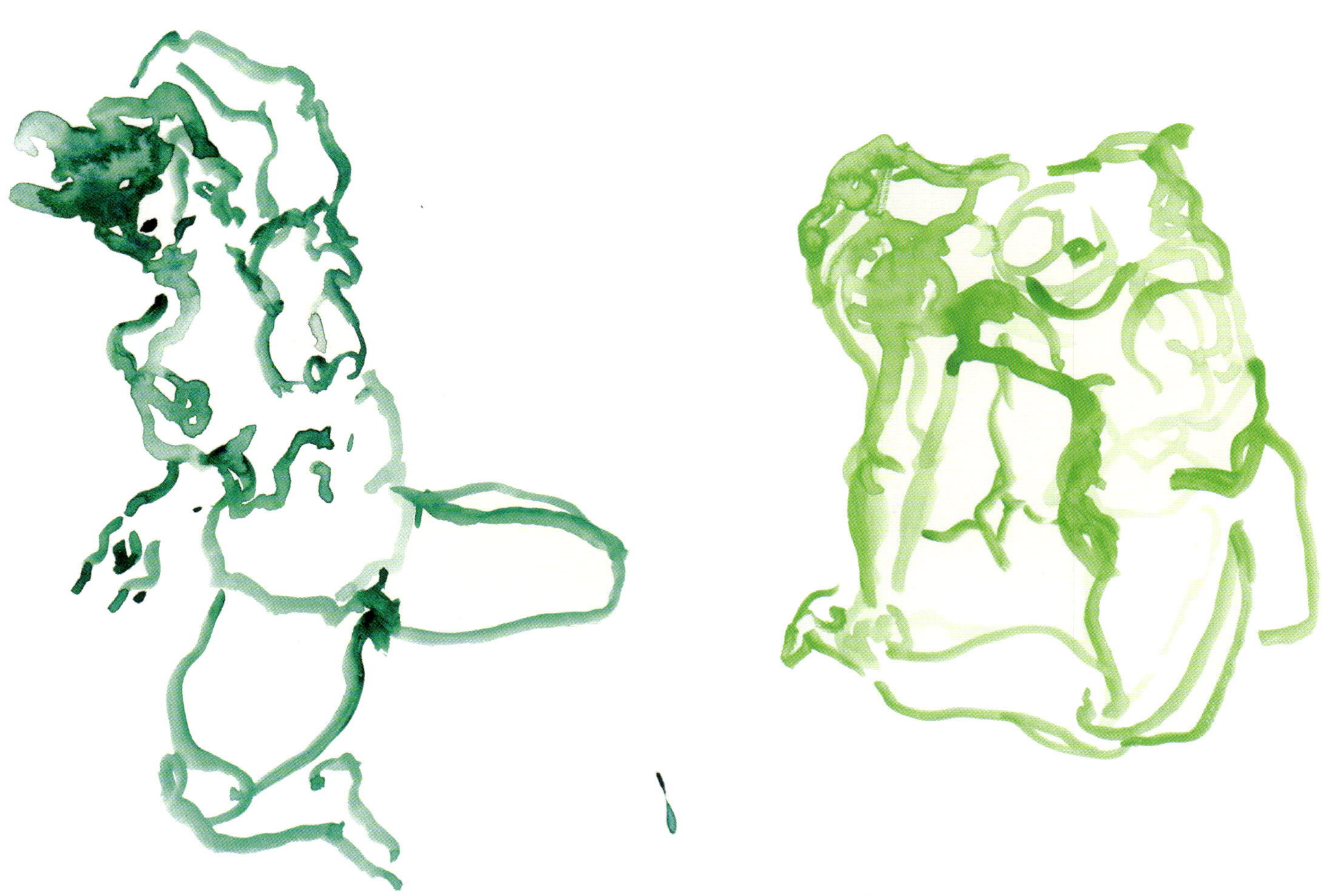

'The human body is not made for being still. The human body is made for being in movement. The most incredible skill is to be still. Being still you feel the movement of your body. Being still is like being too quick because you feel everything inside moving – you literally feel the blood, you feel sometimes also the cells of your skin, you feel all these incredible movements.'

Lidia

Getting Your Eye In

Before speeding off, it helps to get the lay of the land. No matter how short the pose, there is always time to engage your senses, read the model's pose and connect yourself with the moment. You may only make one or two marks to describe the whole pose, but those marks will be the foundations for understanding the particular physique of the model as you continue working together.

Whether I have two minutes or a couple of hours, I observe the figure, allowing my eyes to travel across the form, anticipating the marks I will make with the brush. I'm searching for flow and balance.

- Think of the whole: how the top of the head connects to the toes, via the neck, down the spine, into the hips, through the thighs, knees and calves, to the ankles and feet.
- Discover the relationships between the body's existing paired parts (even if you can't see both of them): hands, elbows, shoulder blades, nipples and so on.
- Feel the distribution of weight in the pose. What's pushing back against it? The floor, a stool, a pillar? It's critical to indicate this in the painting if I want my figure to feel solid.
- Consider the environment and how the figure in the space fits within the rectangle of your page. Use the centre point of the pose to position the model.
- Challenge your assumptions of proportion, seeing this unique figure in three dimensions receding into space.

Scott was modelling online. The high angle of
the camera produced a strange perspective in
this remote digital space. I reduced the figure
and chair to a few lines, flattening it as it was on
the screen. I developed these studies into the
painting you can see on page 27.

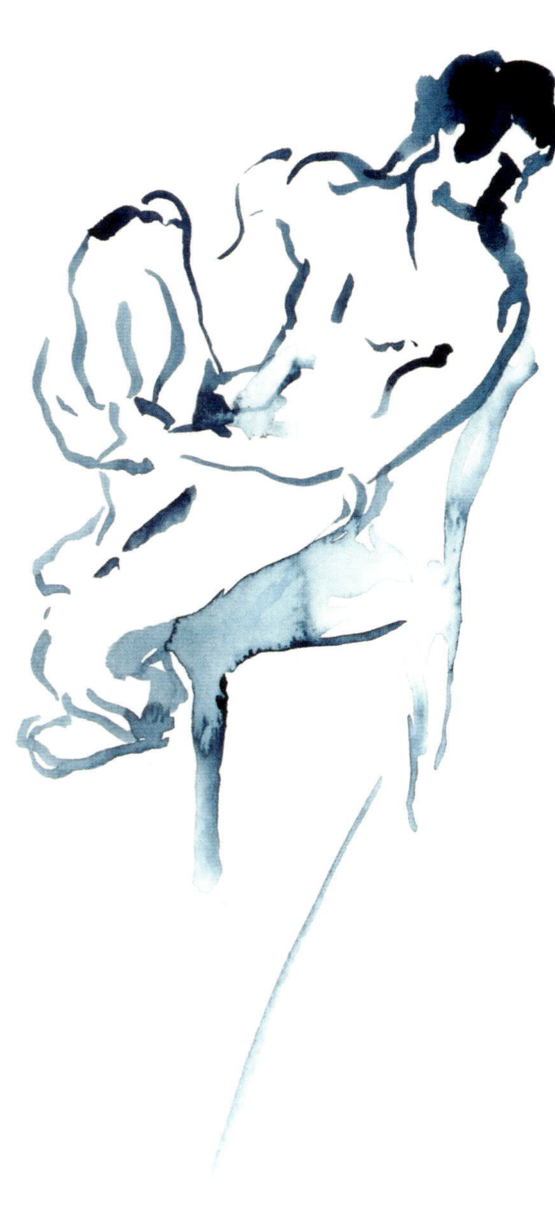

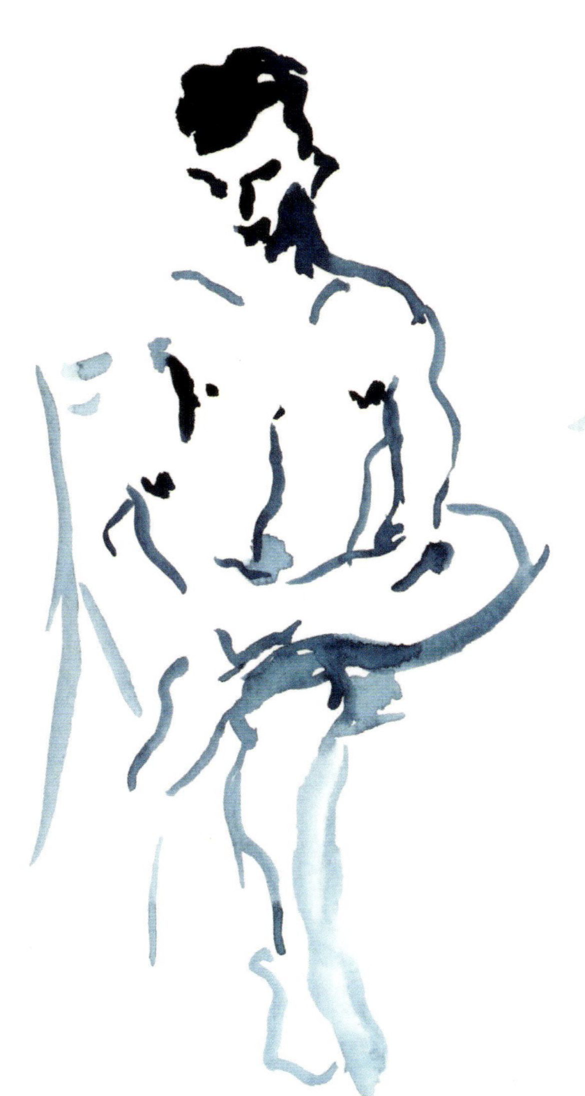

Fast and Free

When your senses are engaged and your observation heightened, it's time to paint. Short, dynamic poses are used to get the model and painter warmed up at the start of a session. It is a liberating experience: there is no time to get stuck or fiddle with detail, and you can produce so many works in a short space of time that it doesn't matter if many of them don't work out.

When the model and I are ready, I set the clock for two minutes. I spend the first few seconds reading the pose, then I load the brush with paint and let the feeling of the pose travel through me onto the paper. When the timer beeps, we move immediately on to the next pose, and the next. I'm aiming for at least a dozen poses so we can truly get into a rhythm.

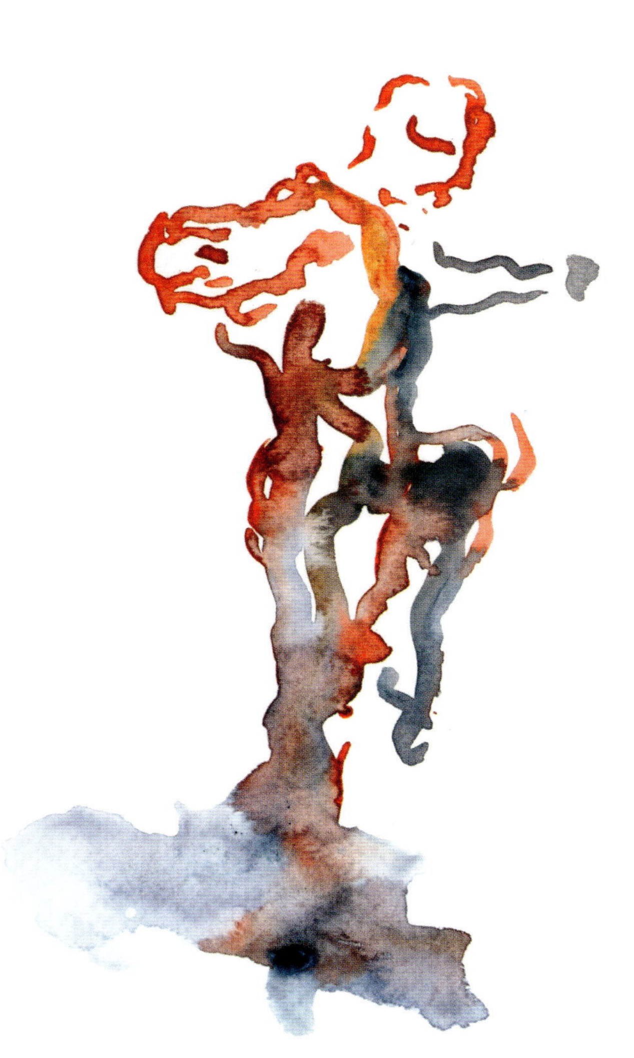

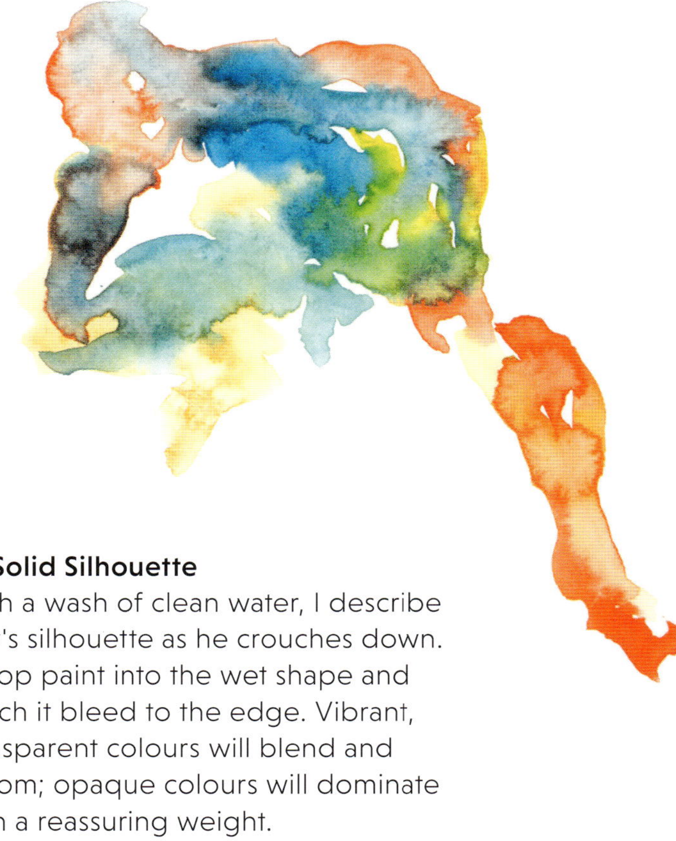

∧ Solid Silhouette
With a wash of clean water, I describe Roy's silhouette as he crouches down. I drop paint into the wet shape and watch it bleed to the edge. Vibrant, transparent colours will blend and bloom; opaque colours will dominate with a reassuring weight.

< The Figure Emerging
For Roy to emerge from the page, I grade the wetness of the paper, so that painted lines soften in one place and rise to a definitive solidity where it is dry.

If I'm feeling adventurous, I will work wet on wet,
liberating the pigment and watching the painting
develop even after the clock has stopped. This is
a space to experiment, explore, fail and perhaps
stumble upon an unexpected delight.

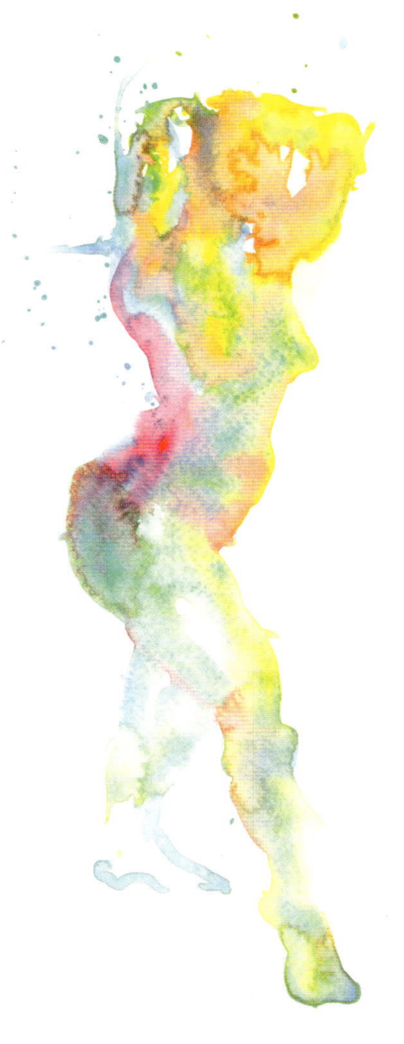

Dynamic Flicks >
To accentuate the movement of
Maya's forward step, I tilt the paper
and blow into wet paint to encourage
drips. I flick paint to add dynamism
and push my painterly mark making
in exciting, unexpected directions.

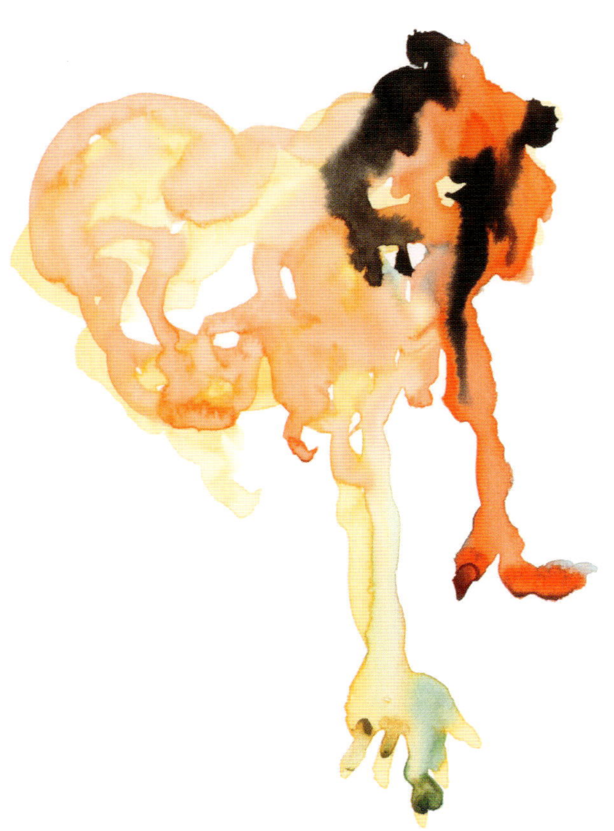

< Emotive Drips
This briefly described form
captures the weight of Lidia's
pose with fluid strokes loaded
with dripping paint.

Typically, a short pose is part of a series. The model is moving from one to another and another. There is an energy that links them. As a painter, you can capture that energy by layering several poses on a single sheet. As a result, unexpected relationships between the figures emerge in a composition full of dynamic movement.

The First Poses >
Roy is giving me two-minute poses. I've prepared a large sheet of paper sized 70 x 50cm (27½ x 19½in), my brushes and paints. I start with a limited palette of ultramarine, viridian and a touch of bright violet. The first two poses fit well together. I leave a bit of space around the third as I'm less sure of its place in the composition.

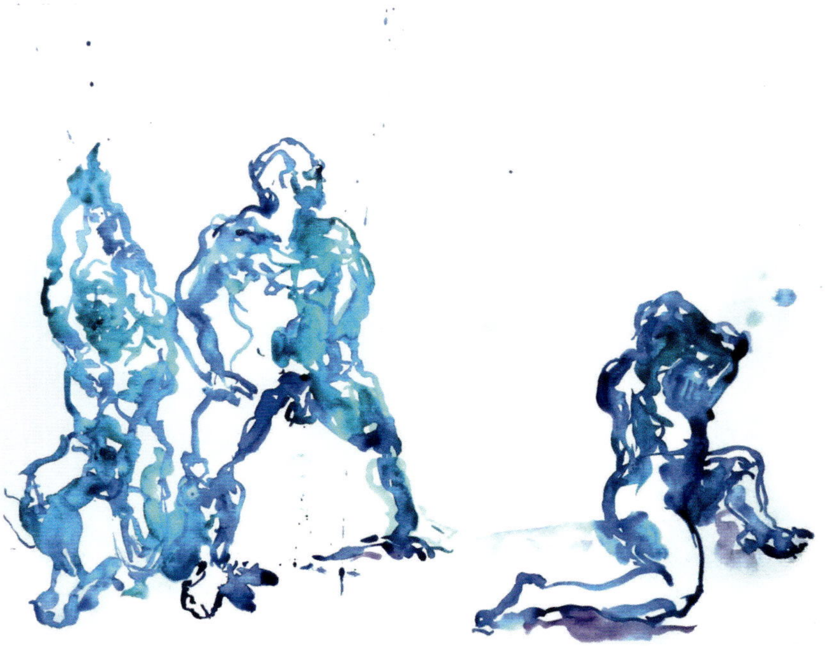

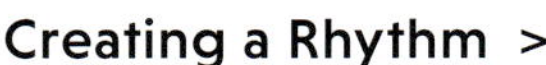

Creating a Rhythm >
Roy then gives me two full-height poses, which I place in the gap. I use the extended arms of the fifth pose as a framing device. I can now feel a rhythm that connects the poses and allows the eye to travel across the page.

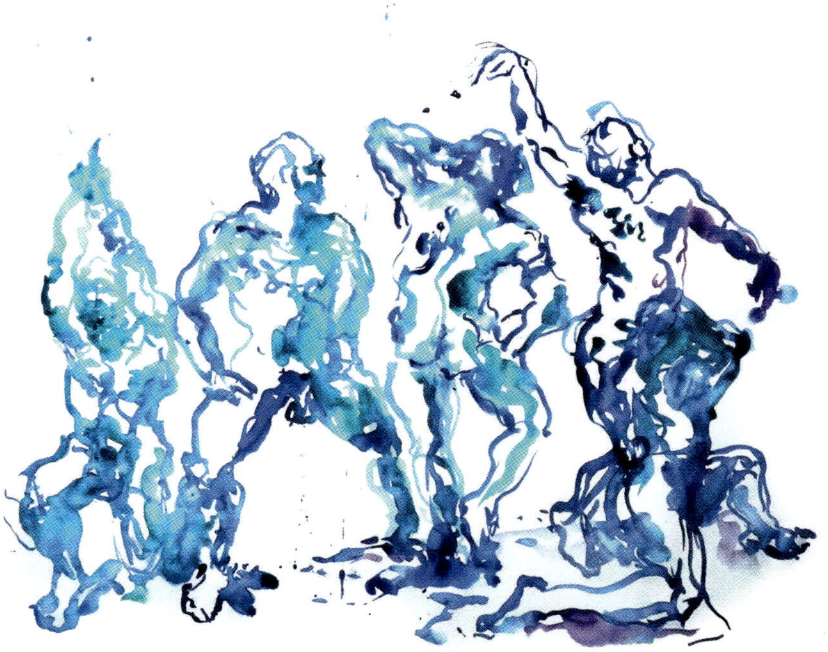

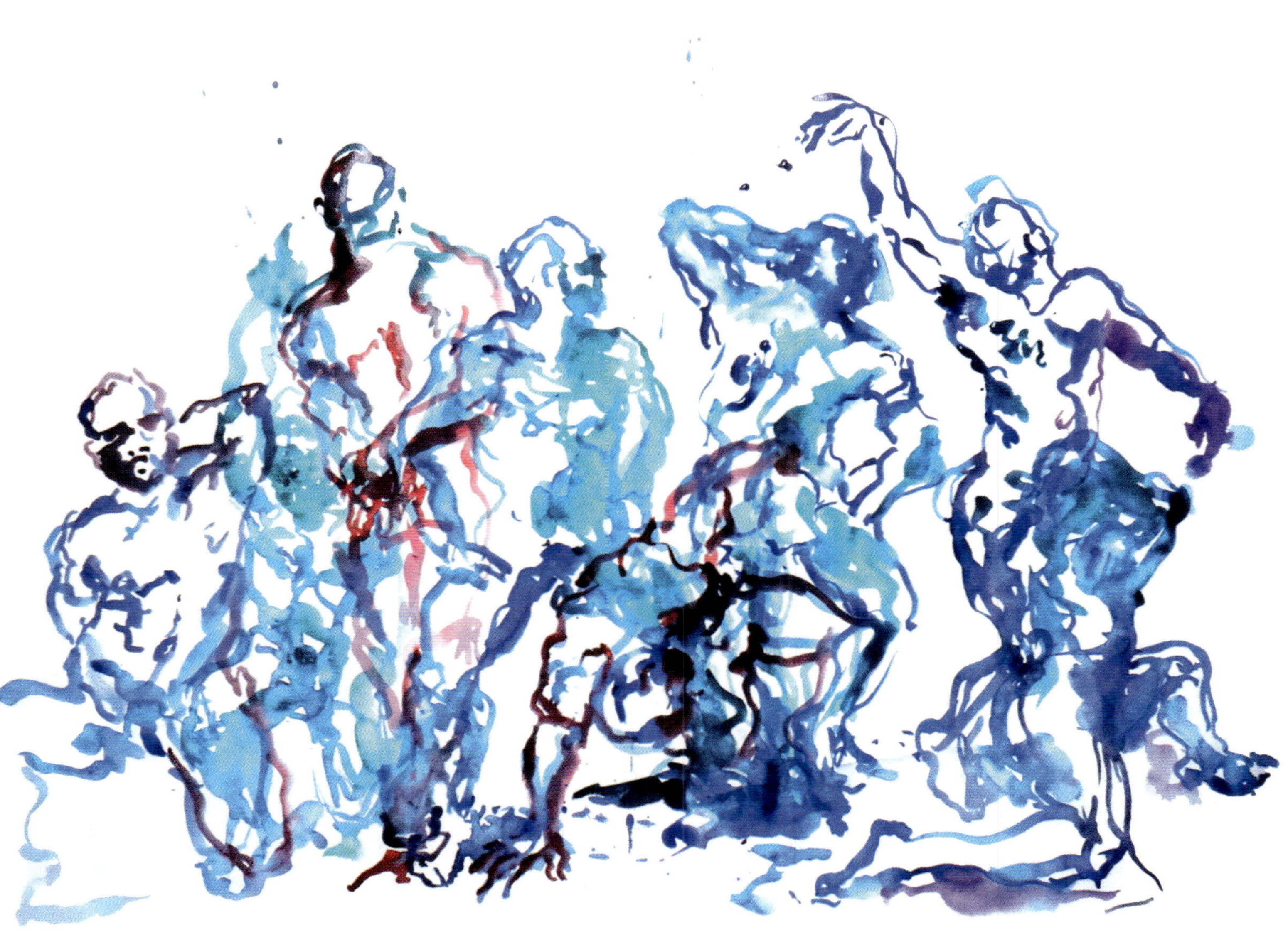

∧ Knowing When to Stop

I place the next pose in the white space on the left, balancing the composition. I'm now overlaying figures, so I introduce alizarin crimson to distinguish them. I'm careful to find a rhythm with this new colour to complement the blue. After eight figures, the composition is full of movement and variety, but not too busy. It's time to call it finished.

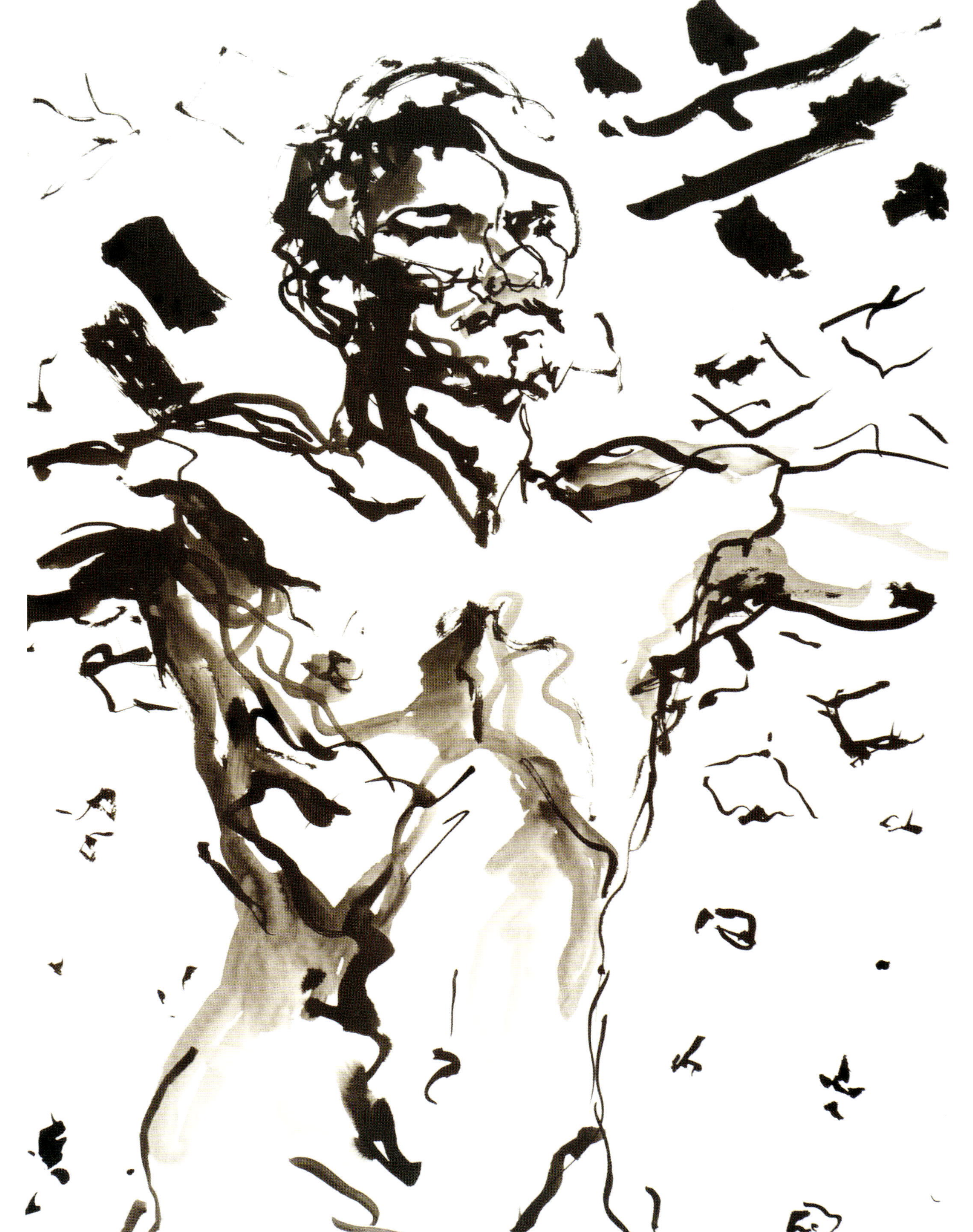

In the example on the previous page, you can see that I have worked with less water to prevent the figures from blending into a single amorphous mass. As a result, the expressive potential of the painted line shines through. It is immediate and intimate – and particularly suited to the nude.

A brush lacks the precision of a pen or pencil, and therein lies its magic. Press imperceptibly harder and the line will thicken; trail across the surface and the paint will dry to a scumble; move slowly to release more paint; move fast for an elegant taper. By continually experimenting, this highly nuanced relationship between you and your medium becomes increasingly personal.

To experiment with line, I like to use a Japanese ink brush with a round head and long bristles. It tapers to a fine point, which means a single brush can create a huge variety of strokes. You only have to look at the ink-painting traditions of China, Korea and Japan to see how expertly this can be handled.

This kind of painting highlights the difference between a natural sable and a synthetic head. The sable is typically made from the fur of the kolinsky, a type of weasel. The strong strands have a good 'snap', which means the brush head retains its shape. Each strand is covered in tiny scale-like fibres, which enables it to hold on to liquids and respond well to shifts in pressure.

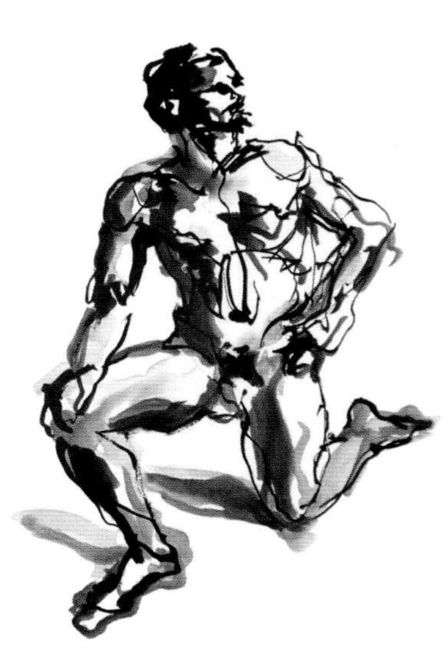

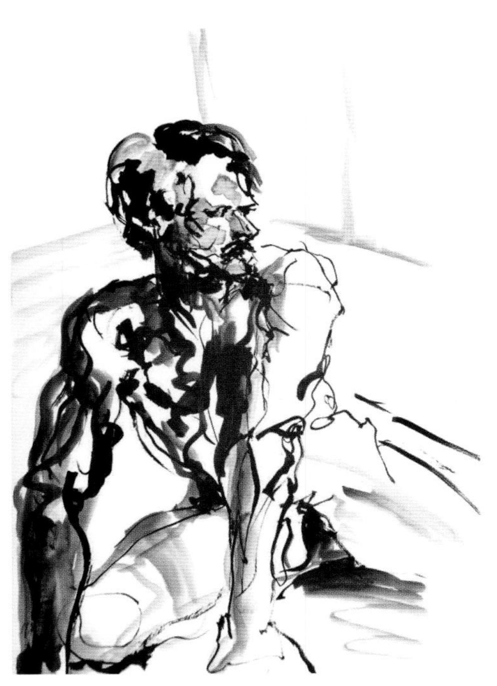

< ʌ Sam in Black Ink

In this session with Sam, I challenged myself to make as many different marks as possible with a single brush. Using black ink and a little water on a large sheet of paper, I let the brush dance over the page. Sam started with five-minute poses, then a fifteen-minute pose. He was standing on a printed cloth, which I used in the longer painting (shown left) to create abstract shapes in the space beyond, exploring more marks as I did so. Throughout, I maintained the same speed of mark making as for the shorter poses.

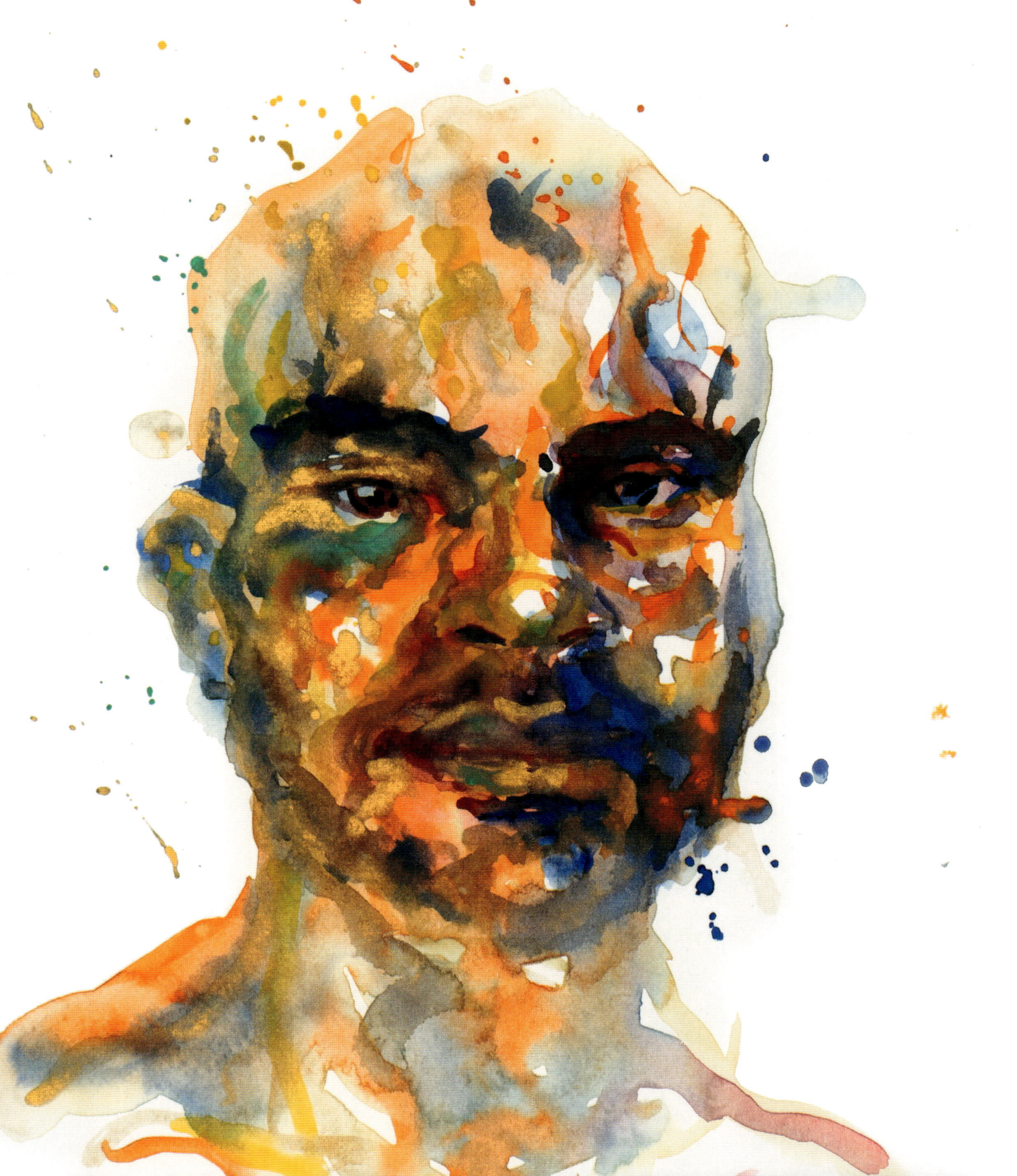

Maintaining Discipline

With quick poses, you have to work fast. With
longer poses, it's harder to maintain that discipline
of fresh observation and instinctive mark making.
There can be a temptation to plan and tentatively
draw guides to help you fill in the right colours
in the right place – and so the magic dissipates.
I find portraits especially dangerous because of
the added pressure of capturing a likeness.

For a longer pose, I like to start out with several
versions and work on them in parallel. I treat
the first marks as two-minute paintings, using
transparent pigments with a generous amount of
water. Over time, I add layers of marks, sometimes
putting one painting aside to dry while I work on
another. If one isn't working, I bash it around a bit
with flicks and risky marks to see what happens. By
the end, I have a series of paintings, some to be
discarded, some unfinished, and hopefully at least
one that captures the spontaneity of the moment,
the medium and the subject.

< Portrait of Roy

For this portrait of Roy, I wanted to combine a
direct likeness with the joy of splashing paint
around. I worked on several paintings side by
side, spending no more than a couple of minutes
on each at a time. I used line to explore the flow
across the surface of his head and wet-on-wet
washes to get an idea of colour balance. The
painting I took forward to completion began with
a light silhouette wash with drips and splashes to
diffuse any sense of an outline. I worked into the
mass of the form to give it solidity, then brought
definition to the features of the eyes, nose and
mouth. The whole thing, including the study
paintings, took no more than half an hour.

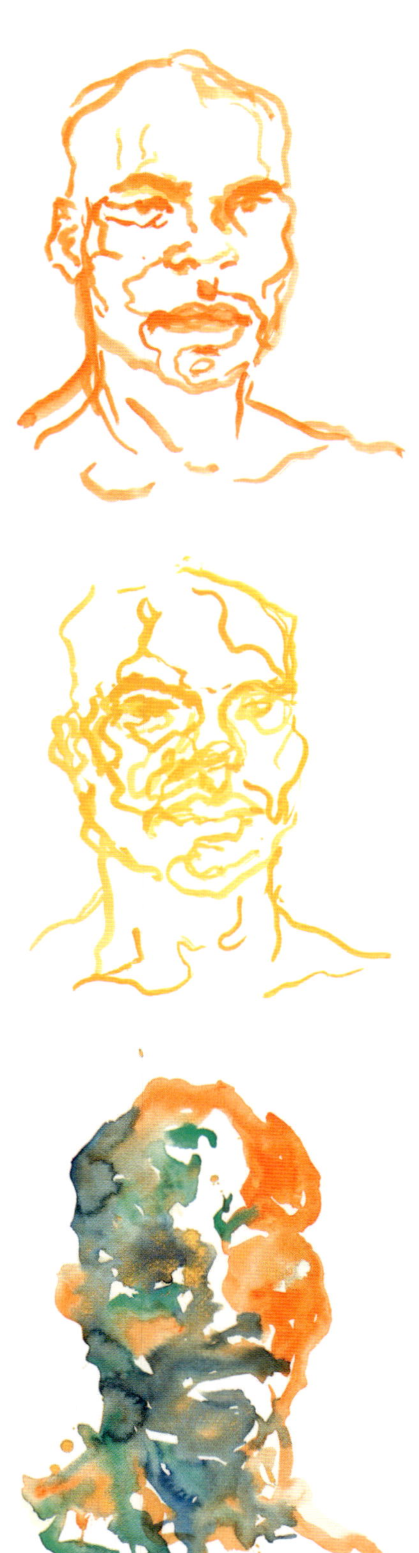

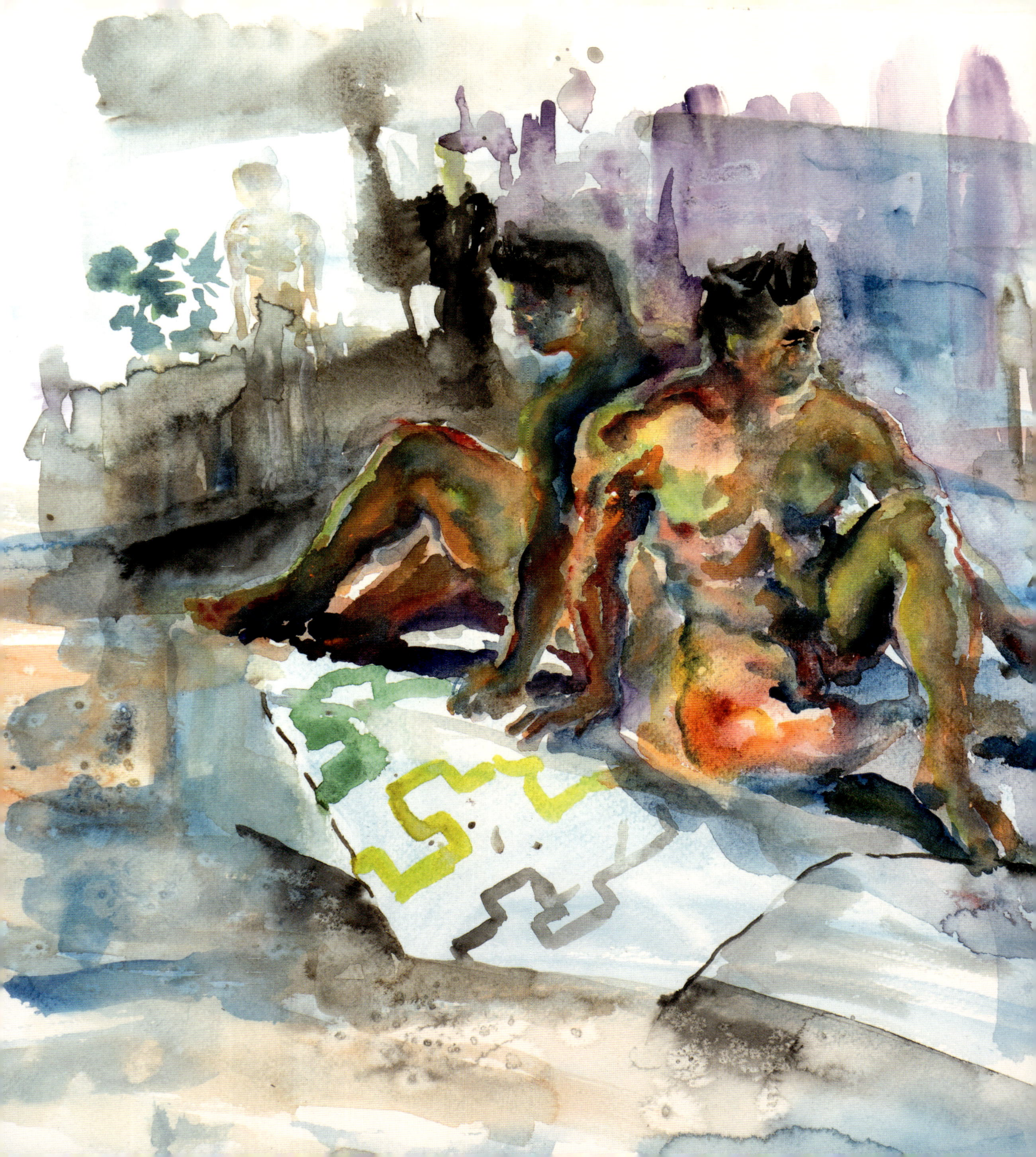

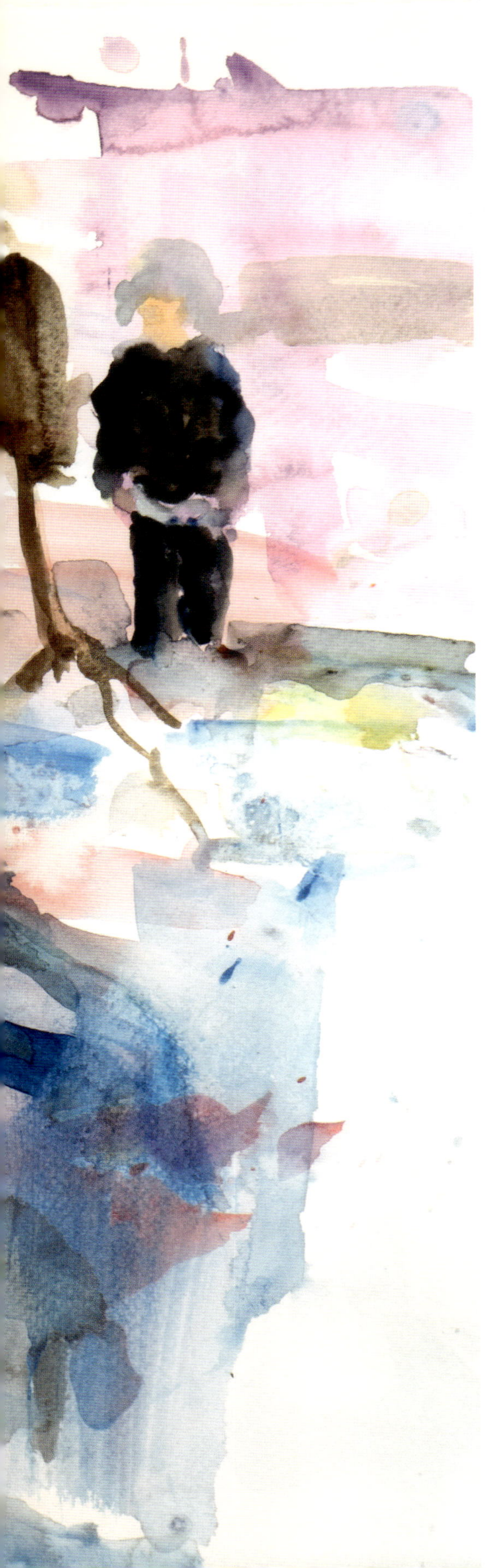

Another way to maintain the discipline of speed in a longer painting is to paint the same model in two poses in a single composition. The model alternates between each pose every five or ten minutes. Each pose must be carefully marked so the model can return to it with minimal delay.

This continued switch between presence and absence forces the painter to feel the impact of the figure on the space. The regular interruptions give little opportunity to become fixated on a detail and provoke a re-evaluation of the composition as a whole. Furthermore, as the two figures develop a presence in the same space on your page, they will reveal a relationship, drawing you into an unexpected story.

< Kam at Maggi's
Kam modelled for our painting group in a seated pose on a plinth. After ten minutes, he moved to a different seated pose facing in the other direction. With Kam alternating between the two positions and my fellow painters working at speed, the room was alive with movement. At one point, a new figure appeared directly in my line of vision. In a few seconds, I included her in the composition on the right, pairing her apparition with the static skeleton in front of the window on the left.

Beware What Pleases You

The more you paint, the more likely you are to chance upon tricks and habits that please you. You'll find shortcuts to represent the figure and techniques for manipulating the paint. With this comes the danger of shifting from persistent observation and truth into complacency.

To fight against this and refresh the joy of accidental discovery, I continually return to quick mark making. If I'm in the middle of a painting and feel stuck, I'll put it aside, shift my perspective and bash out a few quick studies, anywhere from thirty seconds to two minutes each. I'm then ready to go back into battle.

Sometimes, I have a malaise right from the start of the session and don't know how I'm going to find something creative to say. I prepare myself for a series of two-minute paintings. I may use my less dominant hand or paint without looking at the paper. I may start with some splashes and random marks and let the figure emerge from within them. Whichever approach I take, the moment the timer bleeps, I rip up my painting so that nobody – not even I – can judge the result. In this way, I am focused exclusively on observation and connecting with my subject and medium.

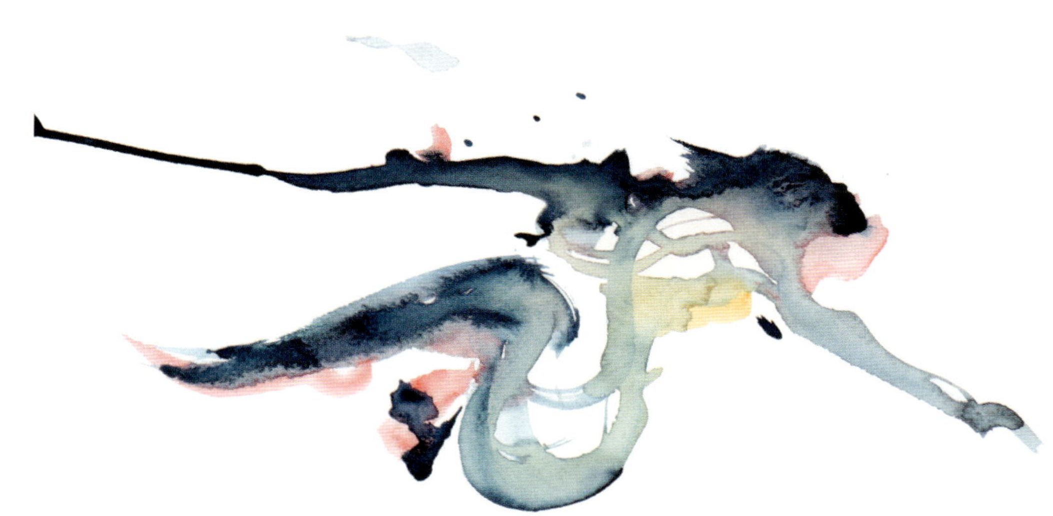

Around the time of this session
with Lidia, I had been animating
a series of watercolour parakeets
(see page 108). As I read Lidia's
gestures, I imagined that she too
was a bird in flight. This gave me
a completely fresh perspective
for my painting.

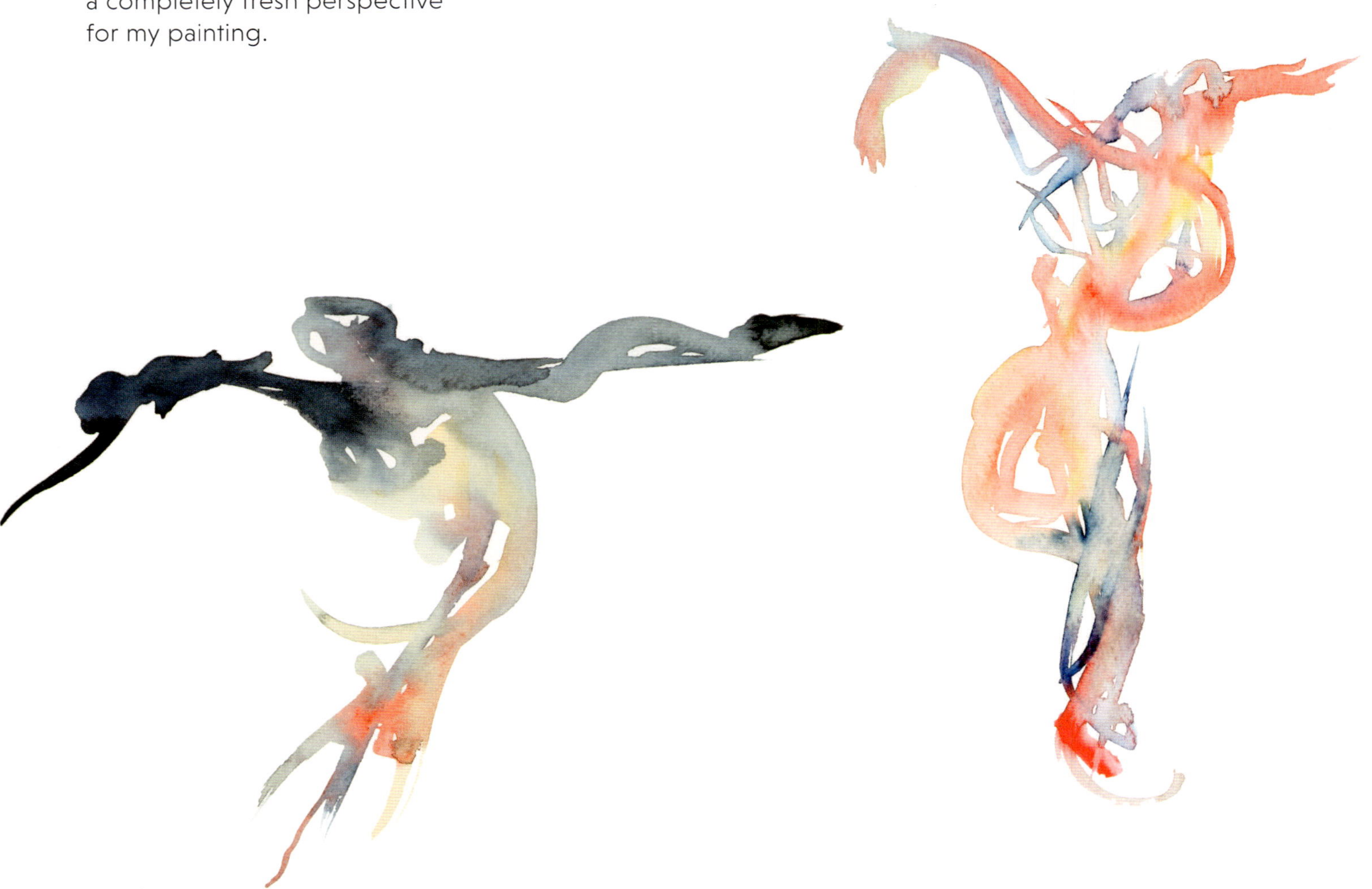

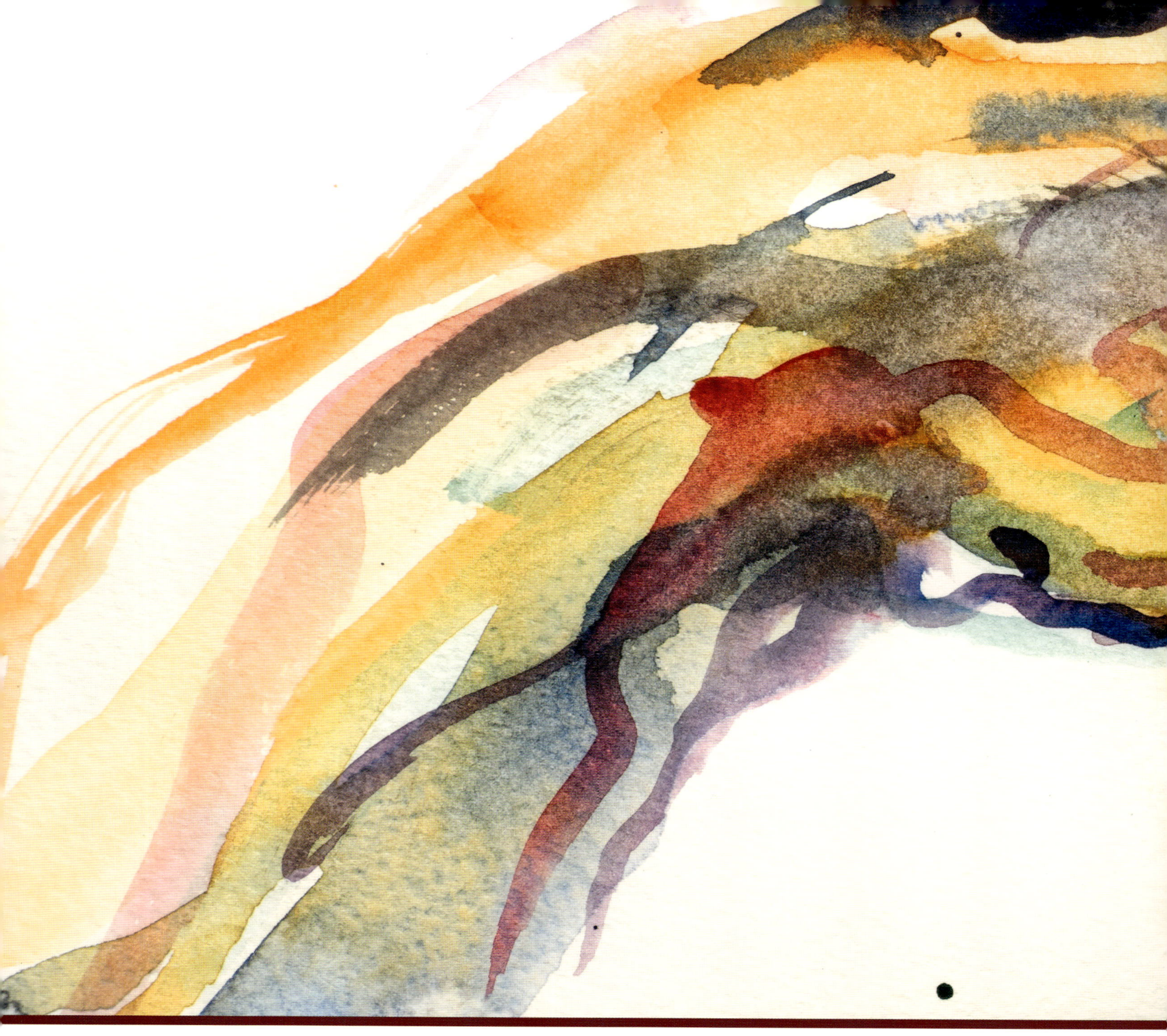

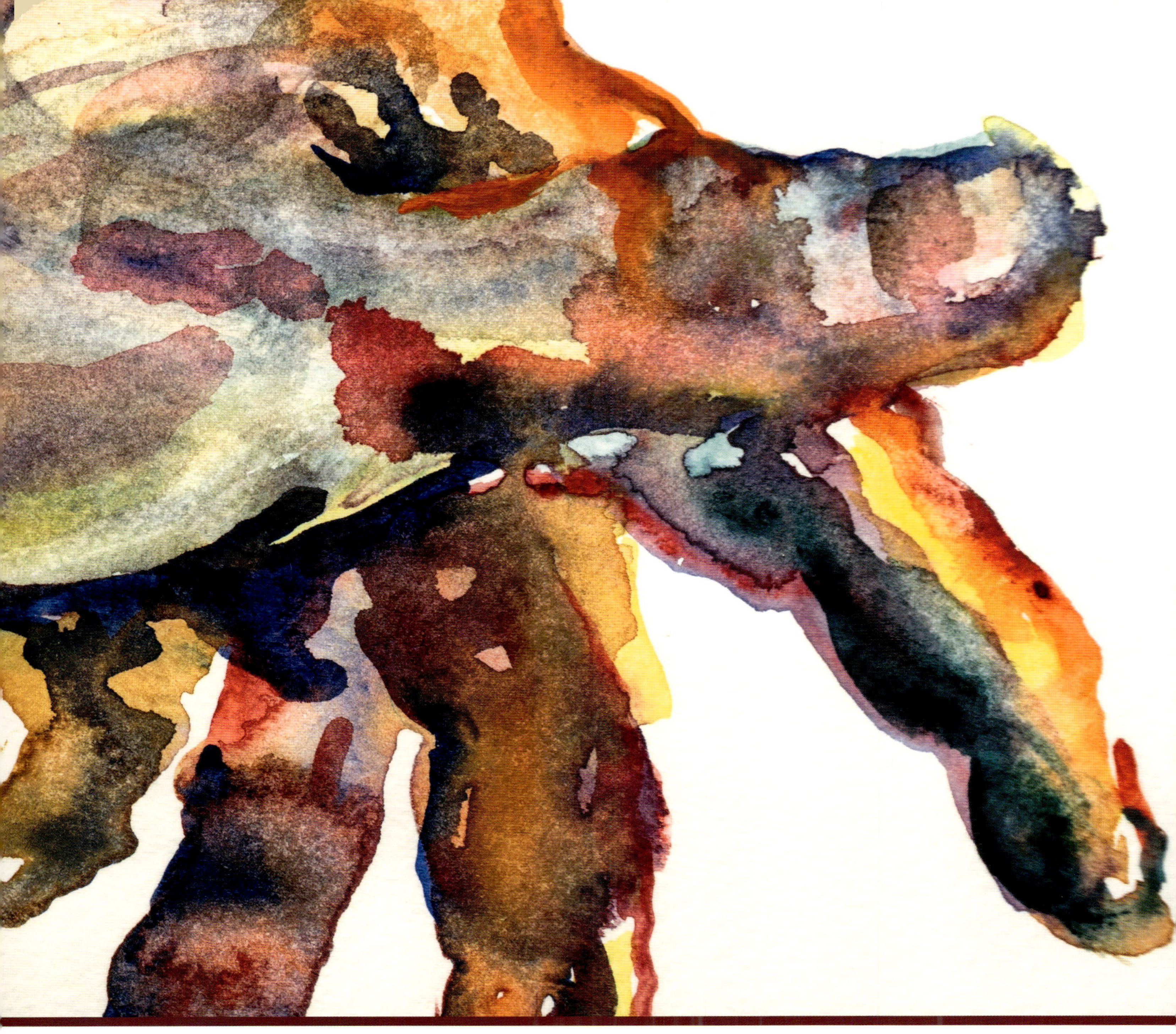

Gesture

The human body is full of expressive gestures, from how we place our feet or tighten our fists to a curl in our shoulders or how we puff out our chests. This tells us the emotional state of a fellow human: are they a threat or threatened, joyful or lost in thought? Real or imagined, starting from this human context can breathe life into a painting.

In this section, we'll explore how to read the gesture of a pose and how the head, hands and feet can accentuate it. We'll also dip into gesture stories and the narrative possibilities of a sequence of poses.

> **Kam Dancing**

In this series of poses, Kam performed a gesture that started low, his weight driving down into the floor. Pose by pose, he unfurled his body into a confident standing stance, arms raised above his head. I layered my paintings to find the relationships between the poses and a fluidity of movement suggesting a dance.

'You feel there is this attention that's focused on you, and you know that you are performing. You know that you are giving something. It feels like there's a kind of an embrace. I'm imagining something from the centre of me and extending out to my fingertips, to the toes . . . I'm really thinking about how the whole body is embodying a gesture or is in mid-motion, and I feel that extending out to my fingertips and to my head and where I'm looking – the direction I'm facing – going out to the artist. Maybe it's a very, very slow kind of dance, but I *am* kind of dancing.'

Kam

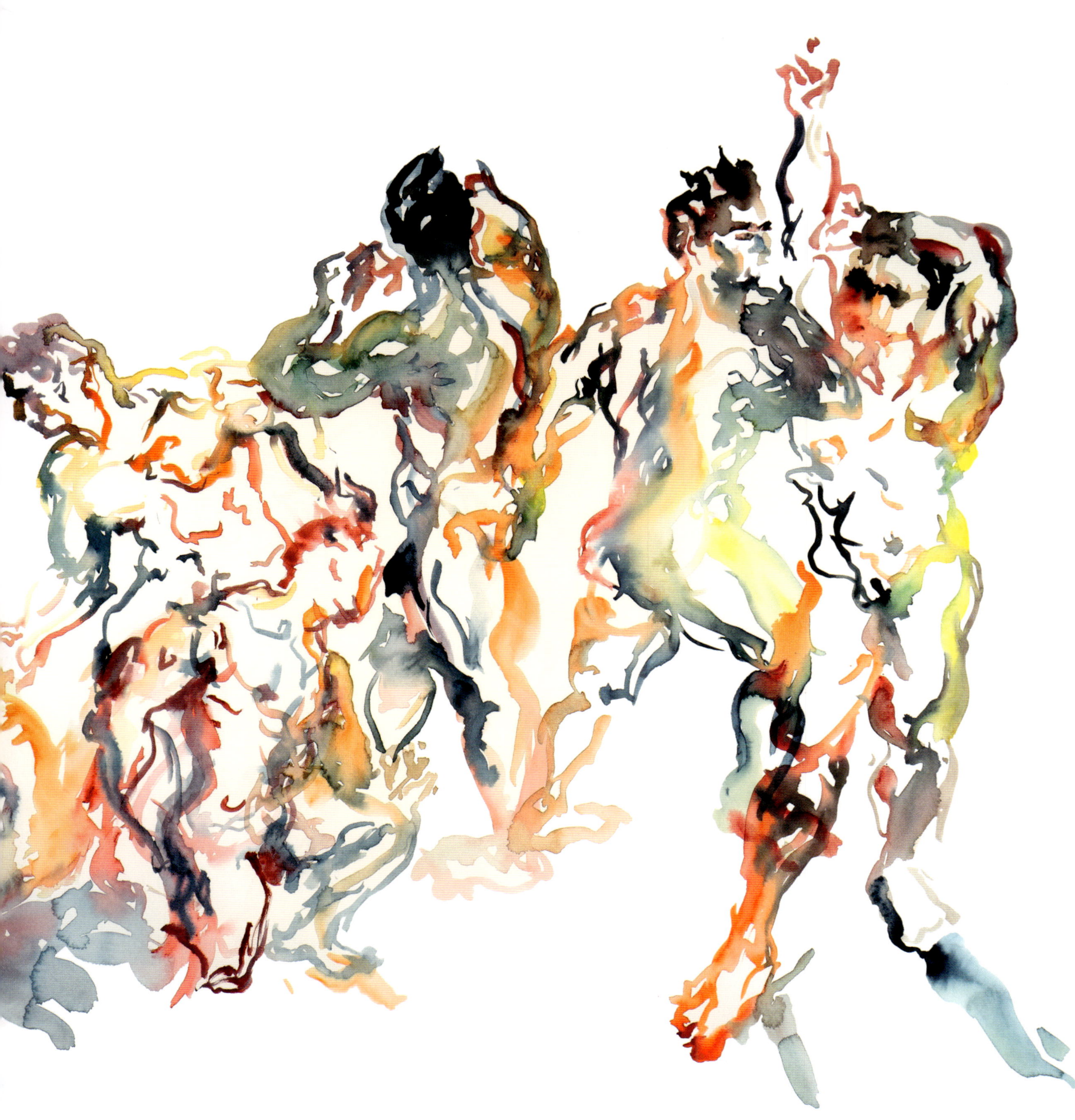

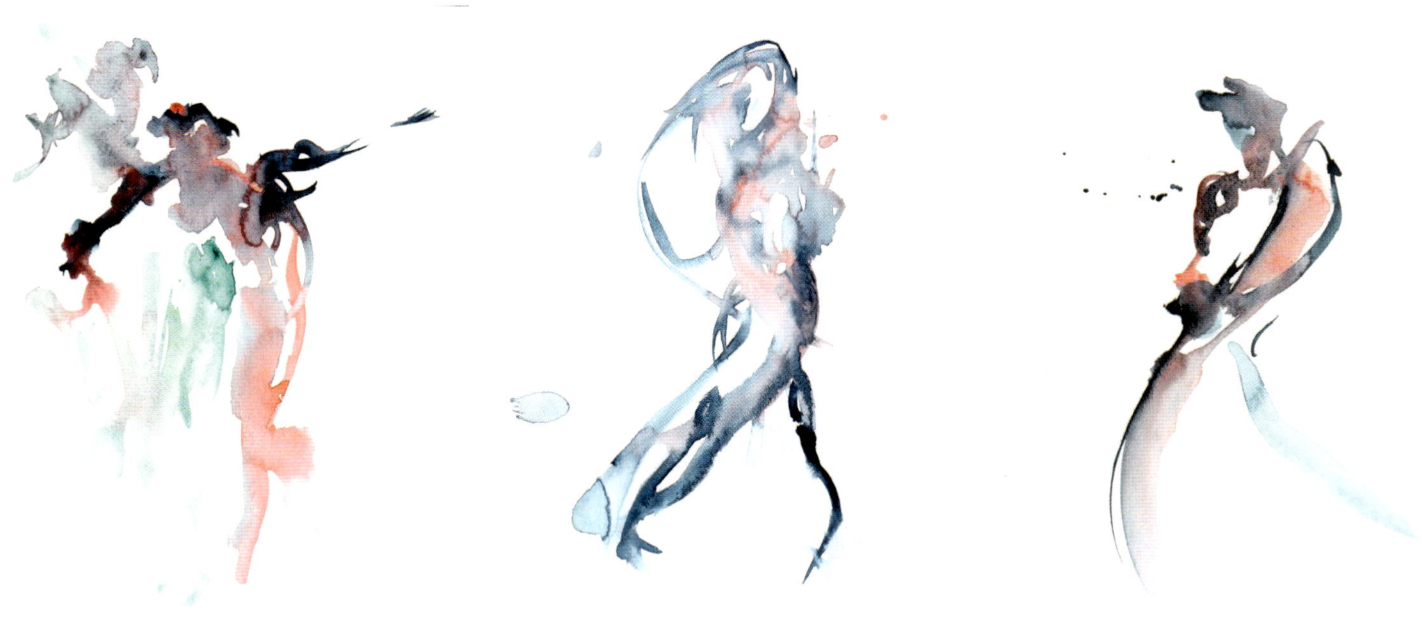

Line of Action

Before I make a mark, I read the pose and feel the gesture: twisting, reaching, reclining, leaning. Energy flows through the body, driven by this action. No longer do I see a collection of anatomical parts, but a purposeful being caught in motion.

This energy flow is sometimes referred to as the line of action. This imaginary line could describe movement, sweeping up as the figure reaches for the stars; it could echo the S-curve of the spine in a *contrapposto* pose (with most of the weight on one leg); or it could emphasize weight or inertia as the model slumps into a chair. The direction of the line is critical: does it lift the model up, weigh them down, propel them forward, pull them back?

To get to grips with this concept, I ask the model to give me a series of twenty-second dynamic poses. For the first ten seconds, I read the pose, imagining it as part of a sequence. If the model is reaching up, have they leapt up to this position, continuing to reach further? Or perhaps they've found the limit of their reach and are about to collapse down. Is this pose the beginning, middle or end of a mini gesture-story?

With this in mind, I use the final seconds to make a few marks representing the line of action.

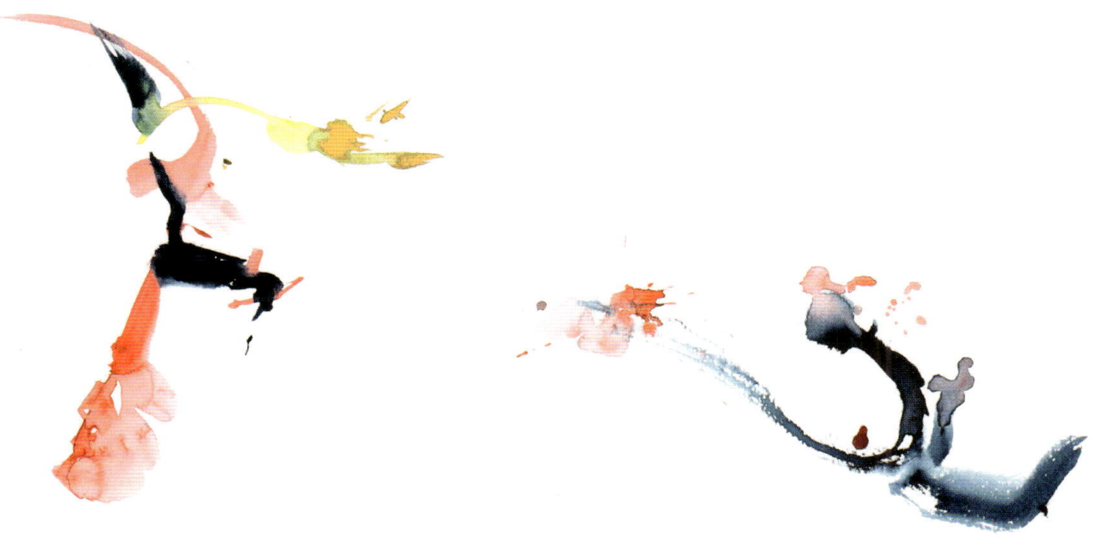

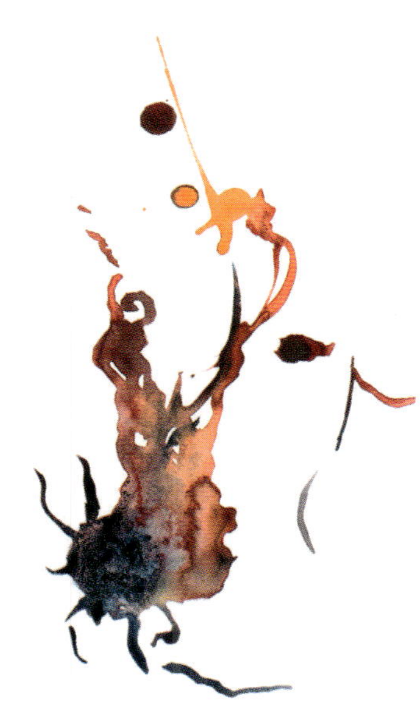

⋀ Abstracting the Form

Working with Lidia is an energetic experience. Her training in physical theatre gives her a particular understanding of her body that transcends anatomy. There is an abstraction of form, which became the focus of this series of gesture poses. You can see how I work through the sequence, progressing from the comfort of figurative shapes to a purer representation of energy flow.

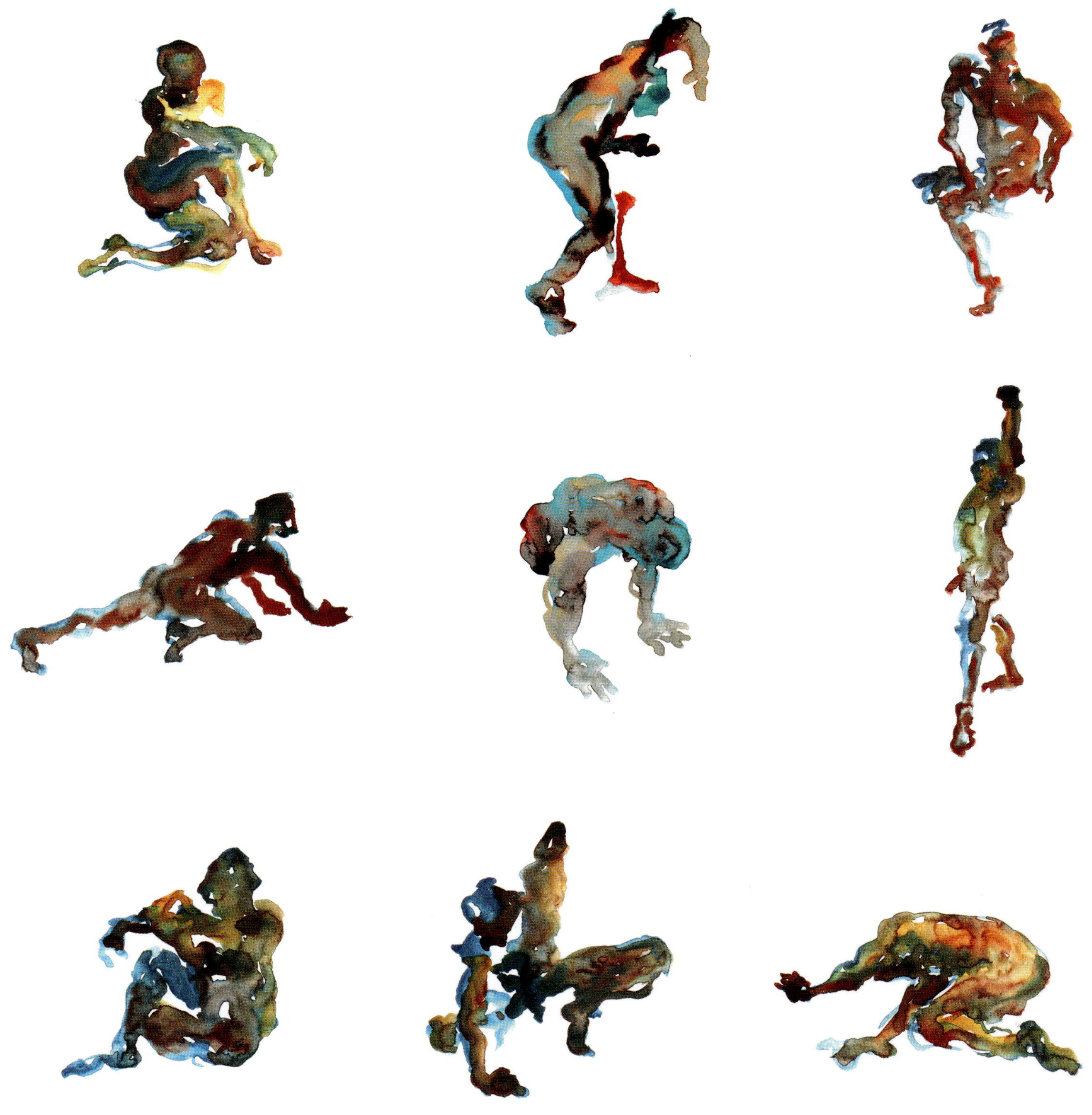

Silhouette

Working in tandem with the line of action is the silhouette. From a distance, the silhouette is our first clue to a gesture. Is the figure standing legs apart, hands on hips, confronting us? Are the limbs curled into the mass of the body in an act of self-preservation?

Sometimes a silhouette can be hard to read as human. Perhaps the head is tucked in and a limb protruding unexpectedly. You can use this to abstract the form or to accentuate a feeling of awkwardness. But if you want to convey a clear action, you can shift your perspective until the silhouette is more legible.

When reading a silhouette, I'm careful not to view it as a shape with a crisply defined outline. It is a container for the body's energy, firm in some parts, porous in others. It should work with the line of action, emphasizing the flow of energy through the figure and beyond.

< Roy Silhouettes
For these two-minute poses, I wanted to explore the power of the solid form. Working wet on wet, I allow a limited palette of colours to bleed into each other. Rather than abstracting the form, I wanted each painting to read clearly as a figure performing an action: twisting, curling, reaching, crouching, rising.

Breaking the Form

As with the silhouette, outlines can be as
dangerous as they are helpful. A crisp outline will
trap the energy of a gesture in a particular spot or
redirect it elsewhere. When used too freely, this
can stultify the energy flow, preventing the eye
from enjoying its journey through the figure. It's
like underlined text: used sparingly, it has power;
too much and it loses focus and rhythm.

To avoid the temptation of drawing outlines, I
deliberately start as far into the mass of the figure
as I can. From here, I work outwards, back in and
out again, following the three-dimensional way
the skin wraps around the figure. I ask myself, if
I shifted my perspective, would the mark still be
valid? The more I think like this, the greater the
sense of depth, allowing the gesture to flow
into the space beyond.

Portrait of Matthew >
I began this painting with a light wash over the whole paper. I made
my first marks to find the silhouette with dilute paint, watching them
bleed into the damp paper. As the paper dried, I concentrated on
the gesture: Matthew leaning in as we chatted about life, art and
everything in between. I made the head dark and solid too quickly,
so I added water, dabbed off some of the pigment and sprinkled
salt to move what remained into little clusters of energy. I added
detail and substance to emphasize the leaning in, concentrating
on the contours of Matthew's face flowing into his neck and right
shoulder. The rest, I allowed to blur off into the distance. The crisp
detail draws the eye, pulling the viewer into our conversation.

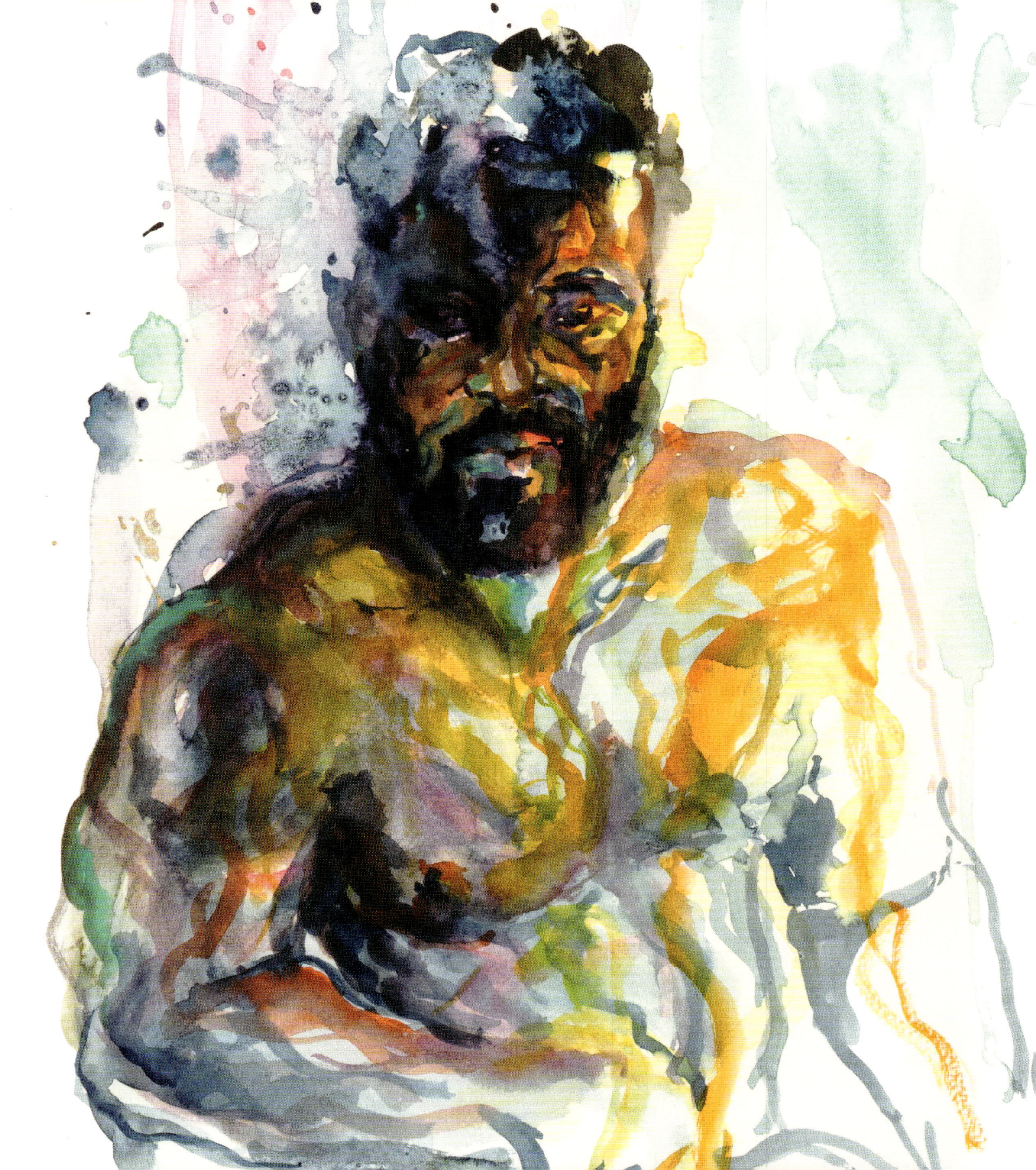

Hands and Feet

The gesture of a pose can be accentuated by the hands and feet. Relaxed, clenched, contorted, extended: they are the punctuation mark of an exclamation, enquiry or quiet statement.

The feet are often the foundation of the gesture: are they planted apart squarely, turned in nervously, or fleetingly on tiptoe? Are they absorbing a heavy line of action or initiating it in an upwards spurt of energy? The way the feet connect with the floor will determine the weight of the pose.

Hands and feet are complex, segmented parts of the anatomy, but should only be as detailed as the rest of the painting – unless you want them to be the focal point of the composition. They are simply extensions of the line through the limbs.

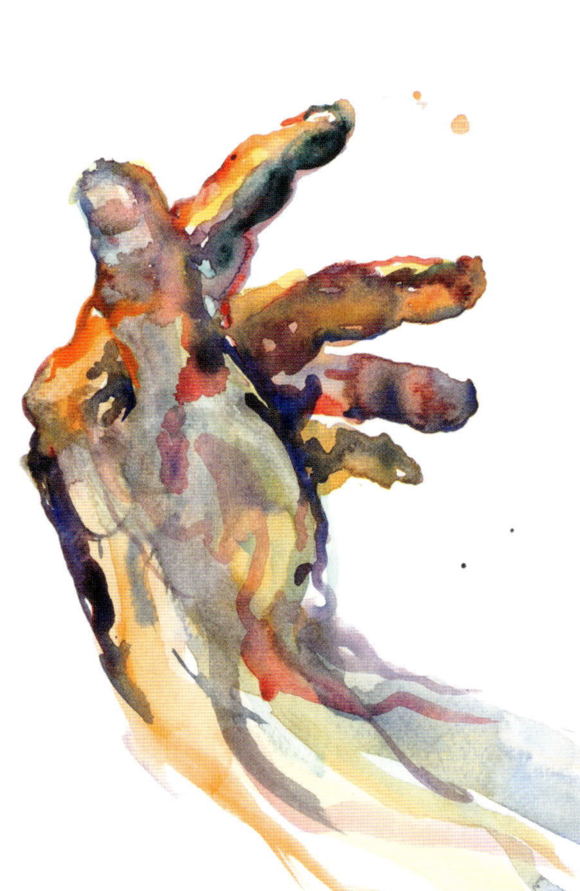

^ Hand Gestures
I made these hand studies with the same attention to gesture, line of action and silhouette as in a full figure. My aim was to find a flow through the wrist into the hand and out through the fingers.

> Poised for Action

Matthew is known for his muscular frame, and yet his poses remain poised and active, like a boxer. I noticed that this starts with the way his feet connect with the ground. I wanted to represent this in a two-minute study.

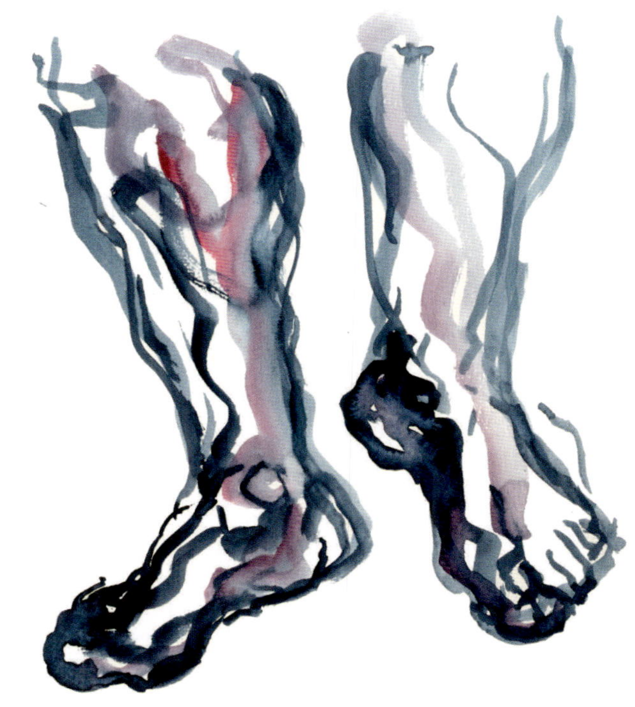

v Dramatic Gestures

In short poses, the model can use hands and feet to increase drama. Here Roy (below left) puts all his weight into his hands, pushing against the floor to raise his upper body. Lidia (below right) embodies a gesture of joyful abandon, her energy flowing through the curve of her body and out through the pointed toes of her extended foot.

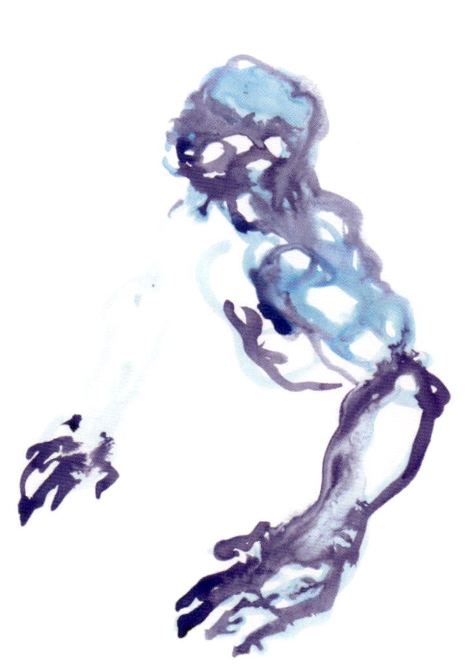

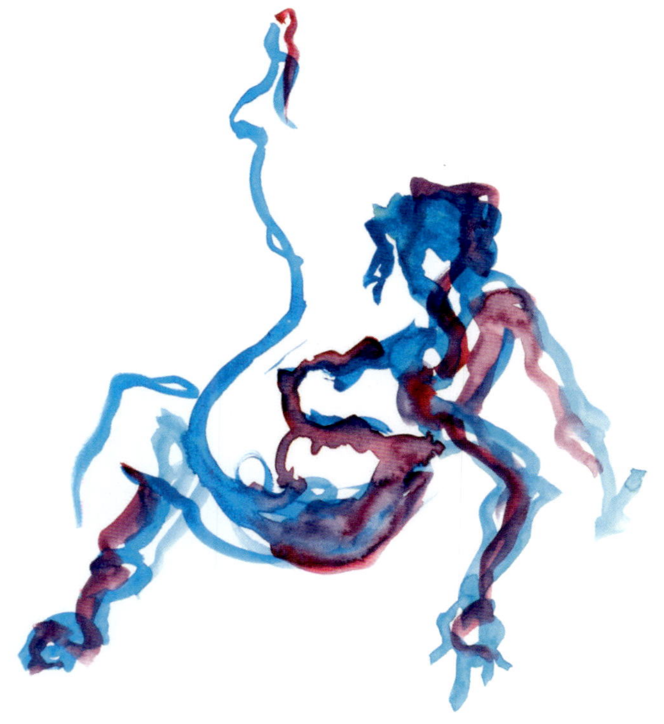

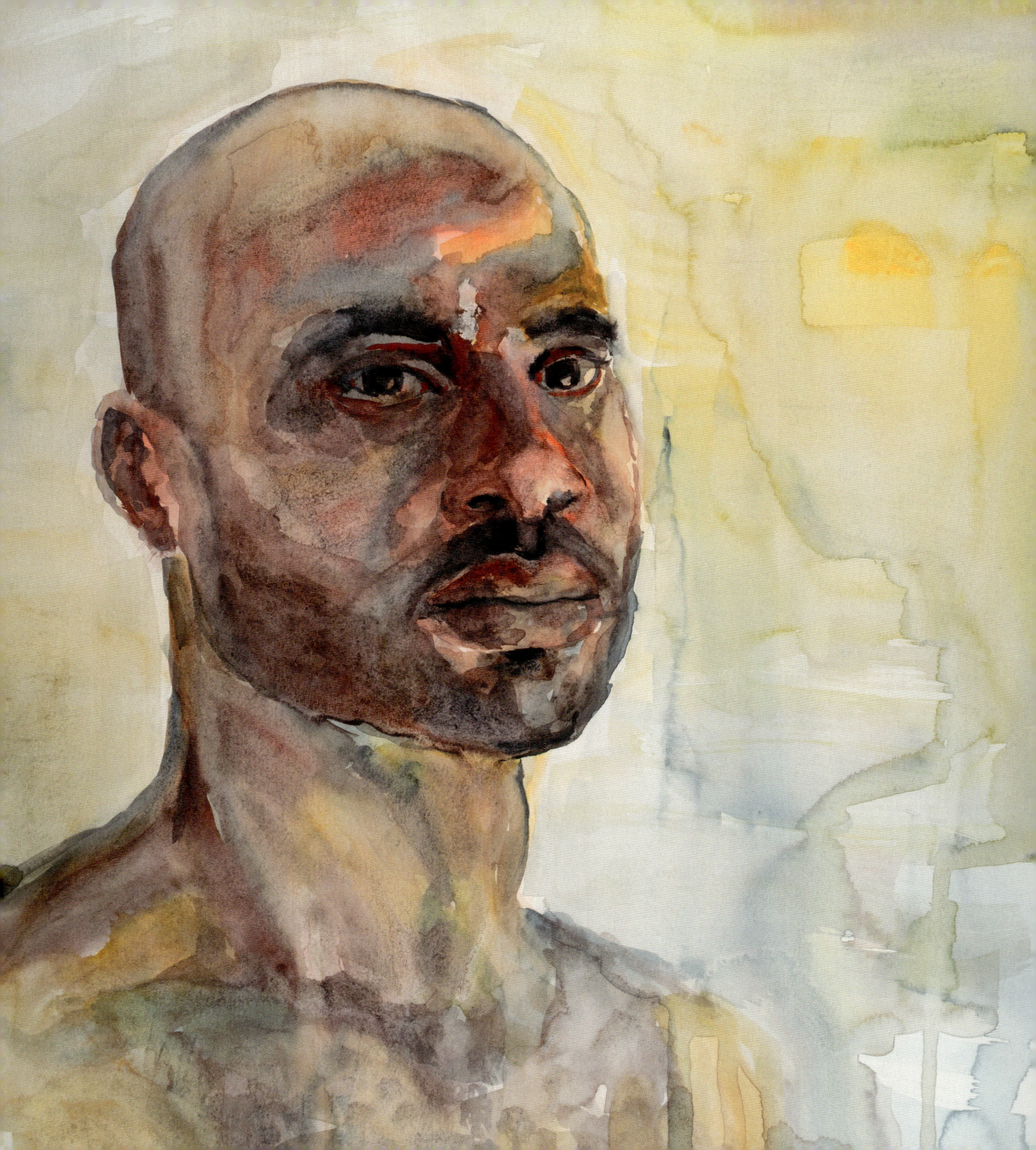

The Head

< **Roy at Whiteford Temple**
The warm sun was streaming through the French windows on a late afternoon in August. There was an atmosphere of calm contemplation as Roy half-turned towards me, gazing into the middle distance. I painted light layers of wash to build up a subtle palette of colours. When the gesture of the head and the neck on the shoulders had emerged, I added the finer detail of the features.

The head is also an important element of the gesture. Often the line of action starts or ends here, flowing through the figure via the spine. This is particularly true if the action comes from an emotional state driven by the head: headlong, clear-headed, heady and so on.

In close-up, the head can convey the most nuanced of gestures. We can read how it sits on the neck and shoulders. Does the tilt imply confidence, curiosity, uncertainty, fear? Does the head confront us or turn away? Then we can turn our attention to the features of the face and the infinite combinations of gestures that communicate emotion.

> **Curling In**
In these two poses, Roy is curling in on himself. The gestures are completed by tucking his head into the mass of his body.

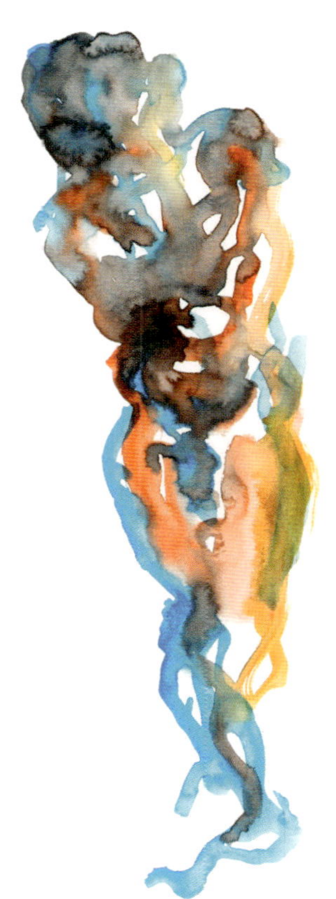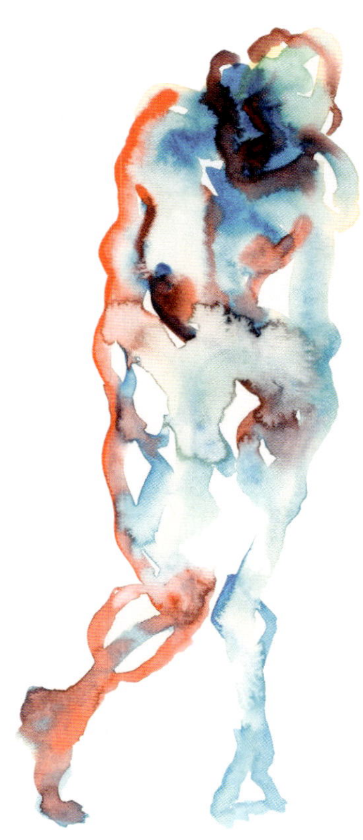

Key Poses in a Sequence

Every gesture has its story. Where did the action start? Where is it going? Is it driven by a particular emotional state? This story can be played out visually with a sequence of poses.

As an animator, this is familiar territory to me: finding the key poses that describe an action. Perhaps the model is undressing, freezing at moments when the limit of a movement is reached: bending down to untie a shoe, or stretching up to pull a T-shirt over their head. Perhaps they are extending pose by pose from a crouch to a stretch, or curling in on themselves.

Connecting one pose to the next also helps me understand the mechanics of the body in space: the extent of a stretch, the rotation of a joint, the re-balancing of weight.

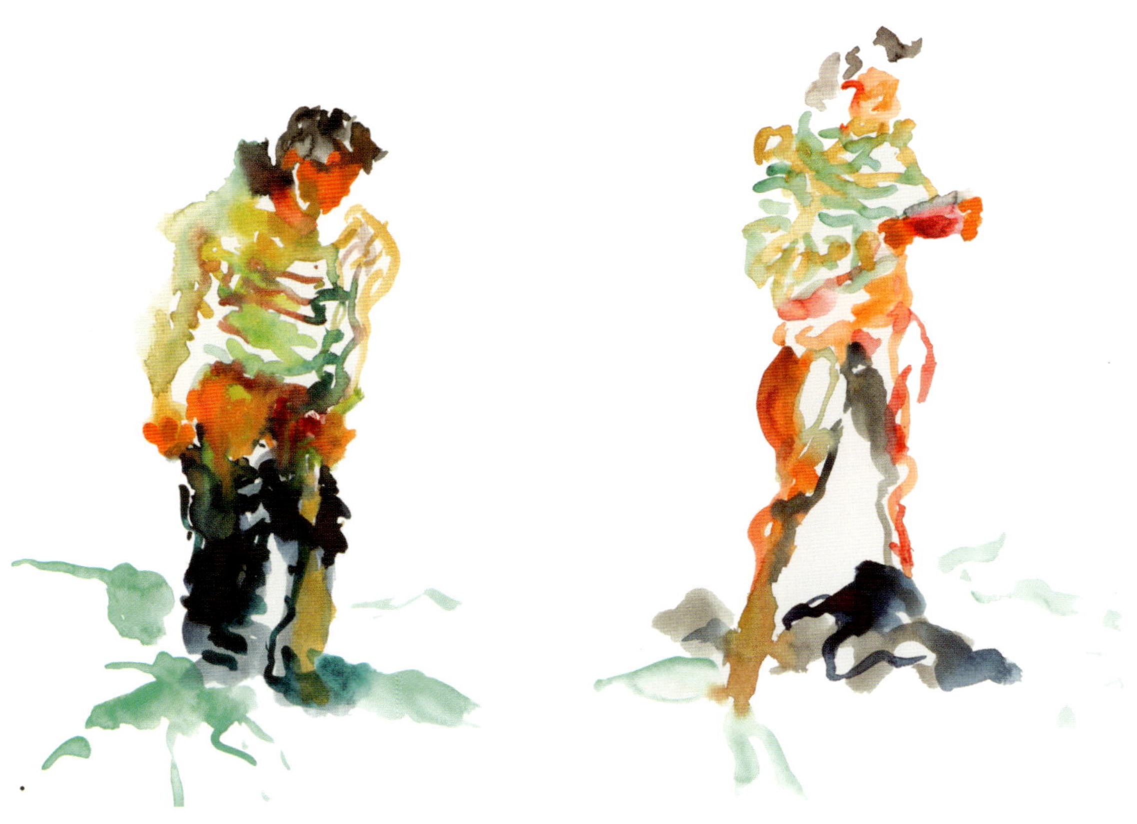

v Lidia Undressing

As we began our session, Lidia used the act of undressing for a sequence of warm-up poses. At each frozen moment, she ensured that the pose had its tension and interest: the stance of the feet, the tilt of the hips, and a purposeful reveal of the bright pink T-shirt under her jumper. You can see in the first couple of poses, I am still getting my eye in, feeling my way around her figure and connecting with paint and paper. By the final pose, I have found confident, gestural marks and am ready to get stuck into the full session.

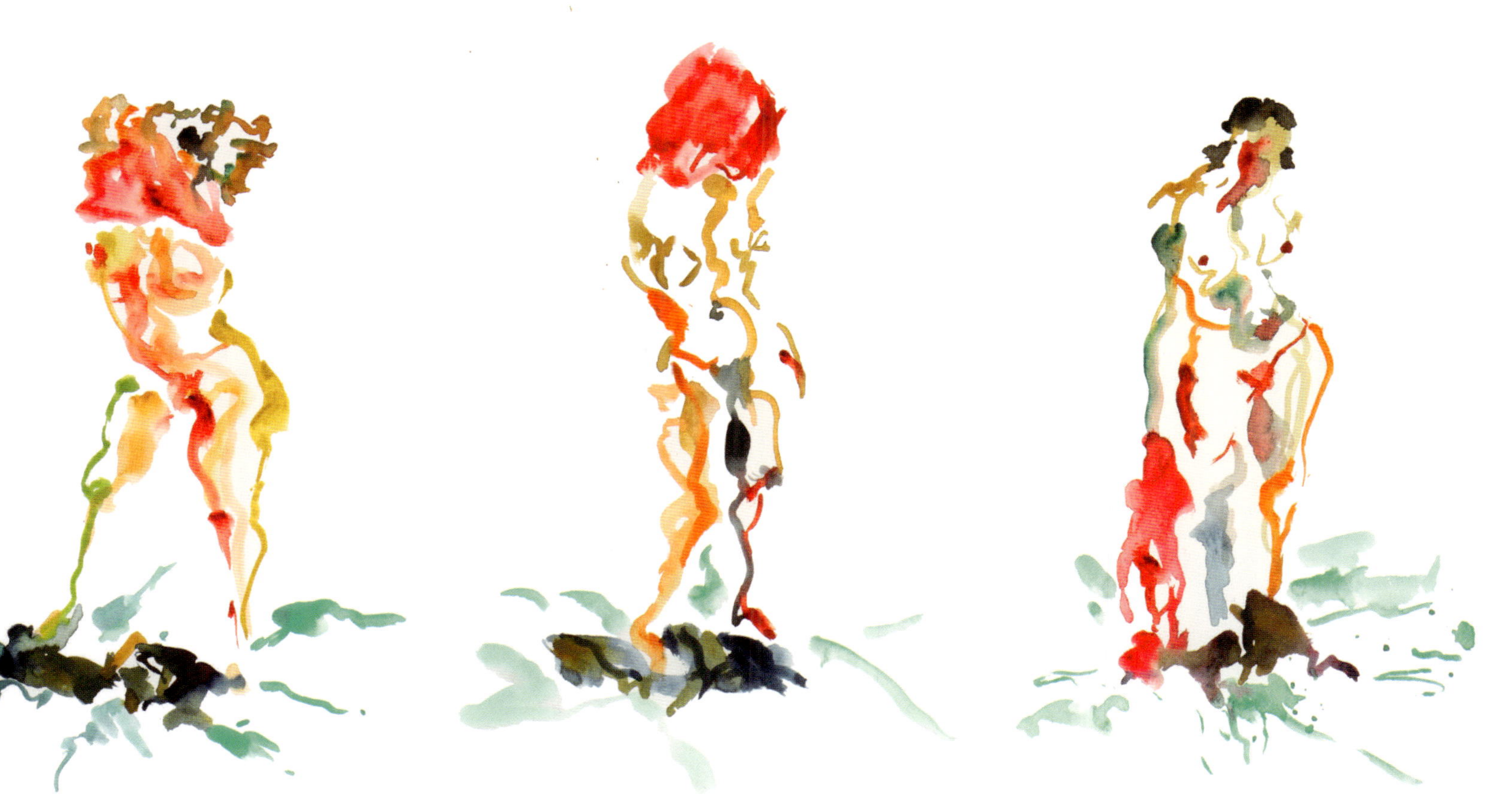

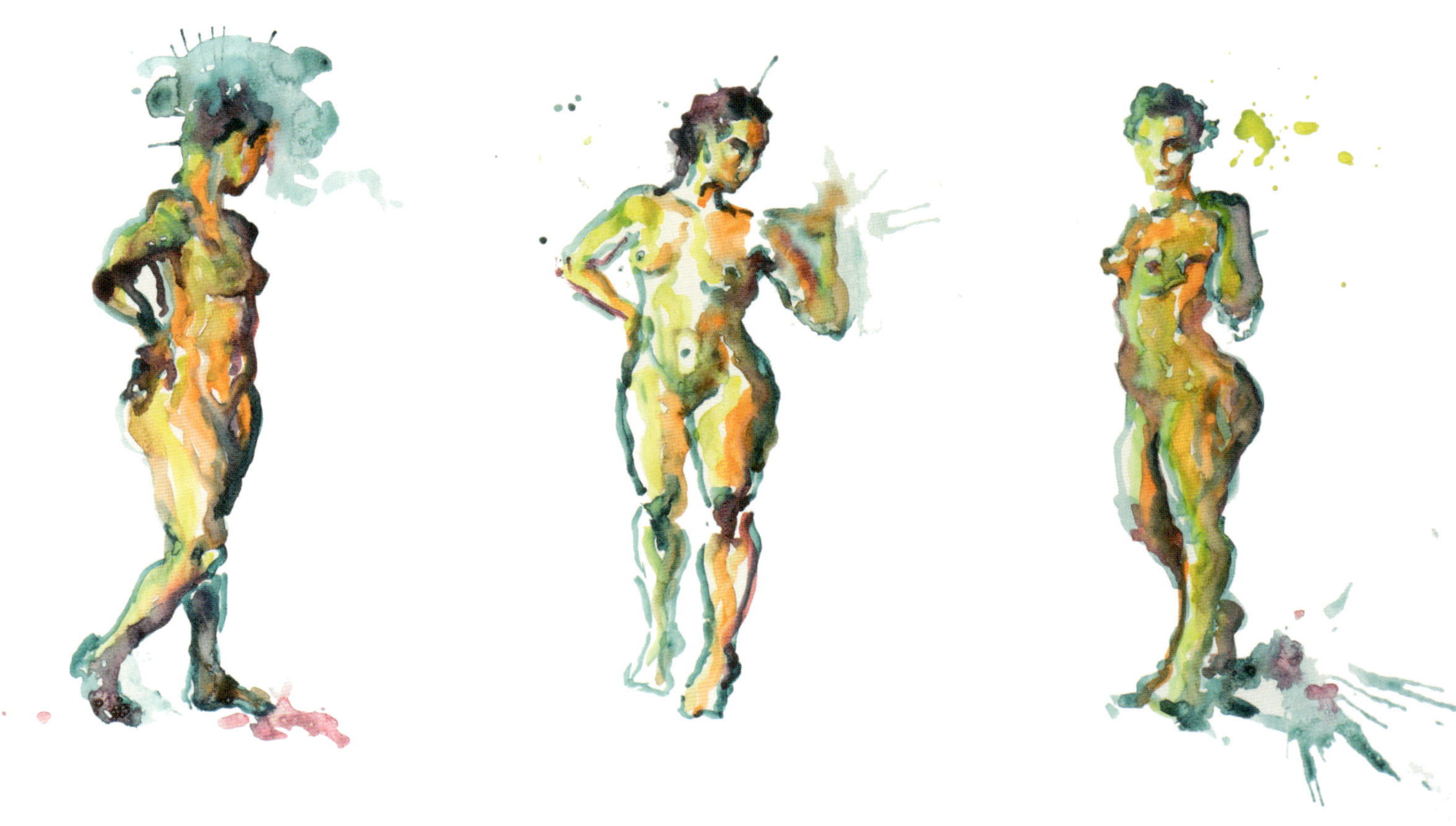

Rotating Sequences

A sequence of poses can be used to delve deeper into one specific gesture. The model adopts a pose and rotates little by little until they have turned a full 360 degrees.

The painter captures the pose from each new angle, seeing how the line of action and silhouette shift according to the perspective.

For this to work well, the model needs to create a pose that works from multiple viewpoints. You can see some great examples in Italian Baroque sculpture, when artists moved from the front-on pose of the Classical tradition to contorted, tense figures to be marvelled at in the round. If you want to re-create these poses with a model, bear in mind that the sculptors often exaggerated the pose beyond what would be humanly possible.

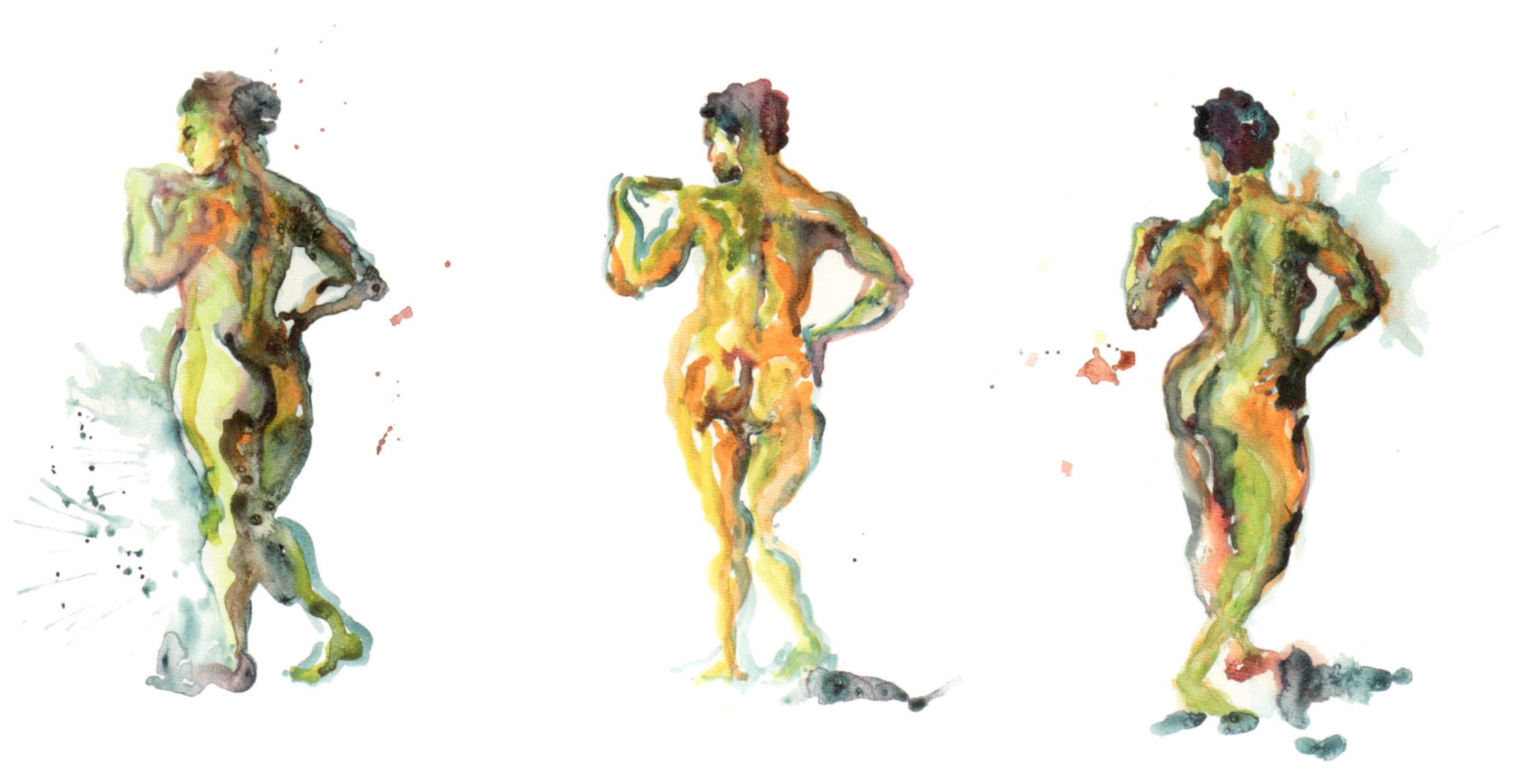

∧ **Maya 360**

For this sequence, I worked with Maya to create
a spinning animation. With a careful balancing of
weight, asymmetrical limbs and turn of the head,
they created a pose that worked well in the round.
Through a series of five-minute poses, they shifted
direction until they had made a complete rotation.
These paintings are animated in the film *Nude
Triumphant*, a still of which can be seen on page 111.

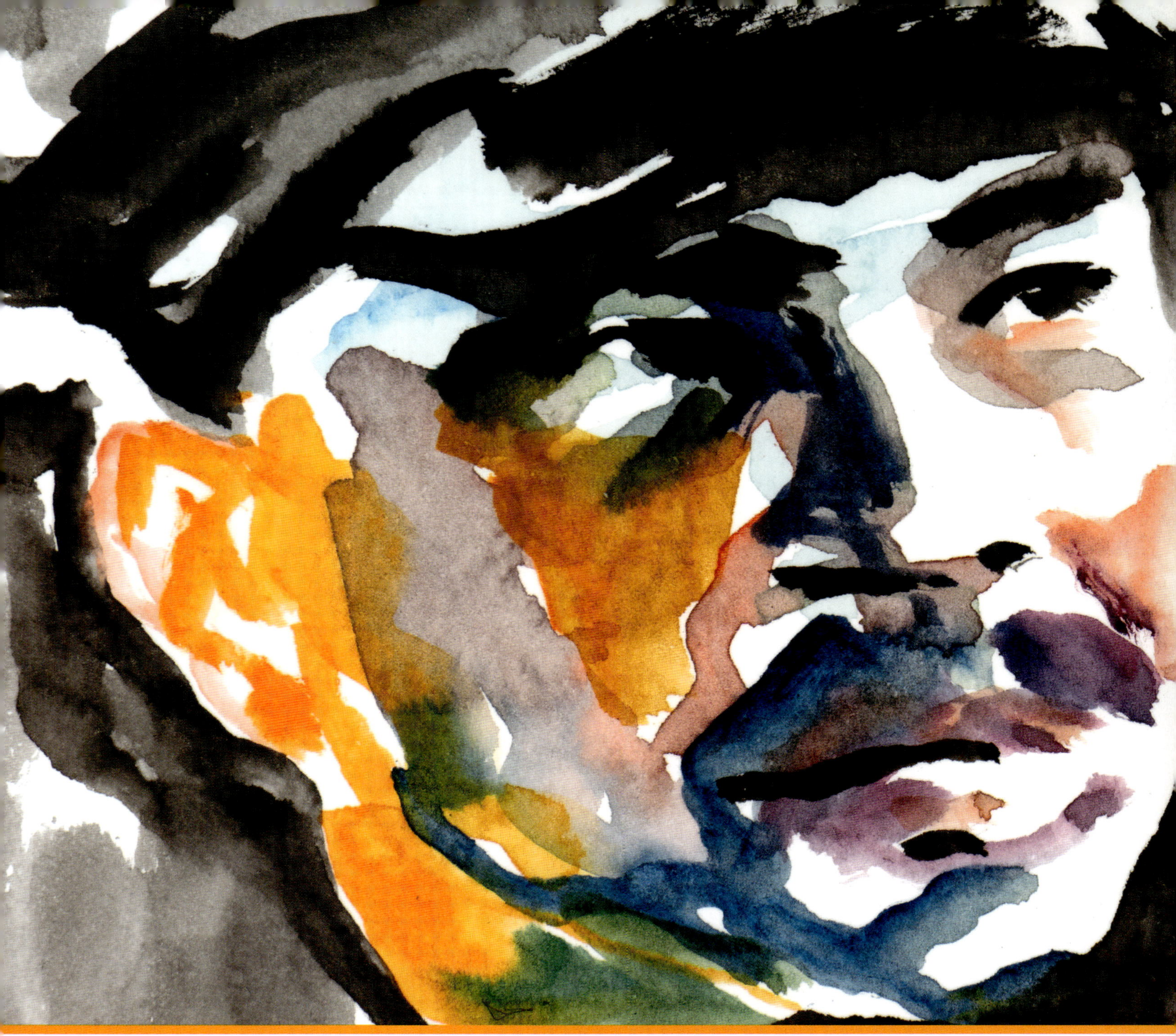

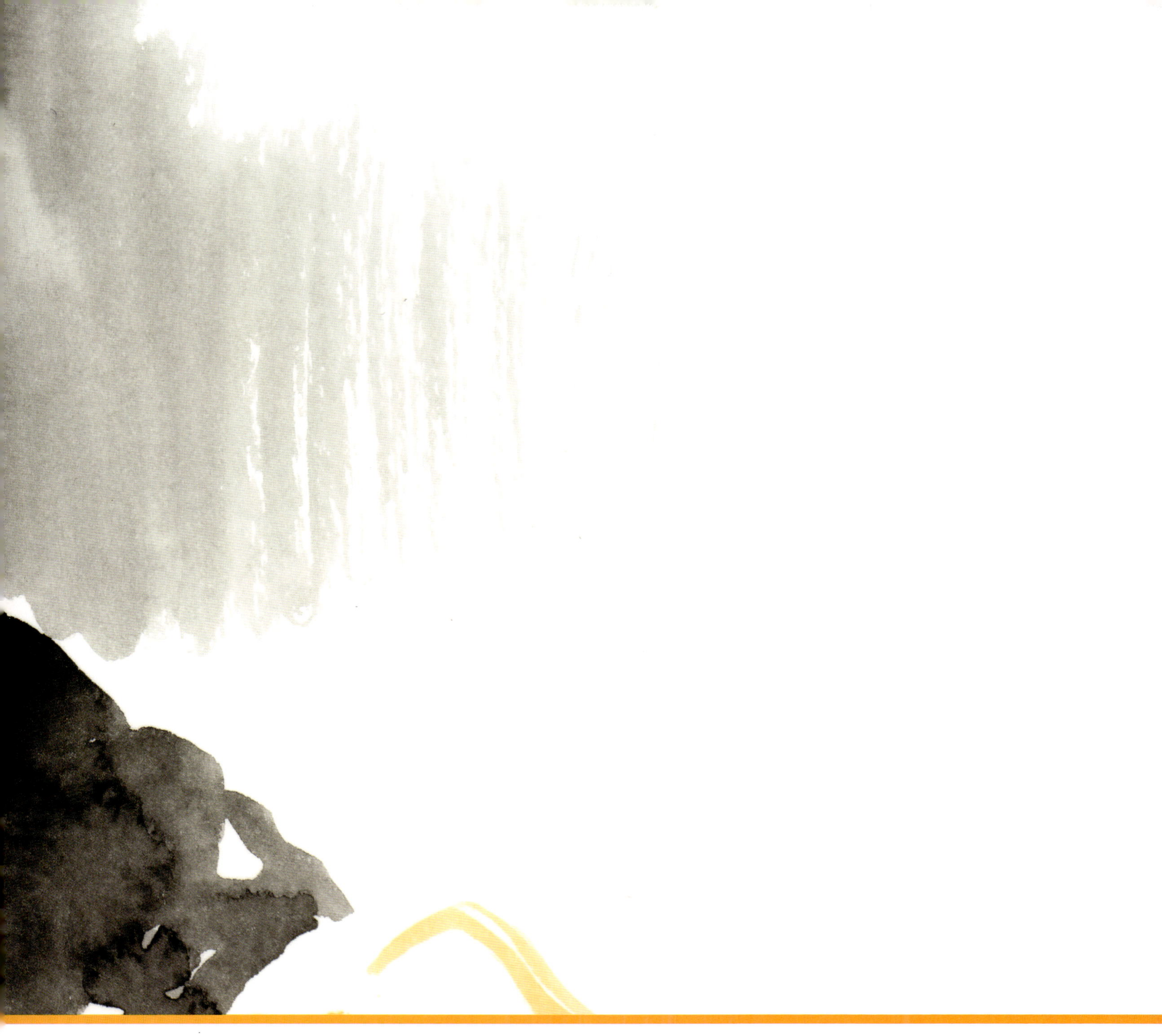

Story

We have seen how a gesture or sequence of gestures can create a mini-story, a snapshot of an action. To extend the narrative, we must turn our attention to the world in which this action takes place and how the model exists within it. This world could be anything from the frame of a blank page to a detailed illustration of a specific place.

In this section, I'll be looking at the relationship between the figure and their environment. I'll explore the composition of the page and how to draw the viewer in, then construct a narrative with the help of costume, memory and imagination.

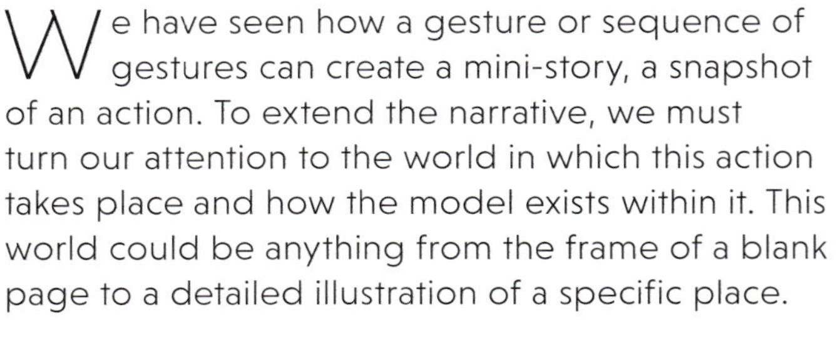

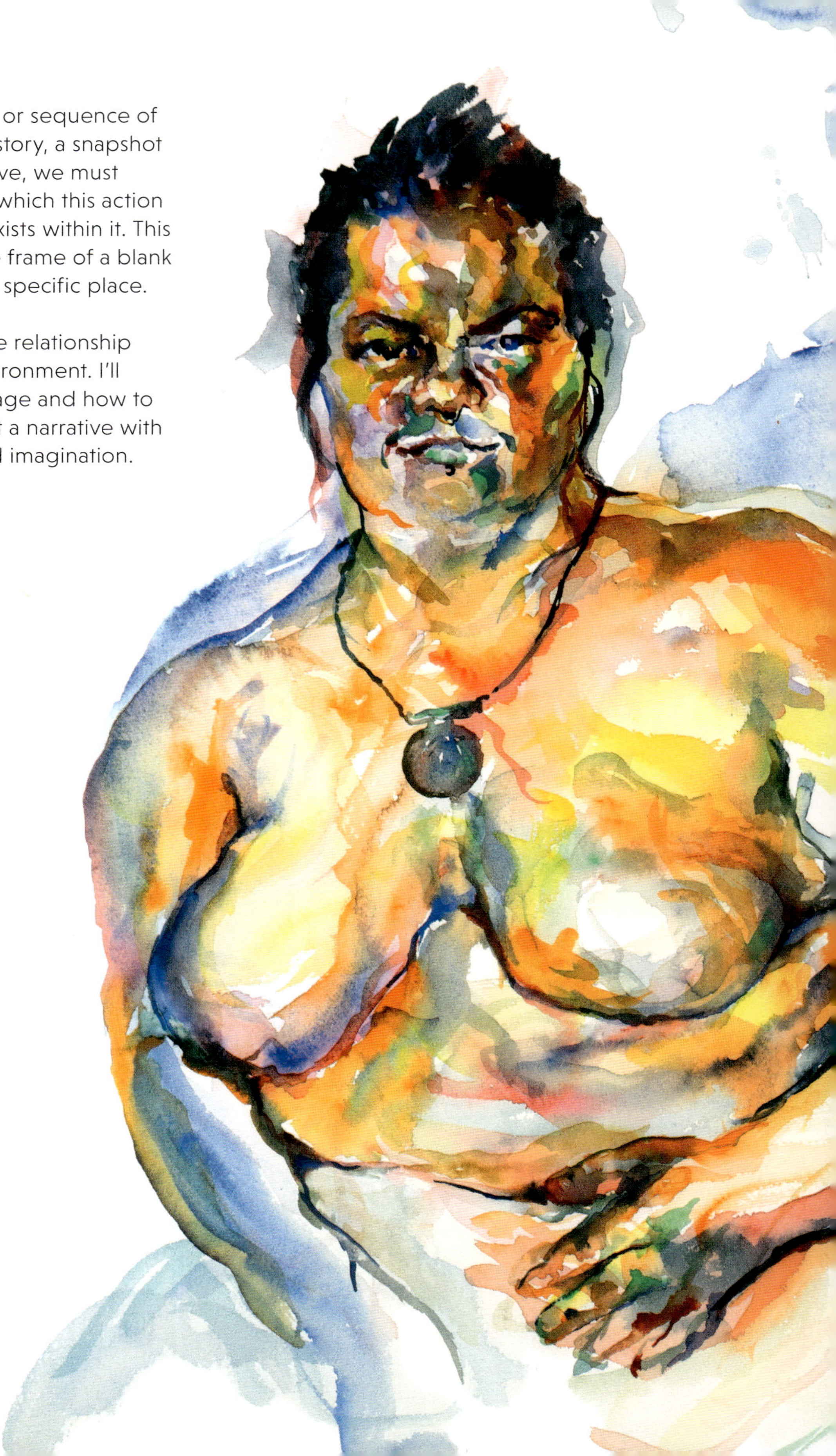

> Leonora's Shadow

Leonora tackles life head on. I wanted to show her confidently occupying the space of the page, indulging in the solidity of her flesh with its dance of colours. The only other presence is her shadow, which stands as a protective spirit behind her.

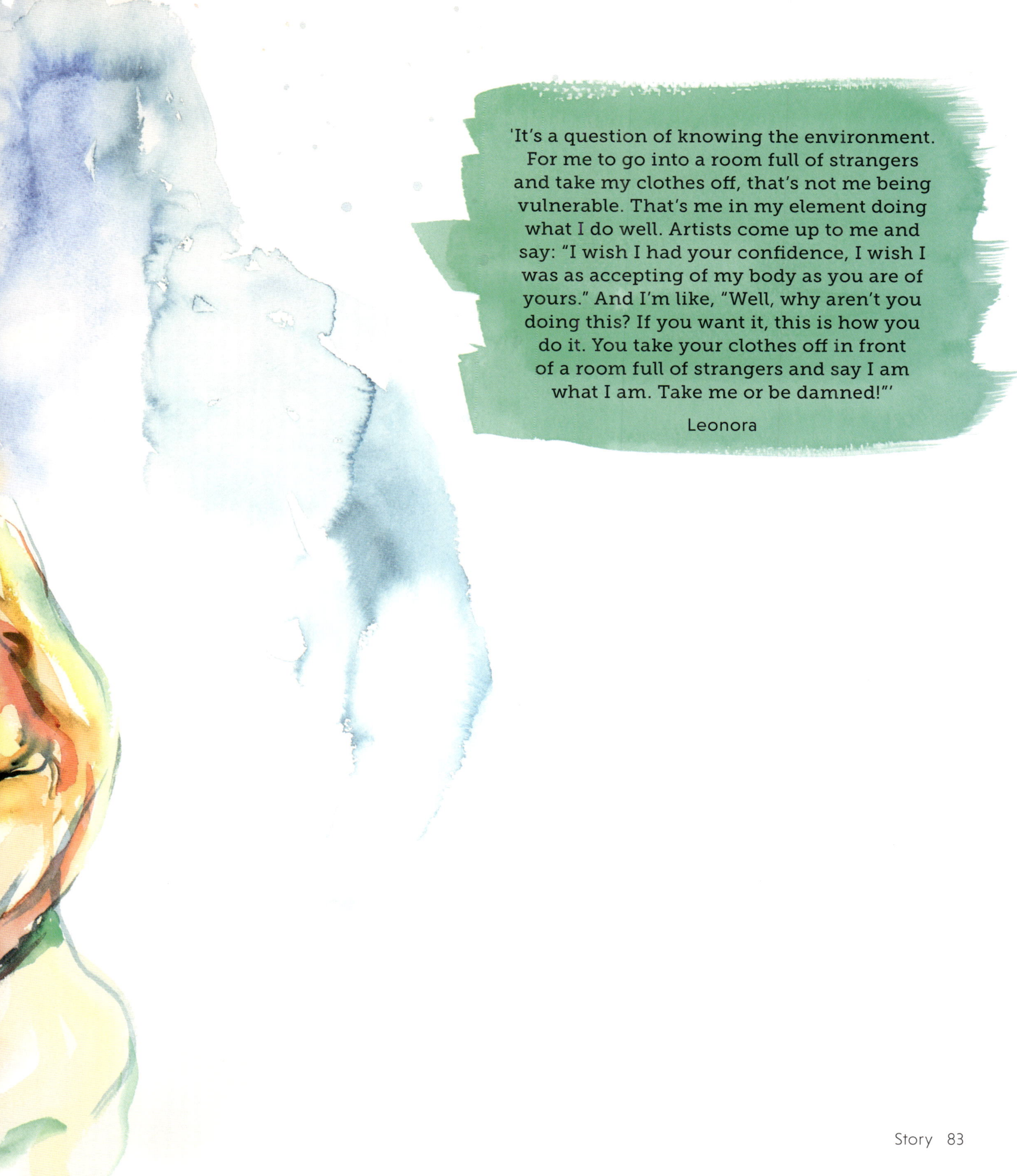

'It's a question of knowing the environment. For me to go into a room full of strangers and take my clothes off, that's not me being vulnerable. That's me in my element doing what I do well. Artists come up to me and say: "I wish I had your confidence, I wish I was as accepting of my body as you are of yours." And I'm like, "Well, why aren't you doing this? If you want it, this is how you do it. You take your clothes off in front of a room full of strangers and say I am what I am. Take me or be damned!"'

Leonora

Composing Your Story

The craft of storytelling starts by placing a compelling character in a context. The story comes from how the figure occupies this space. What are they doing? Why are they there at this moment? Are they large and central, confronting the viewer with ownership and authority? Are they small, almost incidental in the environment? Do they face inwards, inviting us to move into the space with them? Do they face outwards to suggest they are more concerned with their inner thoughts?

Roy on Caithness Beach >
I was watching Roy build stone sculptures on a blustery beach in Caithness, Scotland. While I was inside with a hot cup of tea and a crackling log fire, Roy was enjoying the elements. I used warm yellows and ochres for the interior world, with cool blues and greens for what lay beyond. Through a dramatic difference in scale, I emphasized the contrast between a cosy domestic bubble and Roy in the vastness of nature outside.

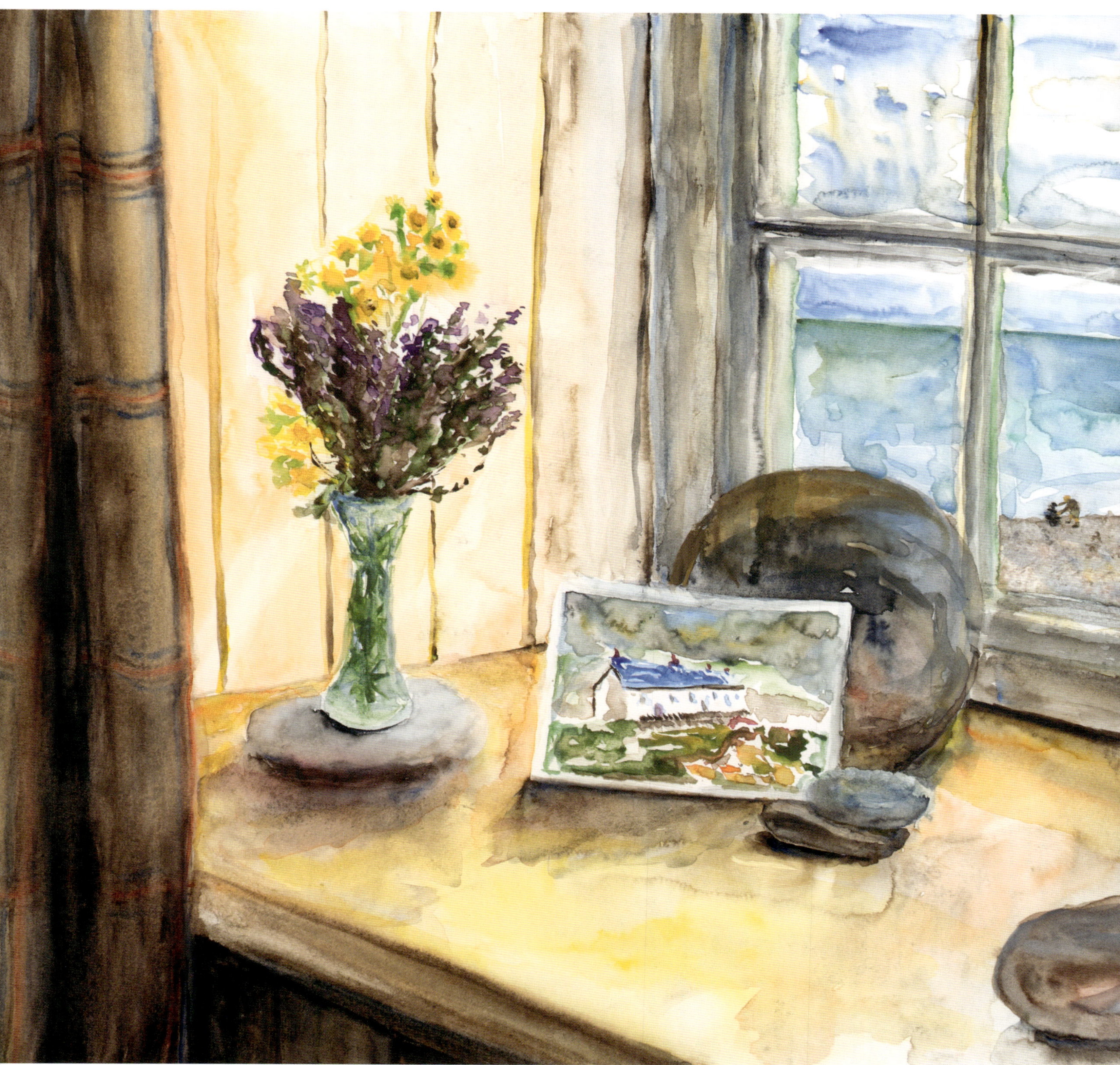

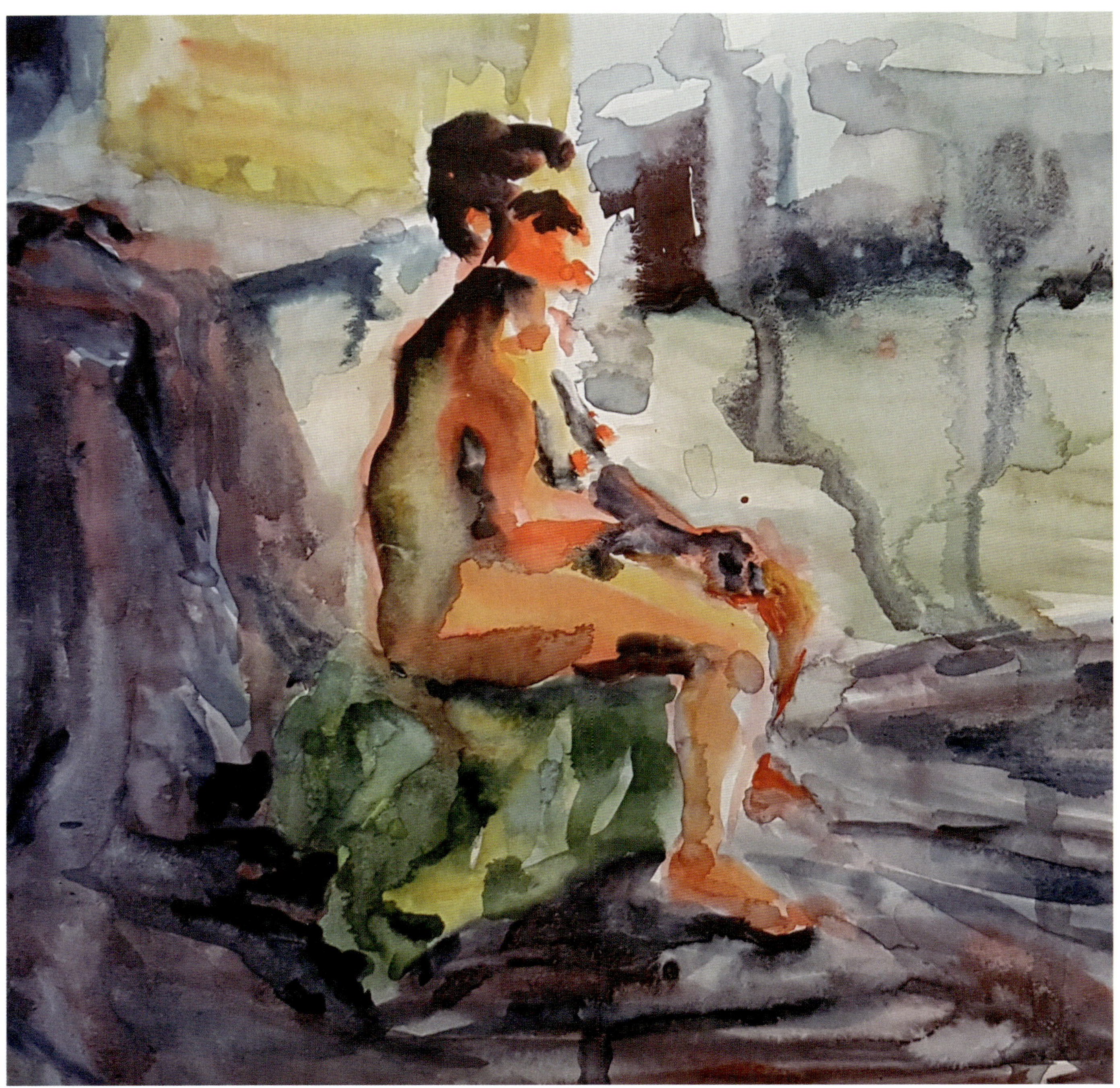

With the figure positioned in the space on the page, I need to ensure that the entire composition is rendered in a singular language. I use different colours and marks to explore the way shadows and light fall on different surfaces, but always in the knowledge that it is the same shadow and light across the whole composition. In the end, I want to convince the viewer that the figure belongs in that space in that moment, connected to the light and air circulating around them.

When painting from life, there will naturally be breaks as the model rests, stretches and rubs feeling back into their limbs. You can use this time to make quick studies of the space without the model. Feel the absence of the figure. When they return, you should have a better sense of the atmosphere swirling around their body into the space beyond.

< Lidia in the Studio
Lidia is always active, even in the stillest of poses, carefully balancing her musculature with a steady breath. In this pose, drapery flowed around her as the fast-changing daylight moved shadows across the room. I painted fast, gestural strokes, standing at my table using my whole arm, even though I was working at a miniature scale. The paint splashed, blended and bled, carried by water. I placed Lidia in the centre of this swirling mass of activity, stable and strong.

Going in Close

Sometimes the story of a painting is in the sensual fleshiness of the model, the sculpted musculature, or delicious palette of shadows. It propels you to fill the surface with an almost abstract interpretation of form. Zooming in on the body can be a liberating exercise, freeing you from preconceptions of anatomy to create a journey of discovery across an unfamiliar landscape.

Start by recognizing the boundaries of the page and the shape they make. Find a section of the pose that you know will be cropped on all four sides. As you paint, allow your marks to flow over the edges and fill the whole page with the surface of the body.

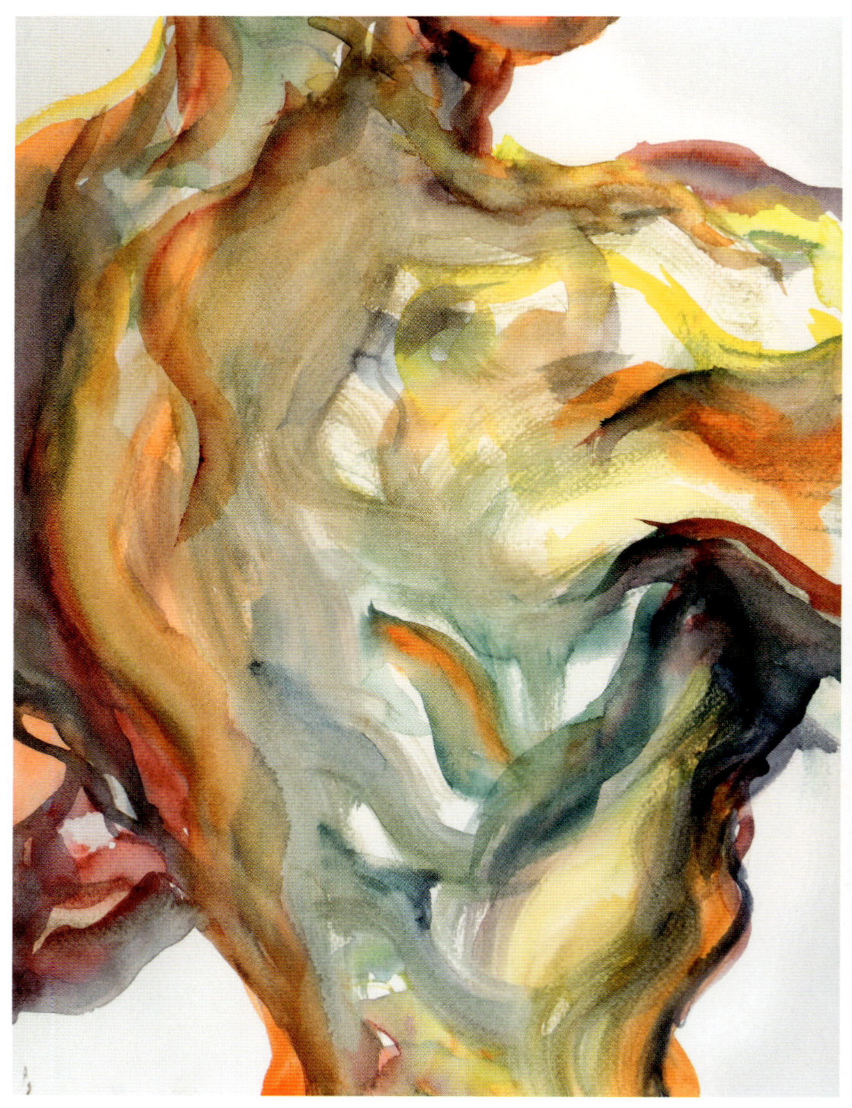

^ The Landscape of Kam
In these close-up studies of Kam, I wanted to explore the flow of the skin across his muscles. By abstracting the pose with an increasingly dramatic crop, it became easier to see the boldness of colour without the preconceptions of 'skin tone'.

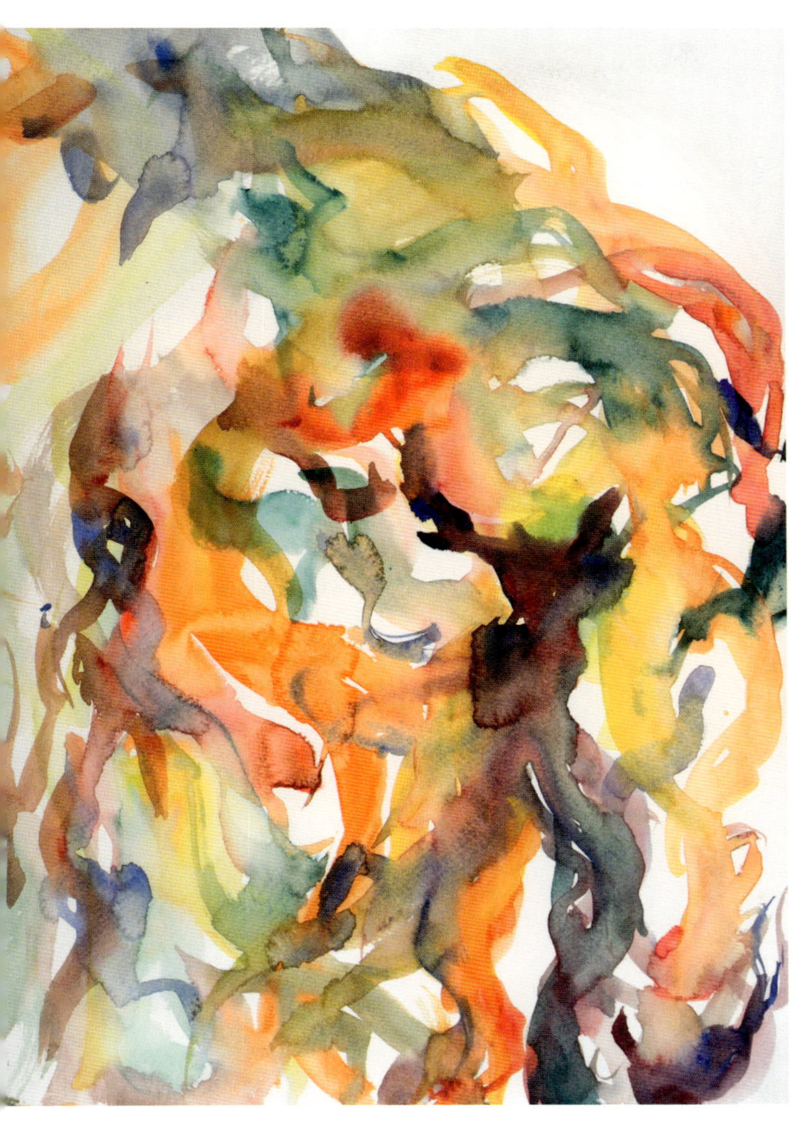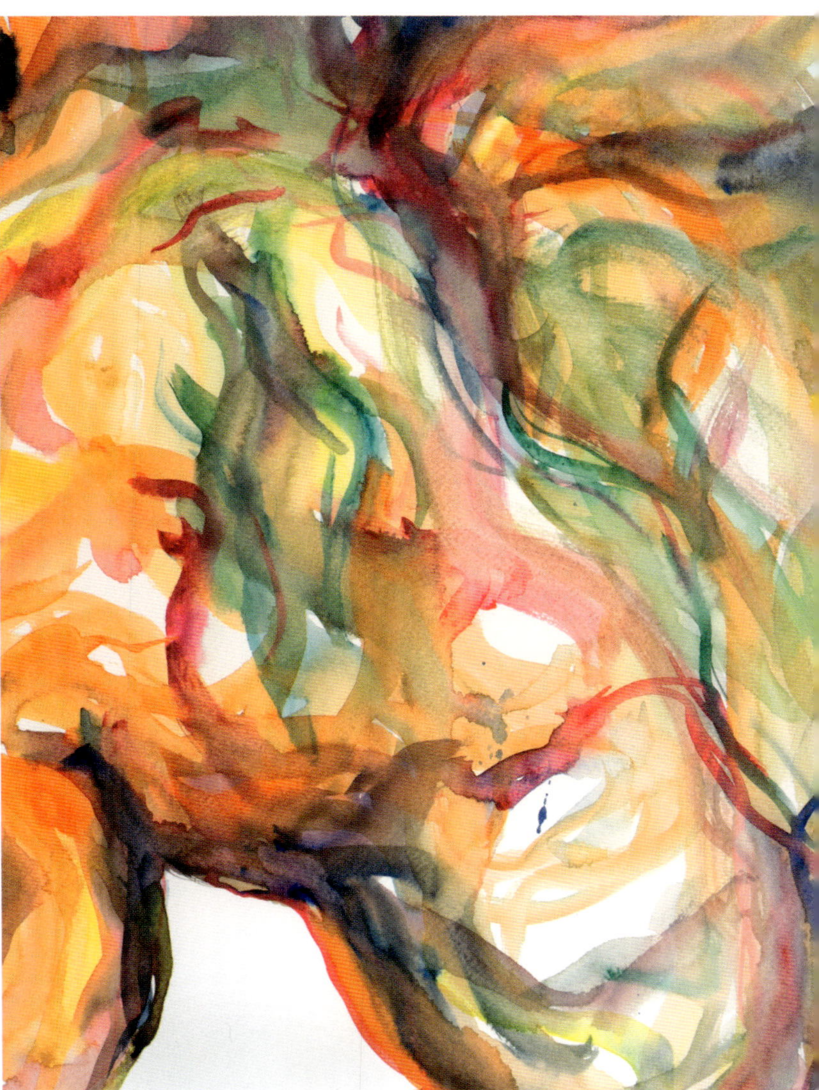

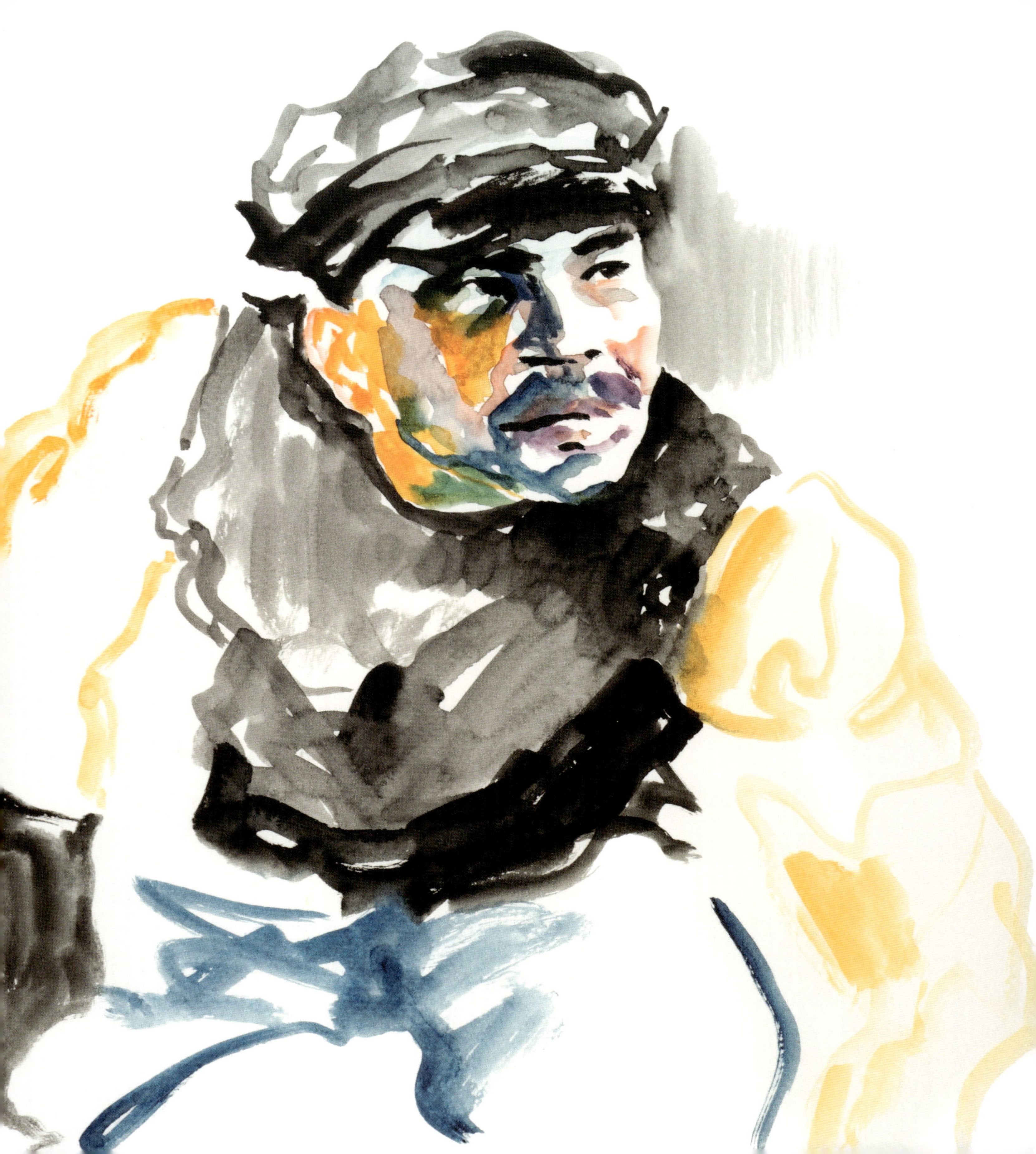

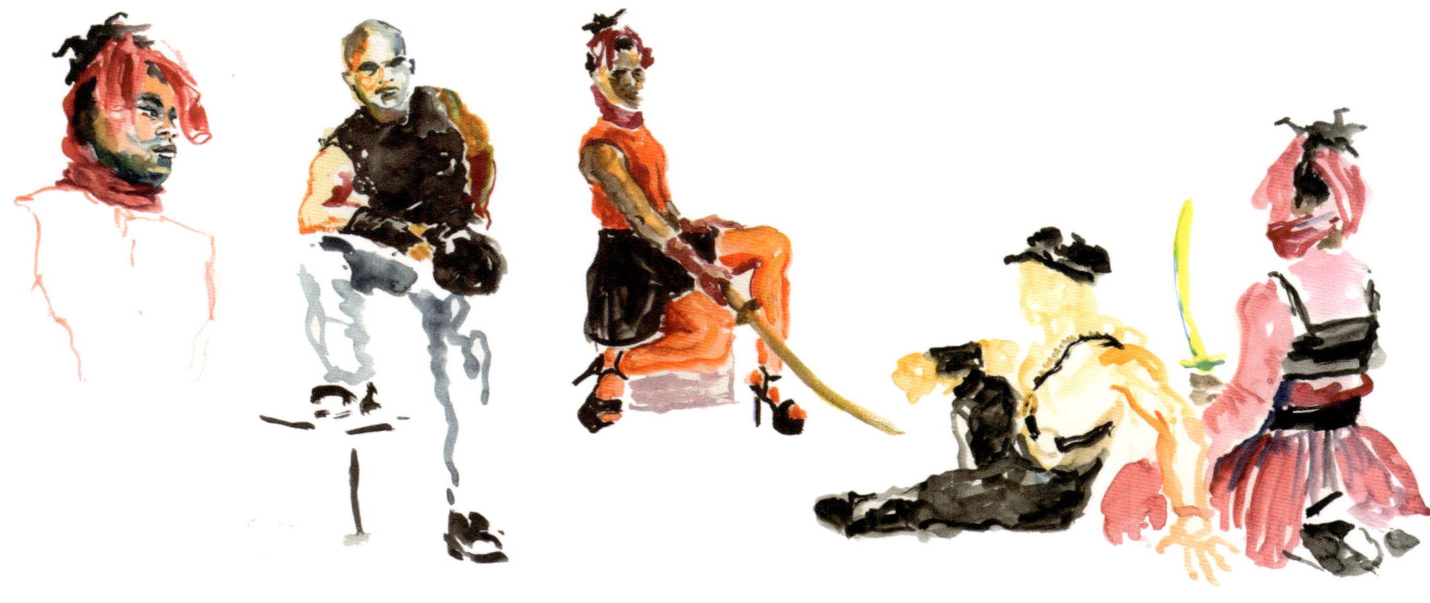

< ∧ **Super Gay Heroes**
Art Model Collective, a
model-run life-drawing
group, produced an evening
at London's Orbital Comics
inspired by the 'Polari Comics'
of artist Villain. Here, Roy
appropriates a leather-clad
'Clone' identity to queer
the traditional superhero
costume. Sakeema looks
on as a gender-fluid Samurai.

Constructing Narratives

Sometimes stories can be deliberately constructed.
As part of a vibrant community of artists, Roy and
I organize and participate in themed life-drawing
workshops. Inspired by exhibitions and events,
these have ranged from contemporary re-
imaginings of Anglo-Saxon tales to a celebration
of queer histories. We've brought books and
films to life and paid homage to the artists who
inspire us.

To do this, we use costumes, props, projections
and music, blurring the boundaries between
art class and art performance. Many models
have a wealth of skills that they can bring to a
session, from design and craft to performance.
Their creativity can transform a workshop into a
theatrical event with an unmistakable narrative.

Filtering Reality

Imagination and memory are intrinsic to storytelling. Every painting will be filtered through the unique lens of the painter, their lived experience and the context of the present moment. Sharpening the focus on to that personal filter shifts the balance away from representation towards interpretation.

Sometimes, there is something compelling about the figure, the energy between us or the relationship with the environment that stays with me long after the session has finished. I can use this memory to fuel a new painting, developing the drawings and paintings I made from life. I don't use photographs as I'm trying to move away from reality to reveal an inner reflection.

Reflection on History >
This painting happened while staying in a historic, family-run hotel on the Isle of Wight. Huge mirrors lined the hallway, the silvered backings blackened and spotted with age like timeless constellations. I imagined myself as one of the many reflections caught there over the centuries.

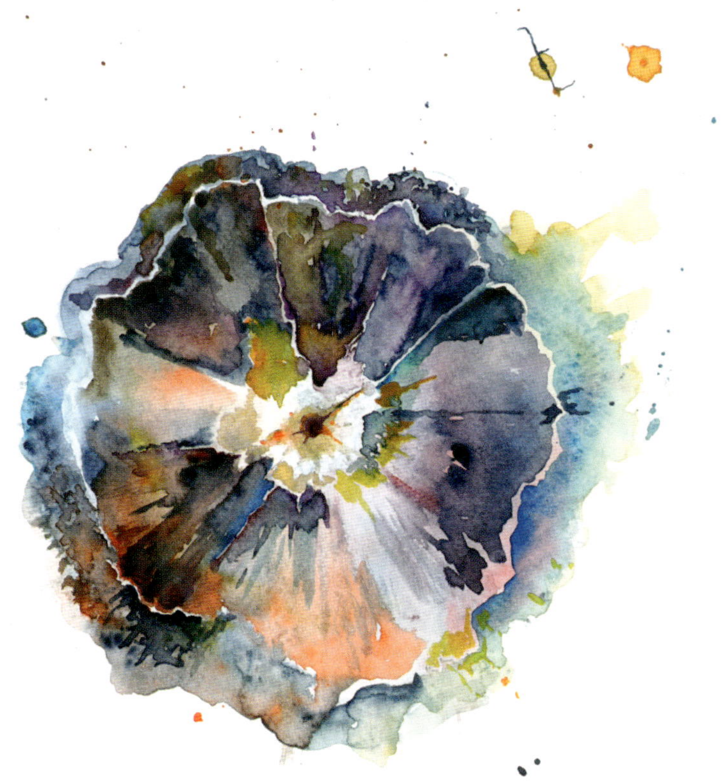

< Galaxy of Glass
I continued my study of the mirror by zooming in on a spot of silvering caused by the oxidation of the antique metal behind the glass. These spots took on the form of a nebulous star or distant galaxy, holding the memories of history.

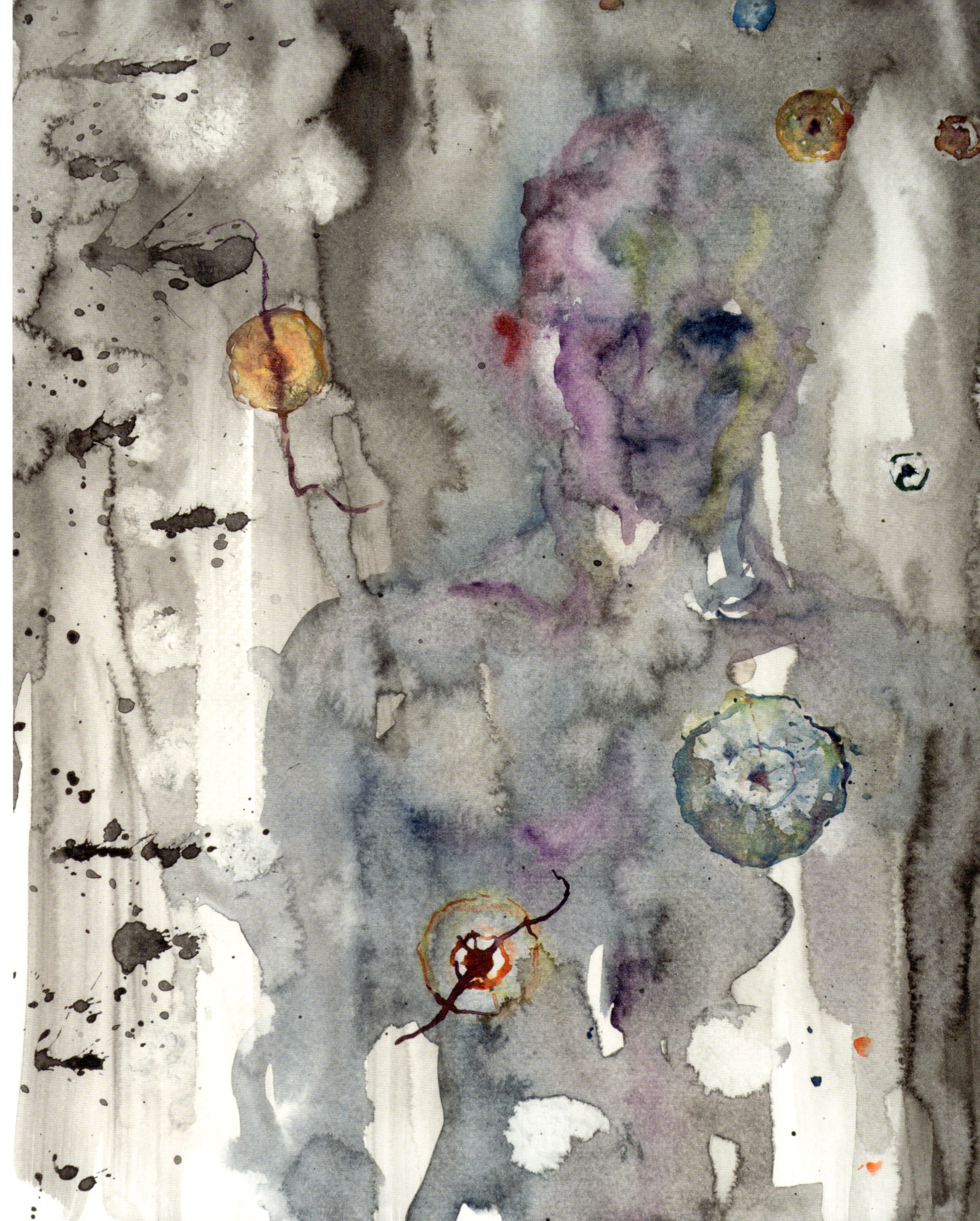

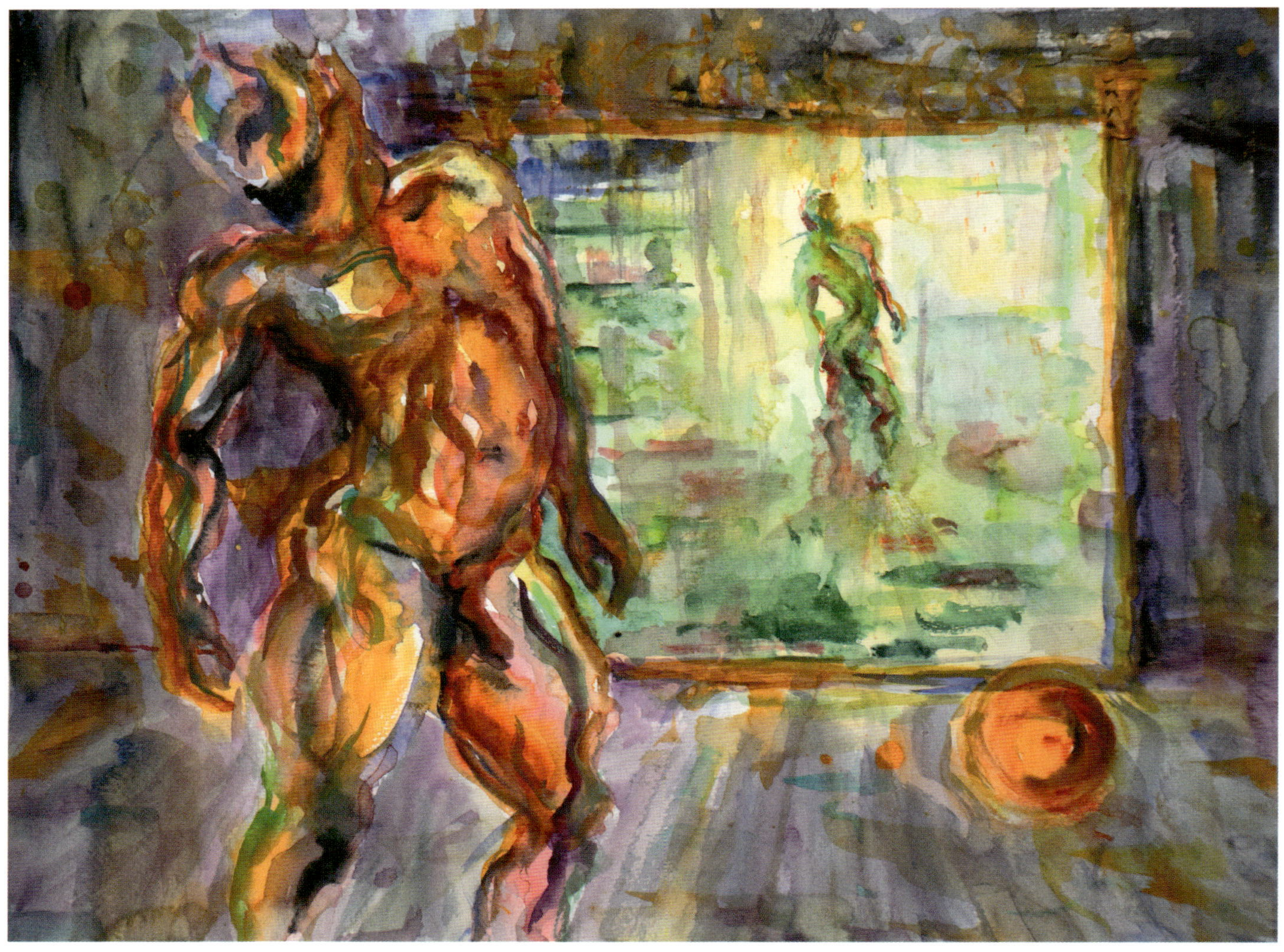

∧ Pip and the Mirror

In preparation for a portrait of Pip, I made a series of charcoal drawings and returned to the studio with the images fresh in my mind. The final work was to be in oil, but I needed to play with colour and flow to help develop the composition. I wanted to draw the viewer through the foreground figure into the mirror world beyond, contrasting the pale light of the far window with a rich palette in the foreground. With the charcoal drawings to hand, I unleashed my watercolours and my imagination.

Gary Online >

I painted this portrait of Gary as part of an online community group. His low-resolution image was flattened by the bright colours of the surrounding digital icons and the warm light in my own living room. I was imagining his world through the filter of my laptop, so I decided to make this the focus of my composition.

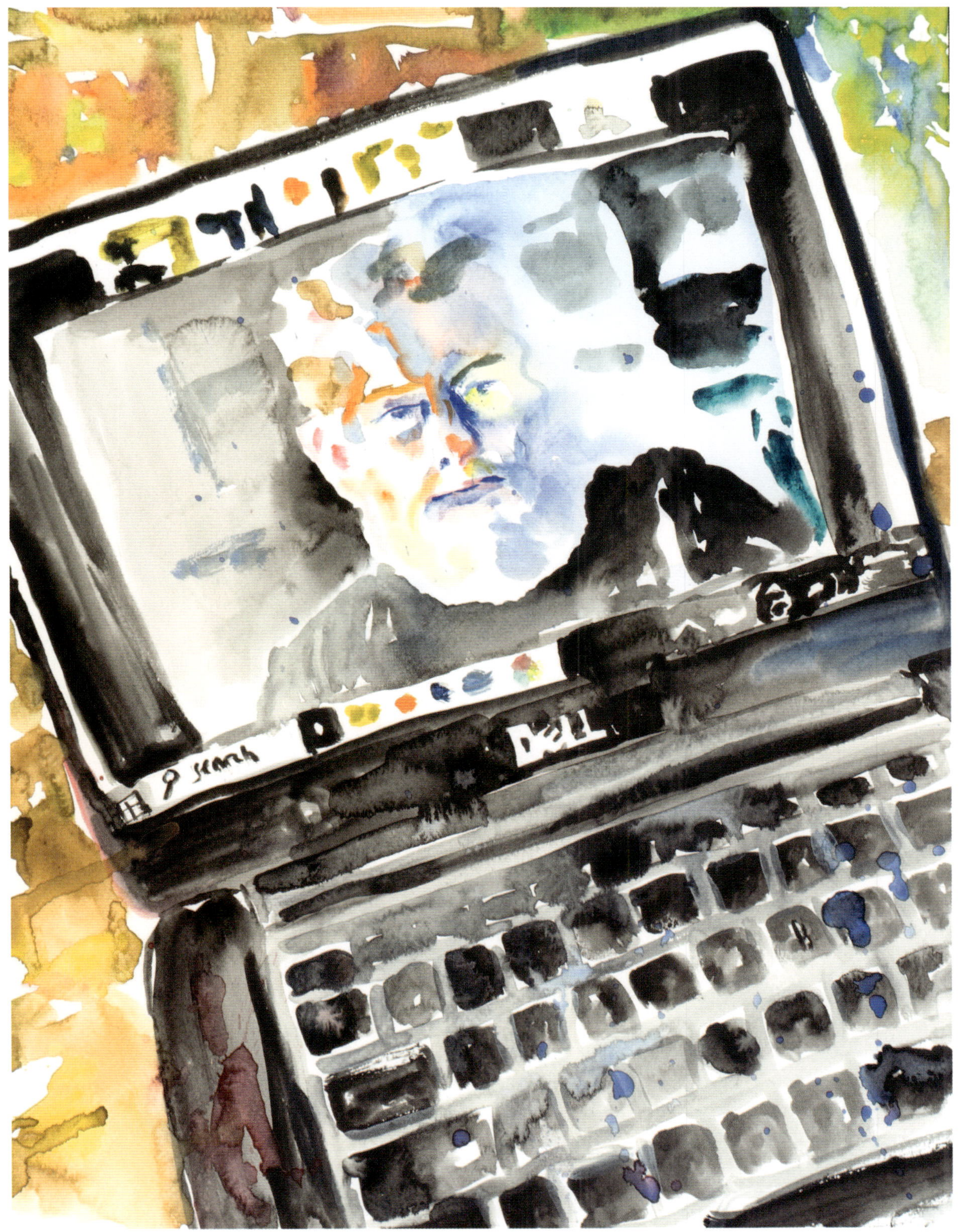

Dell
Search

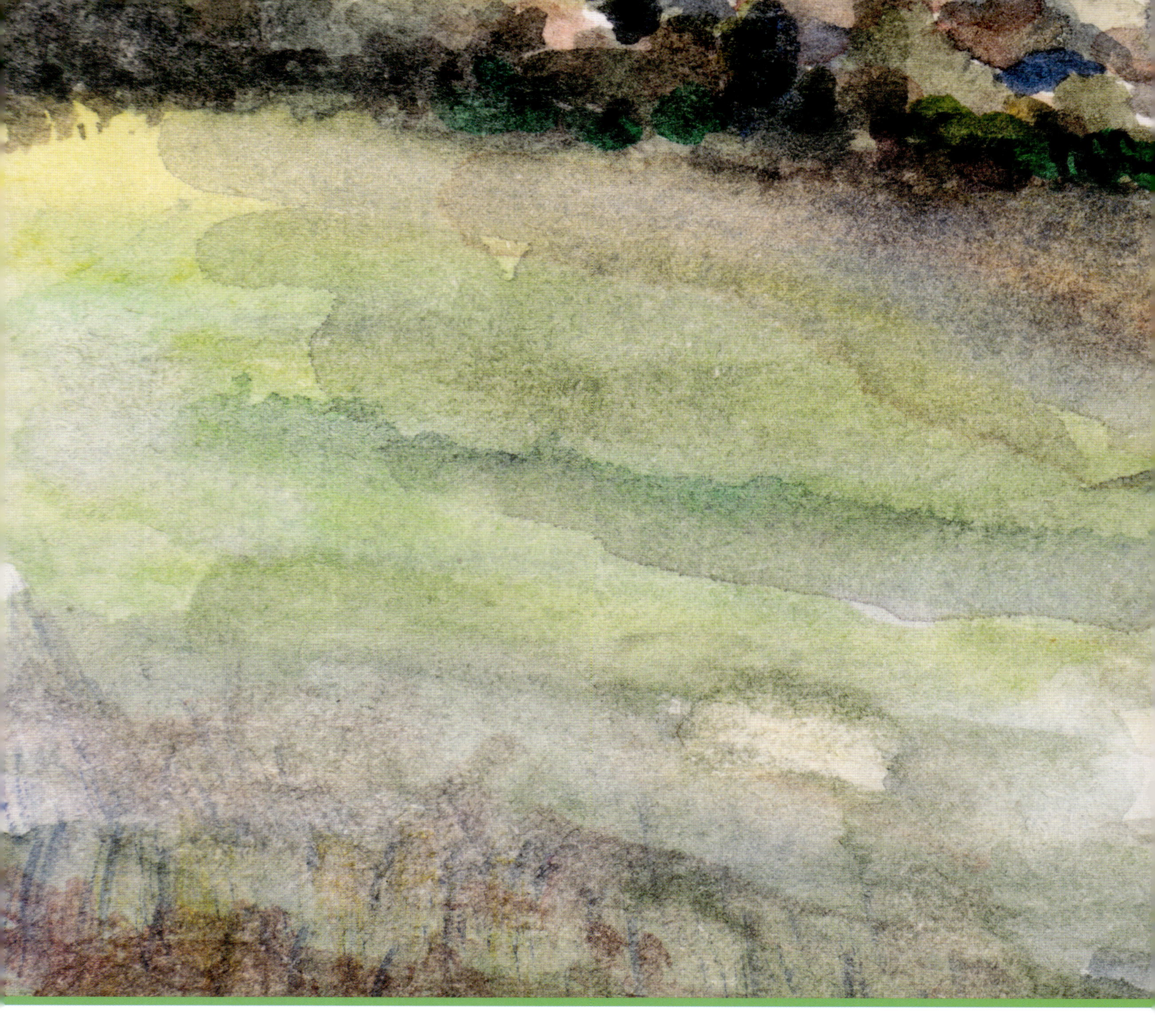

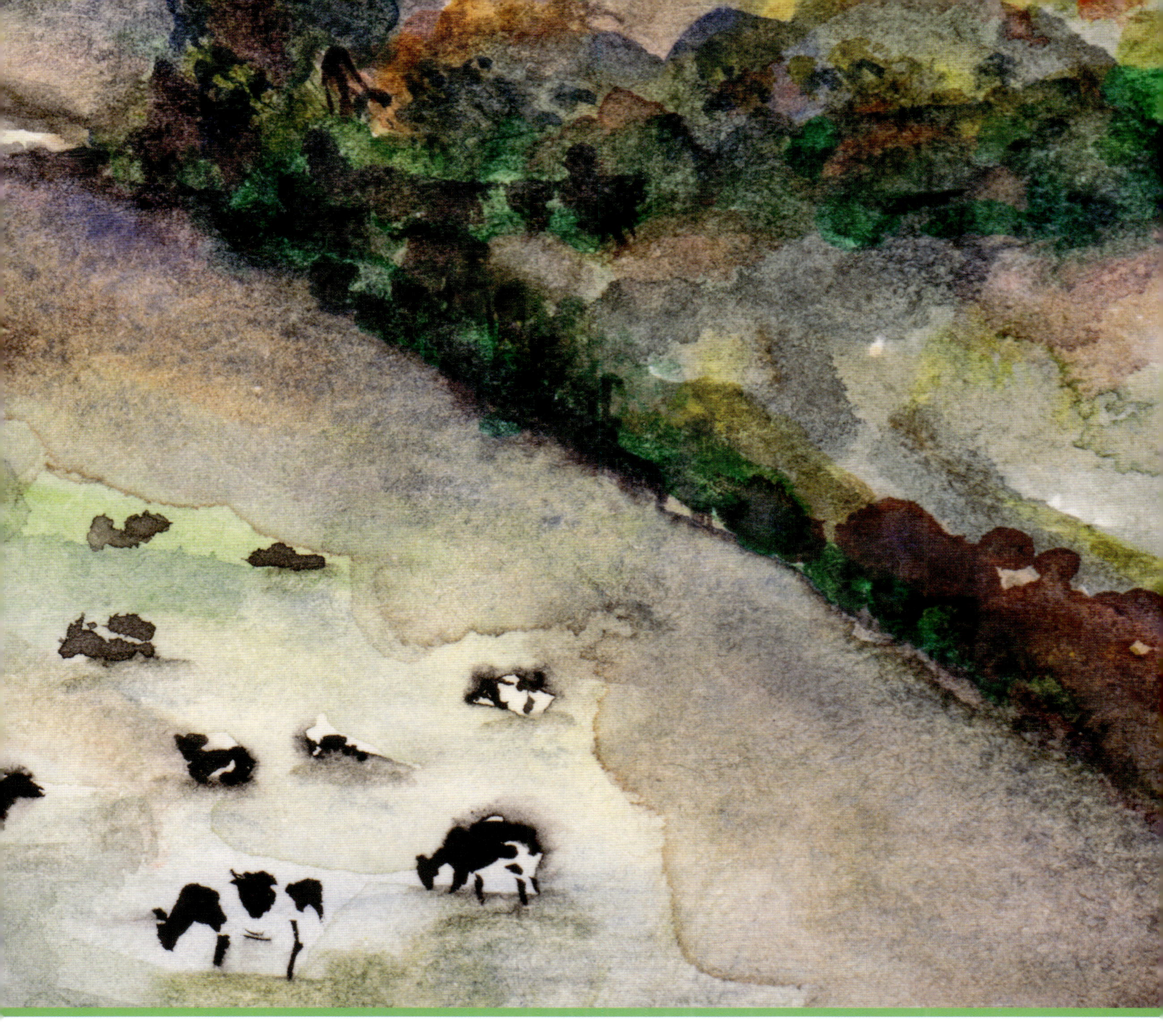

Beyond the Figure

It's natural to try to make sense of the world through our own human experience. We create legends of animals, plants, landscapes, constellations – even an echo – who once had a familiar human form. These stories can entice us to seek out a hidden human identity in anything.

Visual artists tackle this in many different ways: an illustration of an animal in a human role; an inanimate object evoking a Freudian sexuality; a painting transferring complex emotions onto a sunflower. By reading a pose, finding a gesture and seeking out the story of a composition, we can bring a human empathy into the most unlikely of subjects.

In this section, I return to the themes of speed, gesture and story and apply them to animals, still lives, landscapes and even a house.

Black Swan >
This black swan was painted from life in a couple of minutes in busy St James's Park, London. I was struck by the distinctive ruffling of its feathers and the fierce ownership of its space. The deep red beak added to its character.

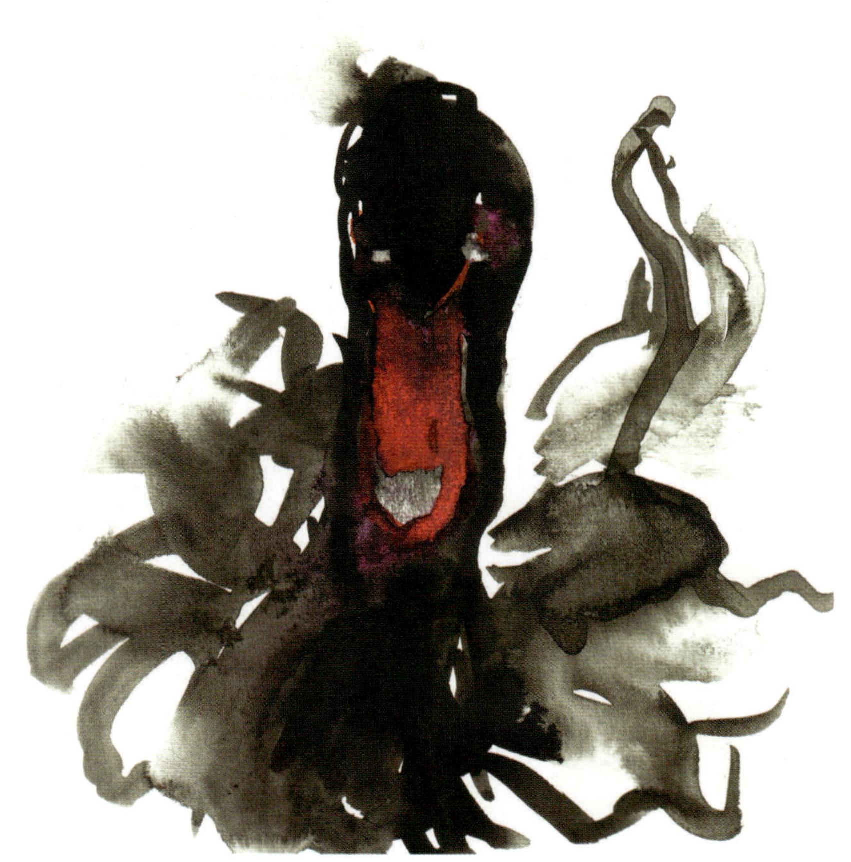

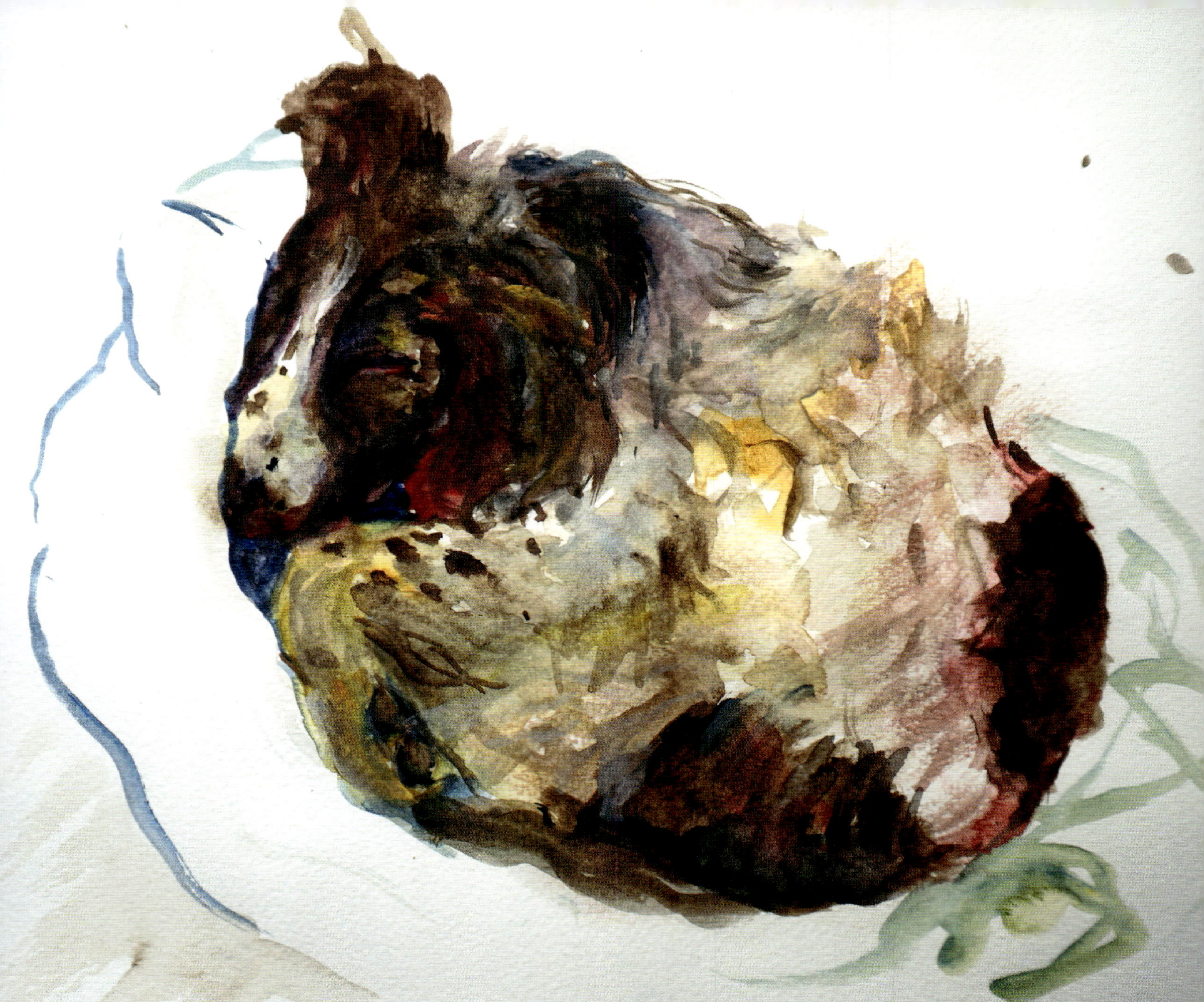

^ Assis Curled Up

With Assis happily snoozing in
his bed, I had time to study and
paint his gesture. The dog's
spiral line of action is echoed
by his round silhouette and
the curves of the bed.

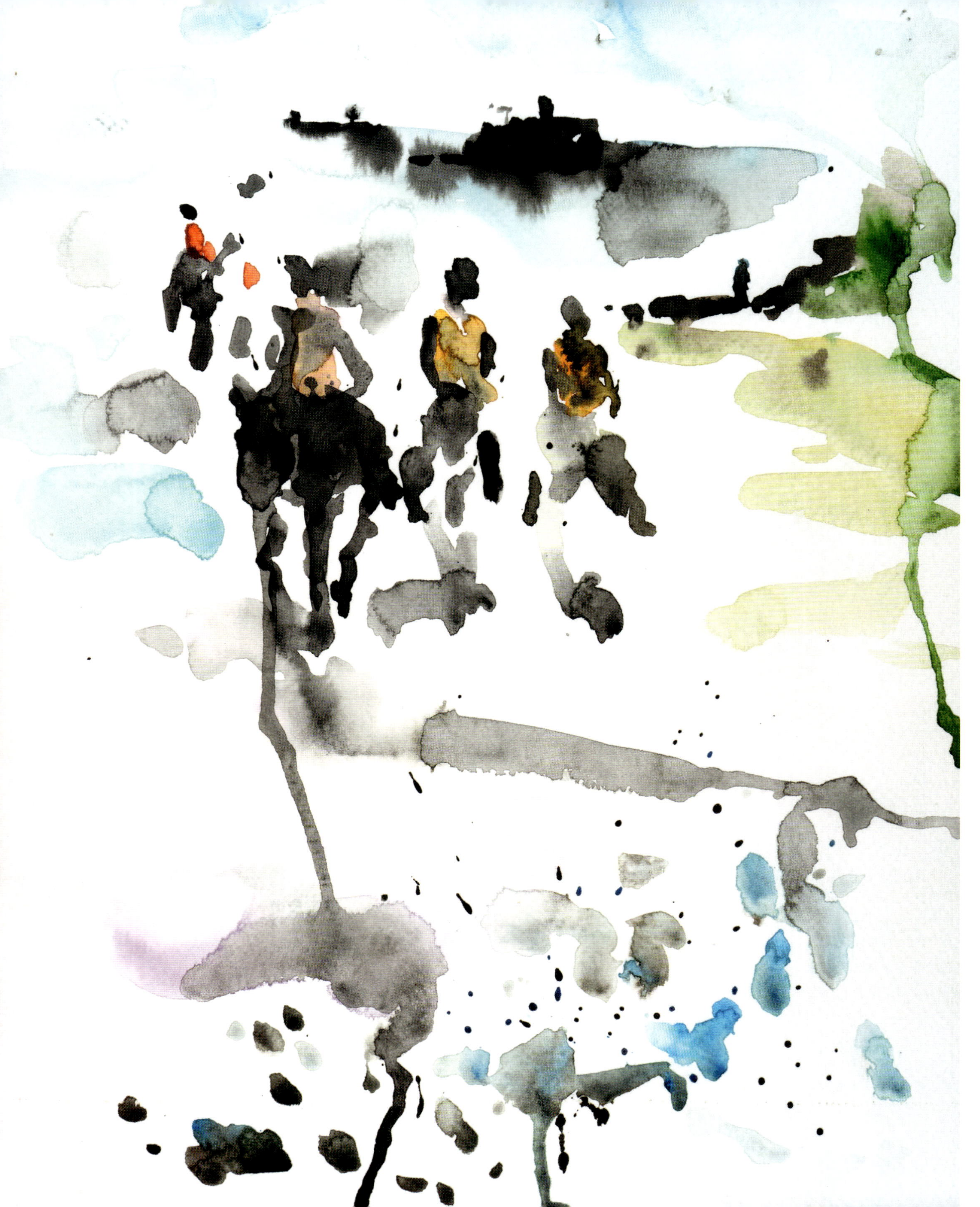

The Bigger Picture

Painting the figure at speed is a solid discipline to prepare you for capturing the big, bustling world from life. Painting an animated group of people, an animal in motion or a fleeting moment of light requires that same combination of heightened observation and fearless mark making.

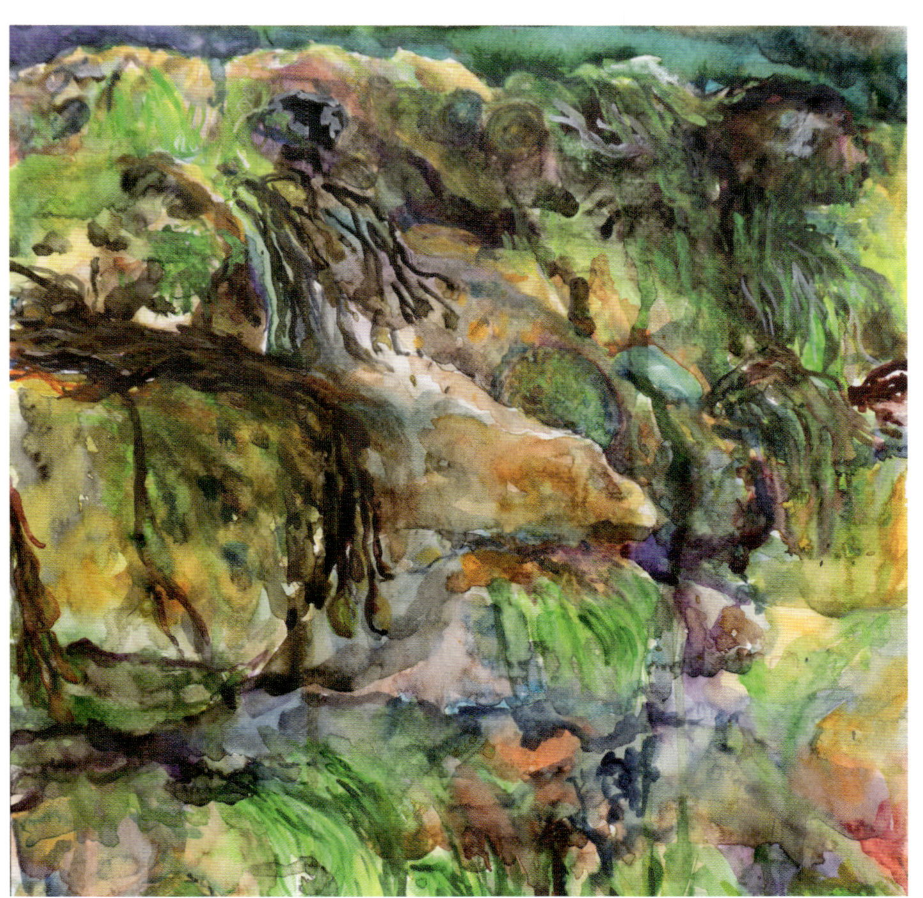

< Priory Beach
On a beach on the Isle of Wight, I was absorbed in a detailed study of seaweed and anemones on a rock. It was laboured and a bit boring. A small group of children on horseback appeared in the distance. I observed them as they trotted closer, grabbed a fresh sheet of paper and in ninety seconds splashed a few marks down before they passed. After the frustration of a representational illustration, there was something alive and joyous in allowing drops and drips to stake their own territory on the page.

^ Seaweed and Anemones (abandoned)
This study of rocks at the edge of the seashore had occupied me for about forty minutes when the horses came by. It was a relief to abandon it in favour of the immediacy of the riders.

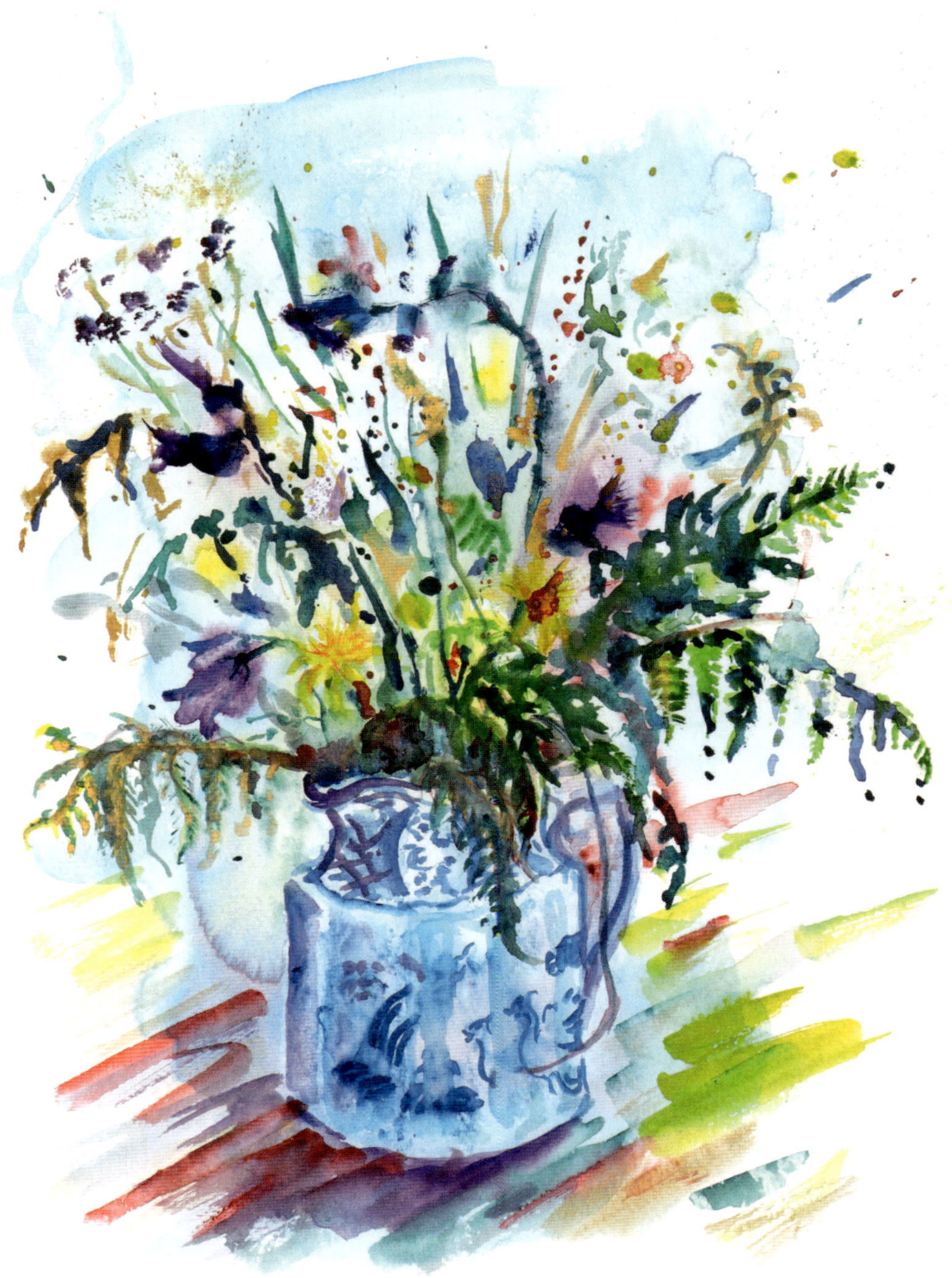

These wildflowers from Galloway were three days old when I decided to paint them: the ferns were drooping, but the yellow gorse and purple vervain were valiantly struggling on. I used drips and gestural lines in sympathy with their ultimate decline.

Gesture implies agency and motivation. By describing the gesture of an object, we turn it into an active being and encourage a connection with our own human experience. A building leans precariously, a rock resists stubbornly, a sapling thrusts itself upwards with determination.

Anneka's Tulips v

By contrast, these tulips were fresh, soaking up the
water in the comfort of their wide bronze bowl.
I intensified the colours and filled the page with
their juicy presence.

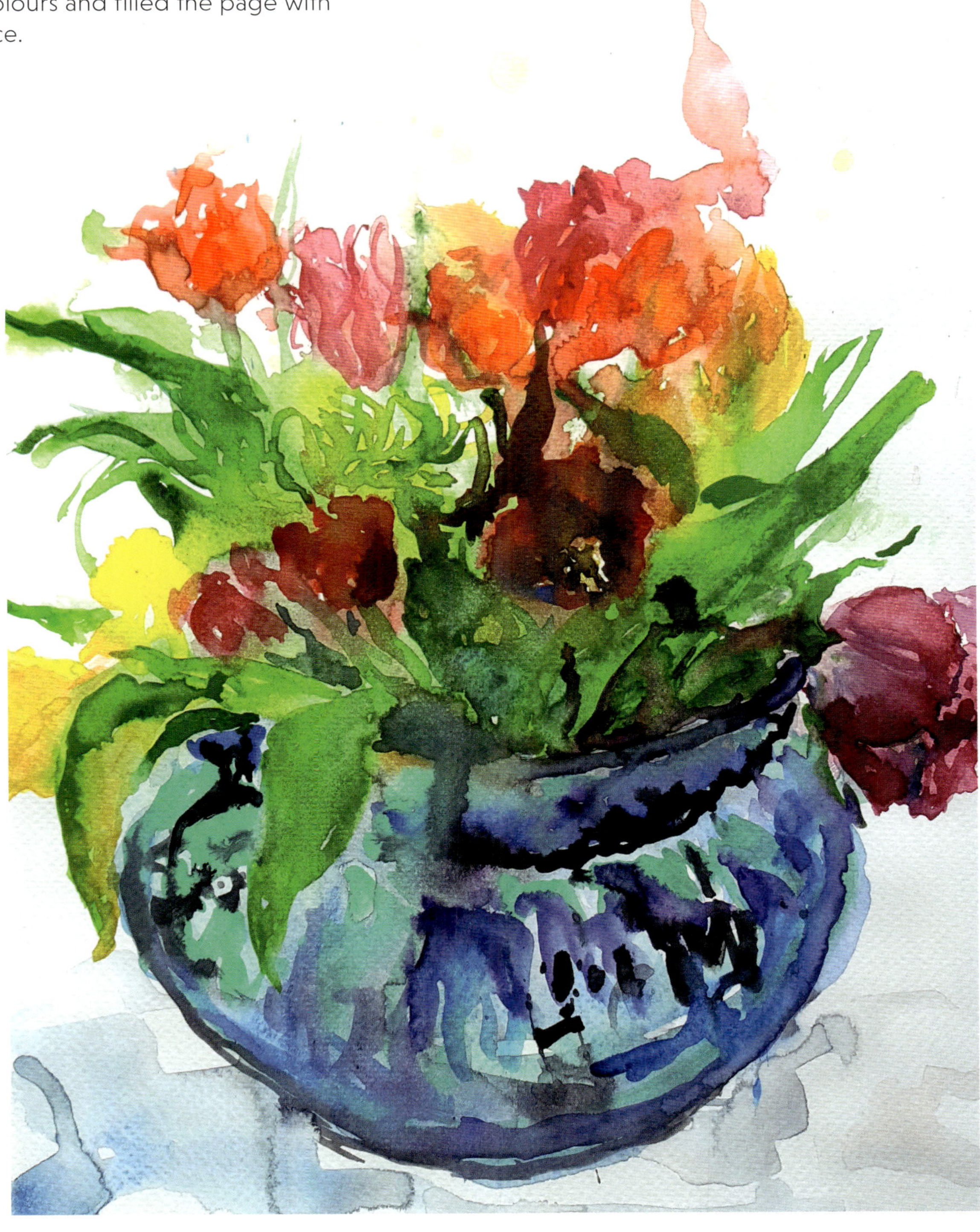

Making Connections

We've seen that the figure must always exist in space, whether this is a rendering of the real-world environment or simply the rectangle of the page. Any subject must have this kind of relationship with its space. How this is described tells a story, directing the eye and forging an emotional connection between viewer and subject.

Dark Pines >

I was commissioned to paint a house as the owners prepared to move on after four decades. I needed to capture the personality of their home, which had become a much-loved part of the family. Rather than a single, static view, I decided to invite the viewer into a timeless fairytale: a lush garden of mature trees and hidden spaces where the family had enjoyed long summer evenings. Tiger, the family cat, proudly stands guard.

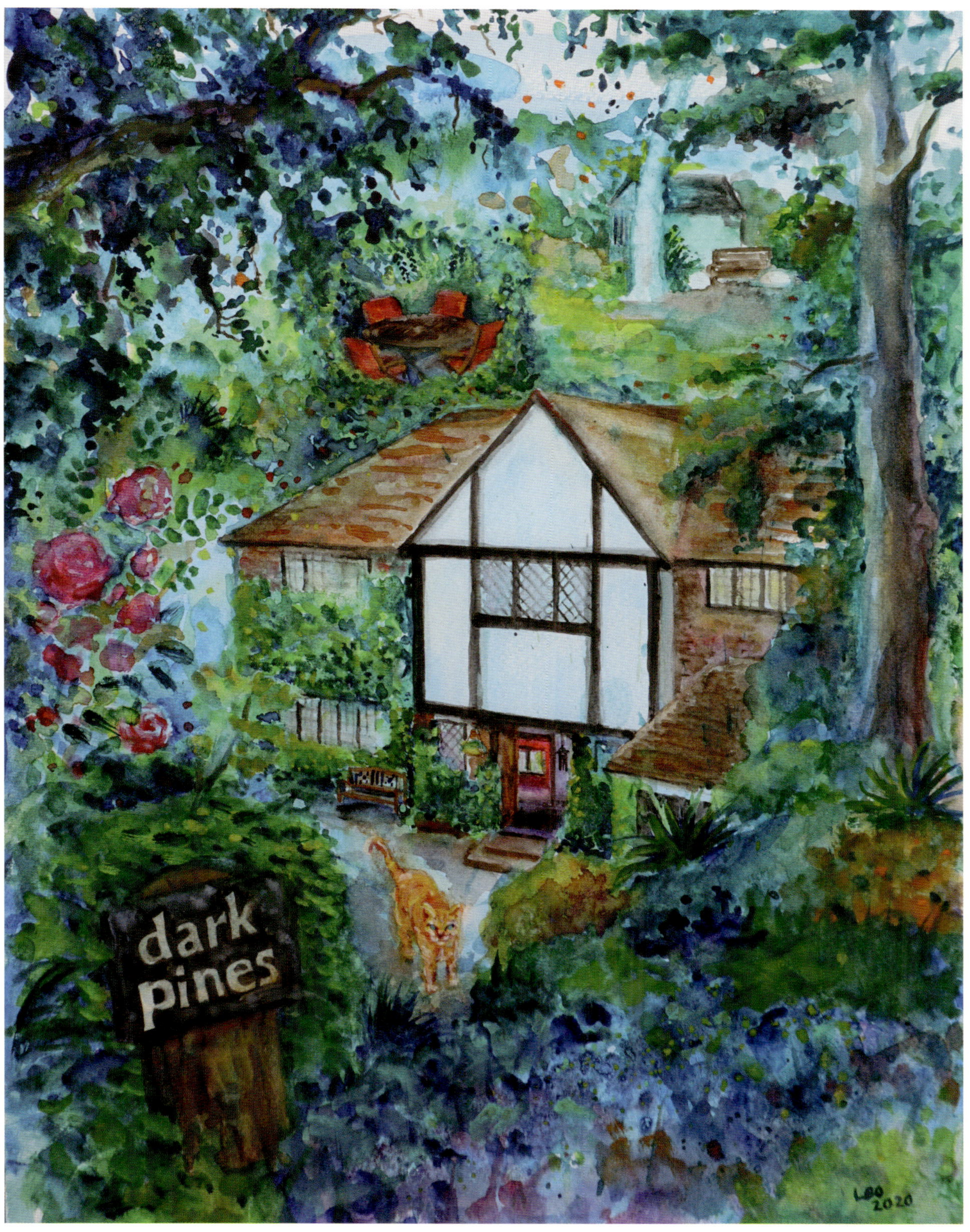

dark
pines

Reclining Landscapes

For many artists the human form is akin to the undulations of a vast landscape, and vice versa. Hills recede into the distance like curves of flesh, woodland nestles in crevices like patches of hair, mist settles like gentle perspiration.

These two Cornish landscapes were painted shortly after dawn on a misty morning in late summer. I imagined the land gently stirring awake, ready to nourish the world for another day. The light was changing so quickly it was almost as if the land shifted and undulated with the tension of a held pose.

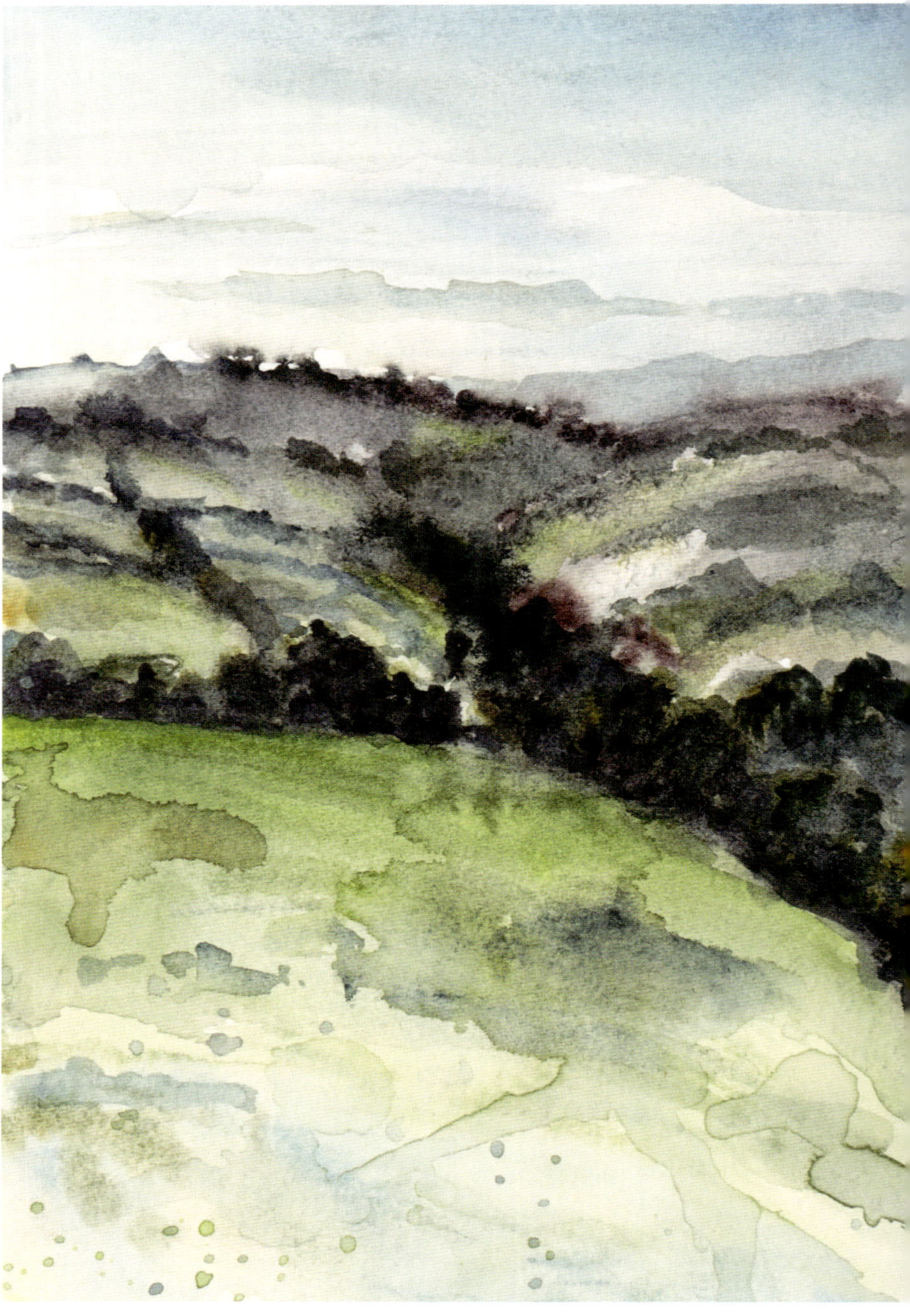

^ Cornish Landscape at Dawn
In my first painting, I worked with the paint as wet as it could be to describe the rising mist. Following a diagonal line of action, I dabbed deep pigments into the crevices to represent the trees at the borders of the fields.

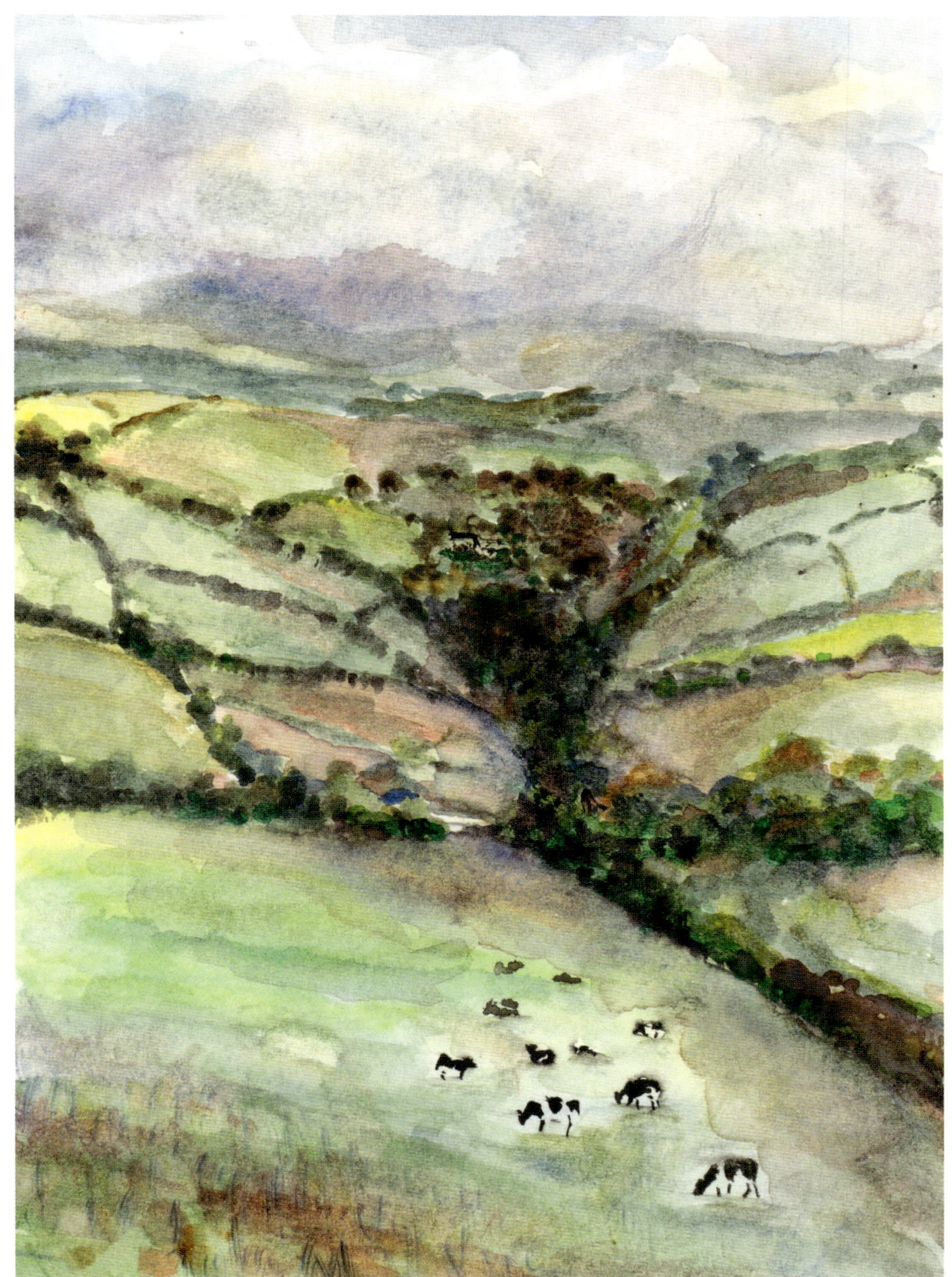

< Cornish Landscape with Cows

Minutes later, I shifted perspective and started the second painting. Colours were already flooding into the landscape and the mist had mostly lifted to reveal finer details. This is when I noticed the cows. By the time I finished, the landscape had awakened into the full light of day and I was ready for breakfast.

Moving Image

Living in my part of south London, I have noisy neighbours: feral parakeets. Nobody knows how they got here: did they escape from the film set of *The African Queen*? Did Jimi Hendrix release them as a symbol of free love? In any case, they're here to stay. We've grown fond of their distinctive squawk and flash of green, dominating the treetops.

London Parakeets ∨ >

When I began experimenting with watercolour animation, I chose the parakeet as my subject. I wanted to capture an almost reckless confidence and boundless energy. The two most important things were the silhouette and the line of action, together describing the swoop of the wings as the bird flies towards us. These watercolours became the frames of an animated loop, as well as the layers in a series of digital collages. You can see the results at www.leocrane.co.uk/parakeets.

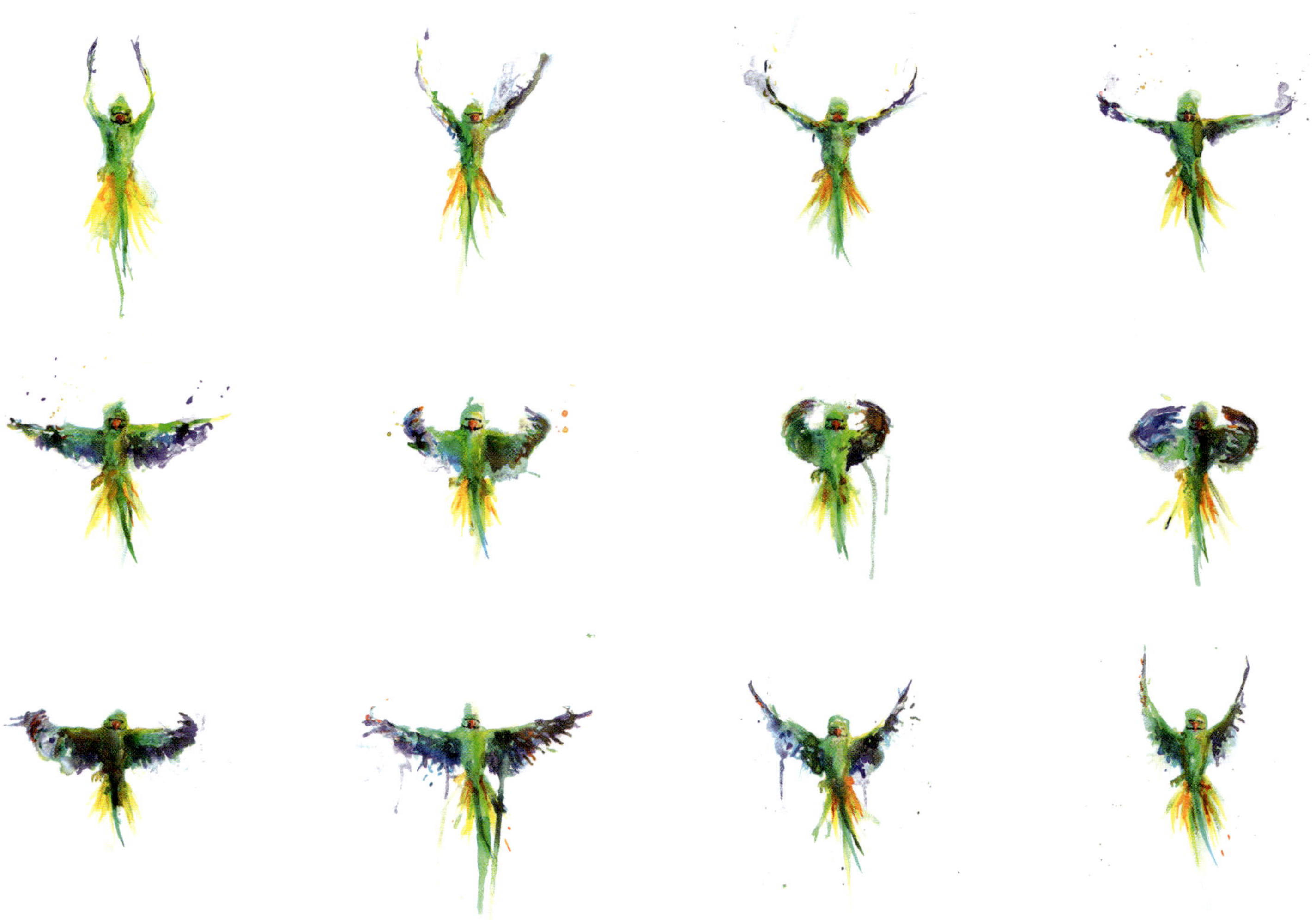

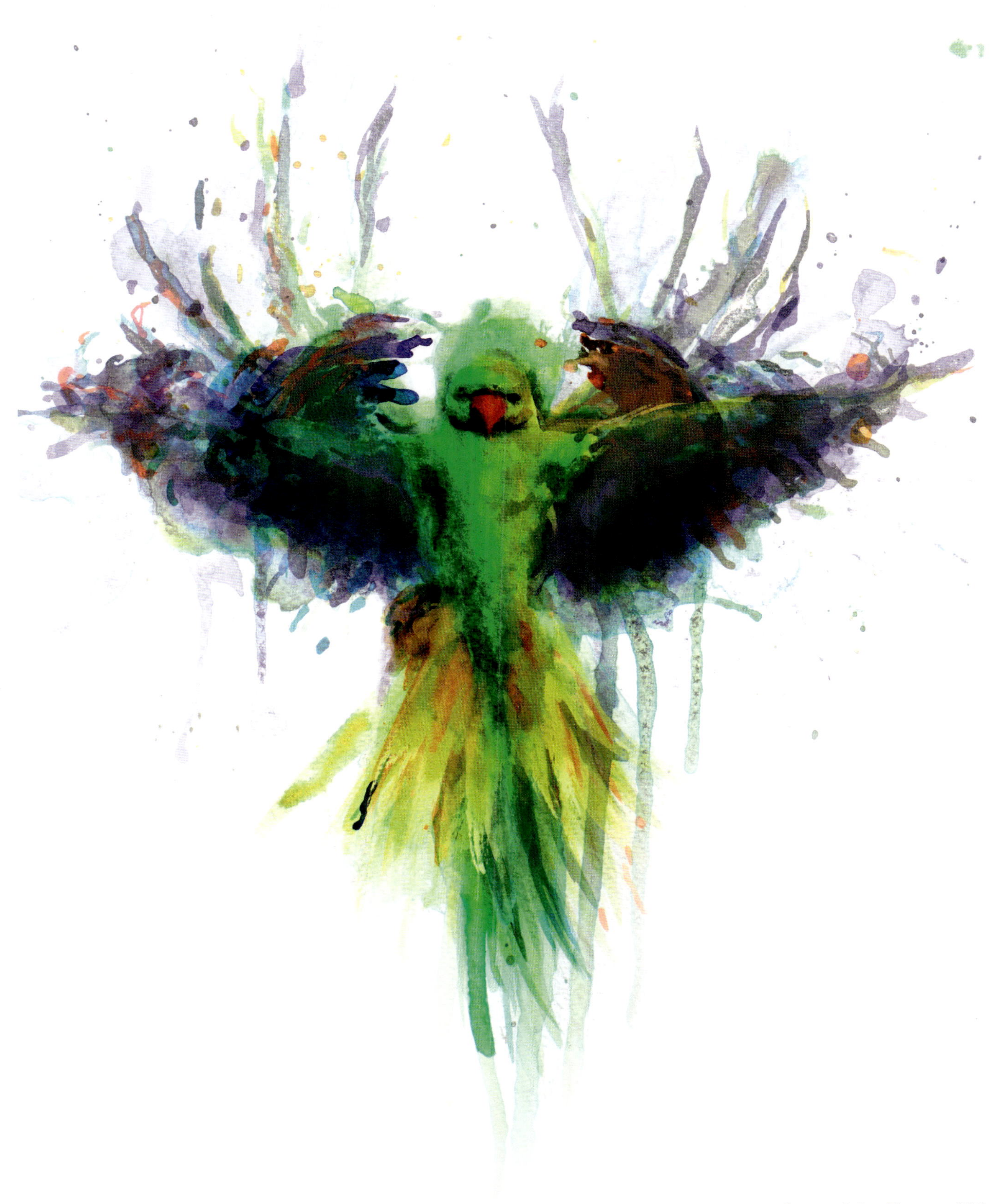

Digital Collage

My creative practice began with computer animation and many years of digital image manipulation. I love watercolour for all the reasons I became disillusioned with the pixel-perfect digital approach: I wanted to feel the contact with a surface, the texture of the medium, how it shifted through time and pushed against my control.

However, like many artists today, my paintings invariably end up as digital images to post on my website or social media. I became curious about what would happen if I gave these versions their own identity through digital collage.

Nude Triumphant v >
These three images are digital collages made for the animation *Nude Triumphant*. Using digital image manipulation, I layered sequences of figure paintings (from life) onto painted backgrounds. The images show Valentina (red), Matthew (blue) and Maya (green). Each model occupies their painted world, alive in their pose and confident in themselves.

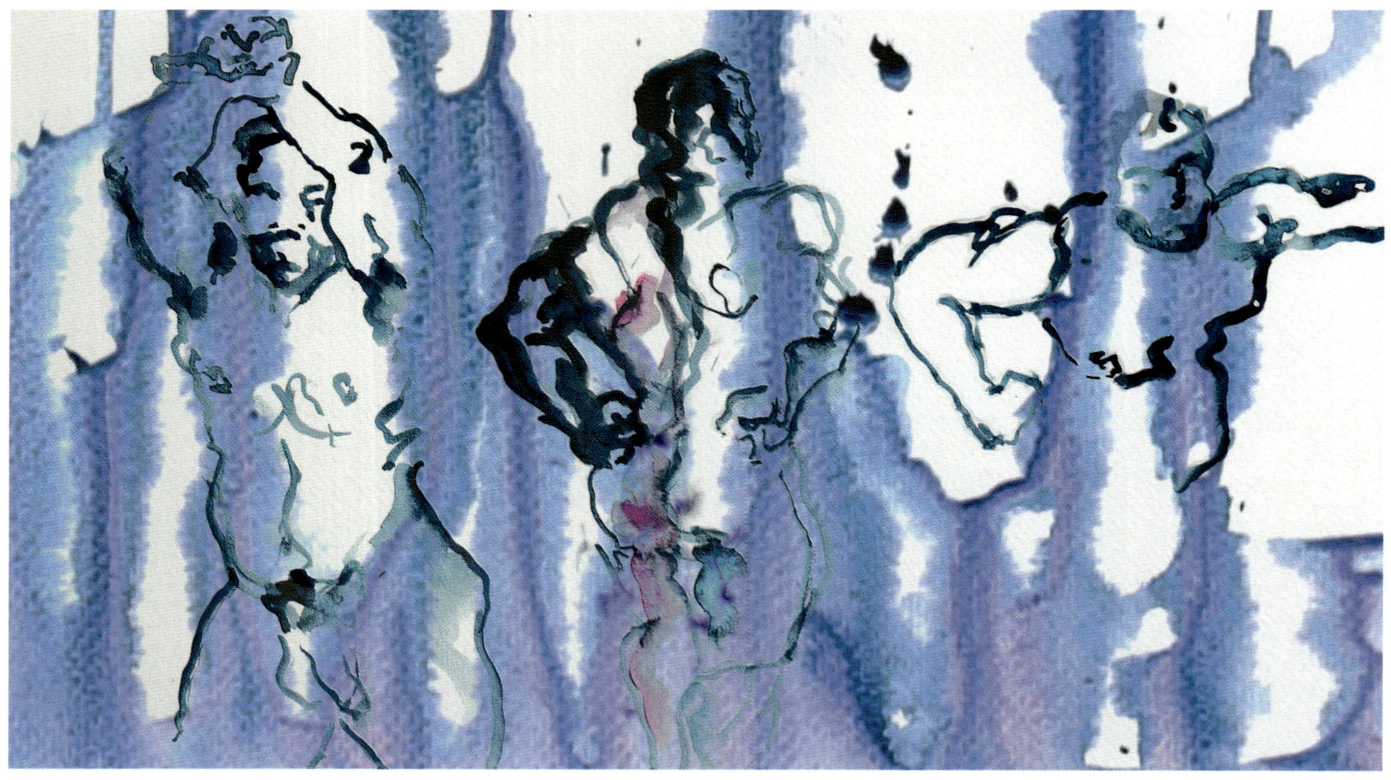

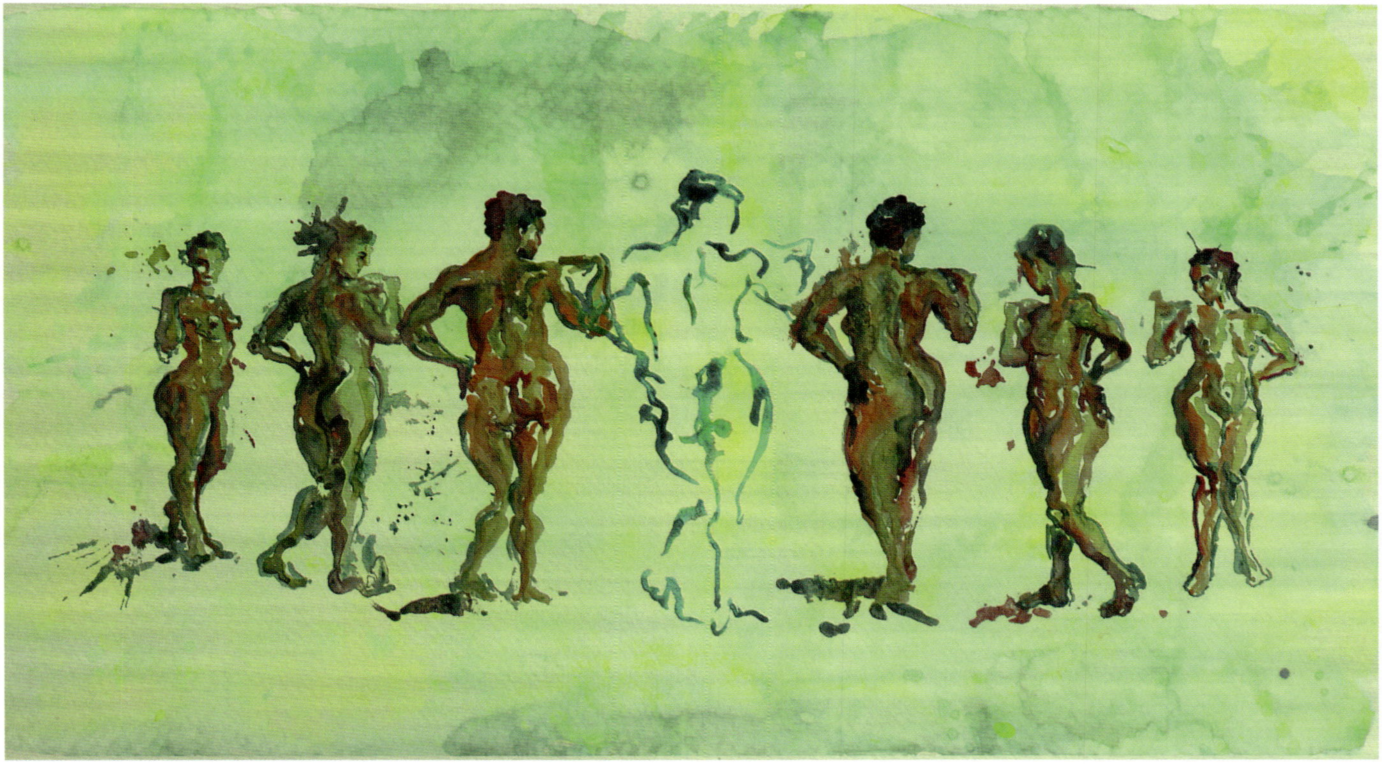

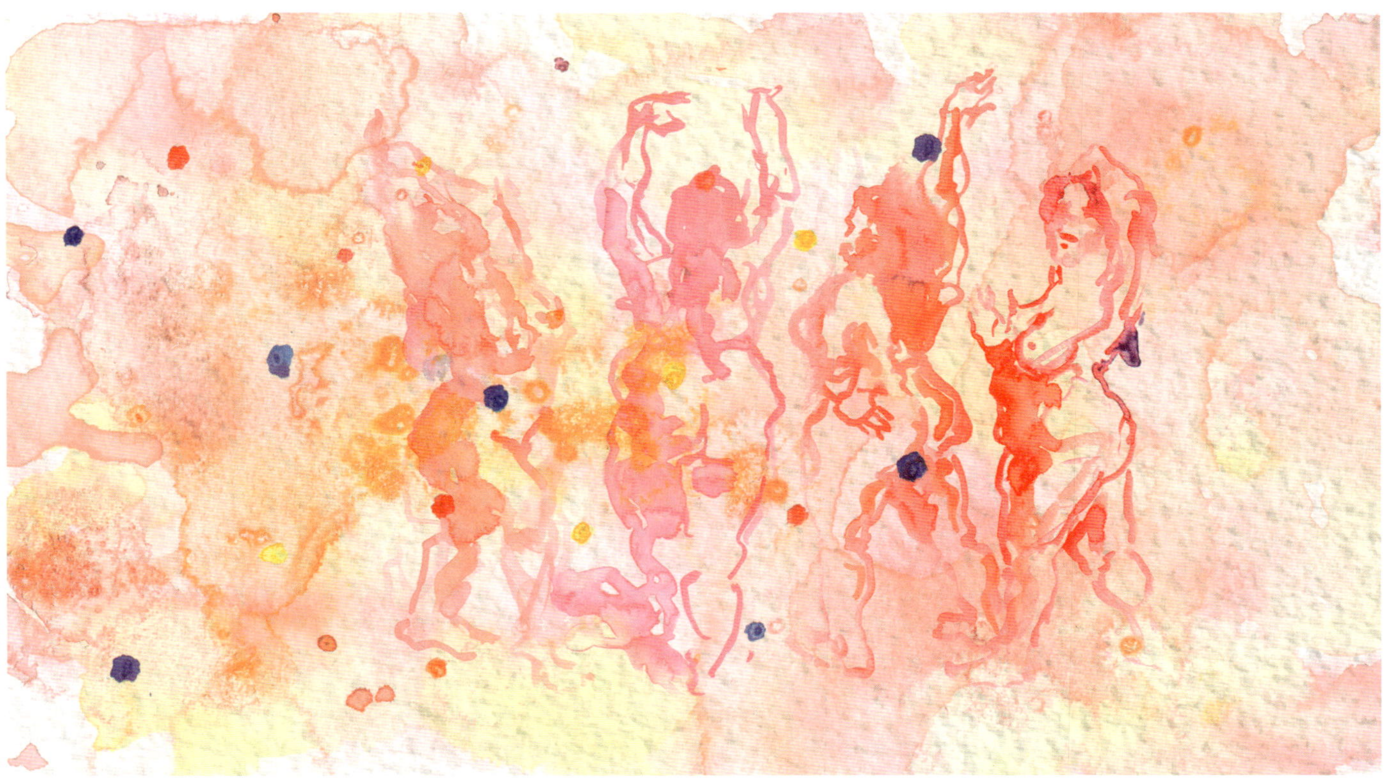

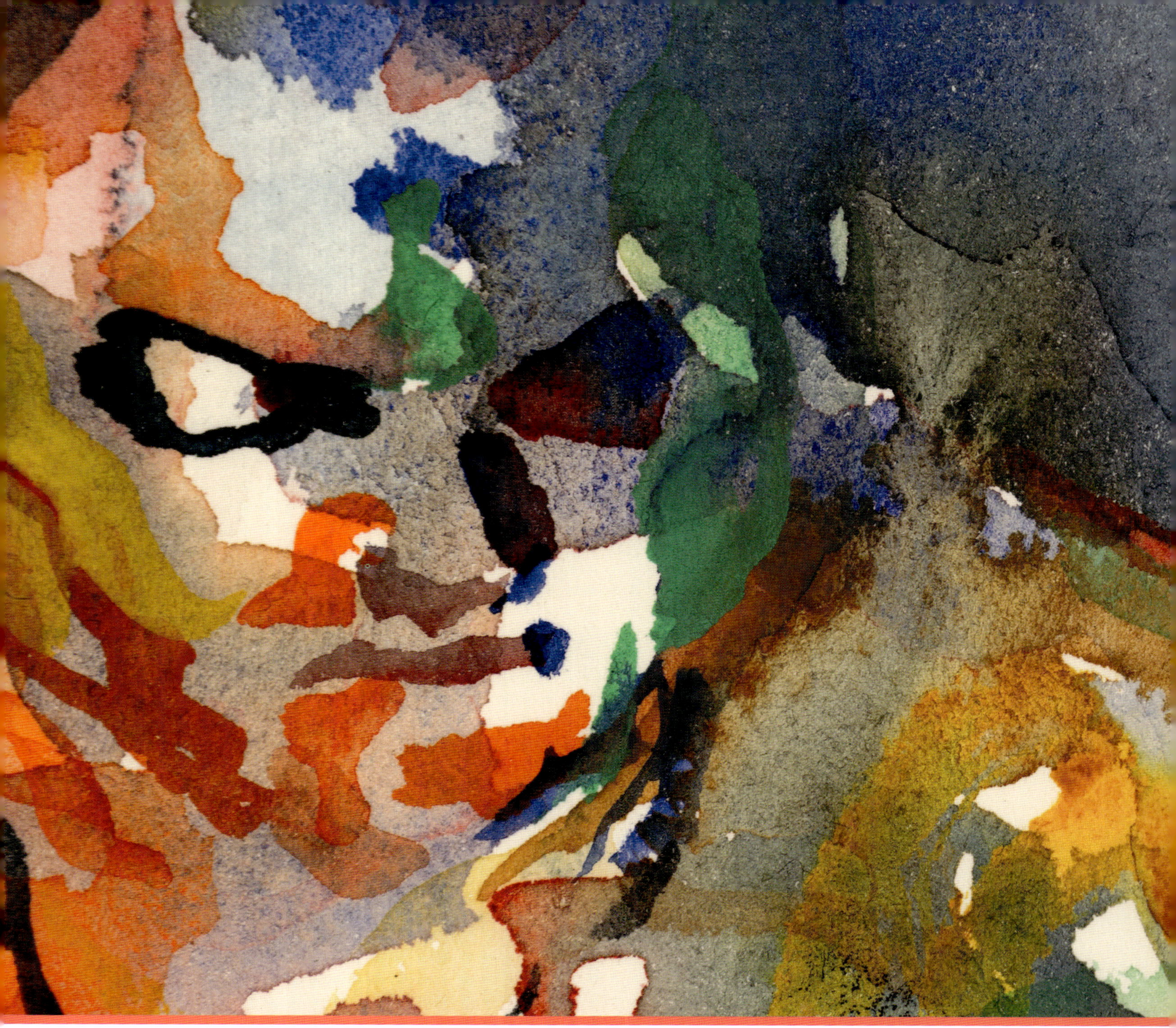

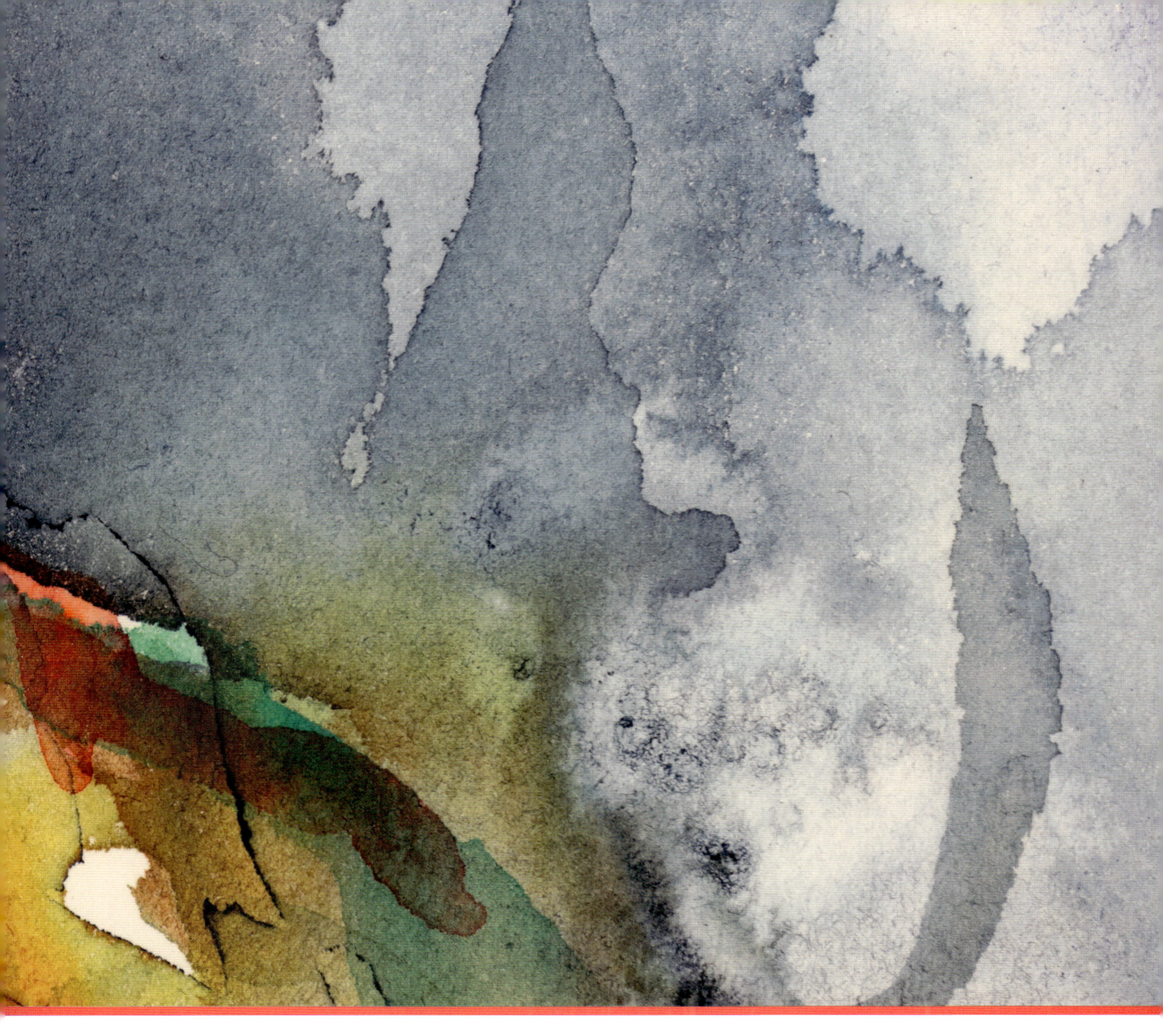

From the Models

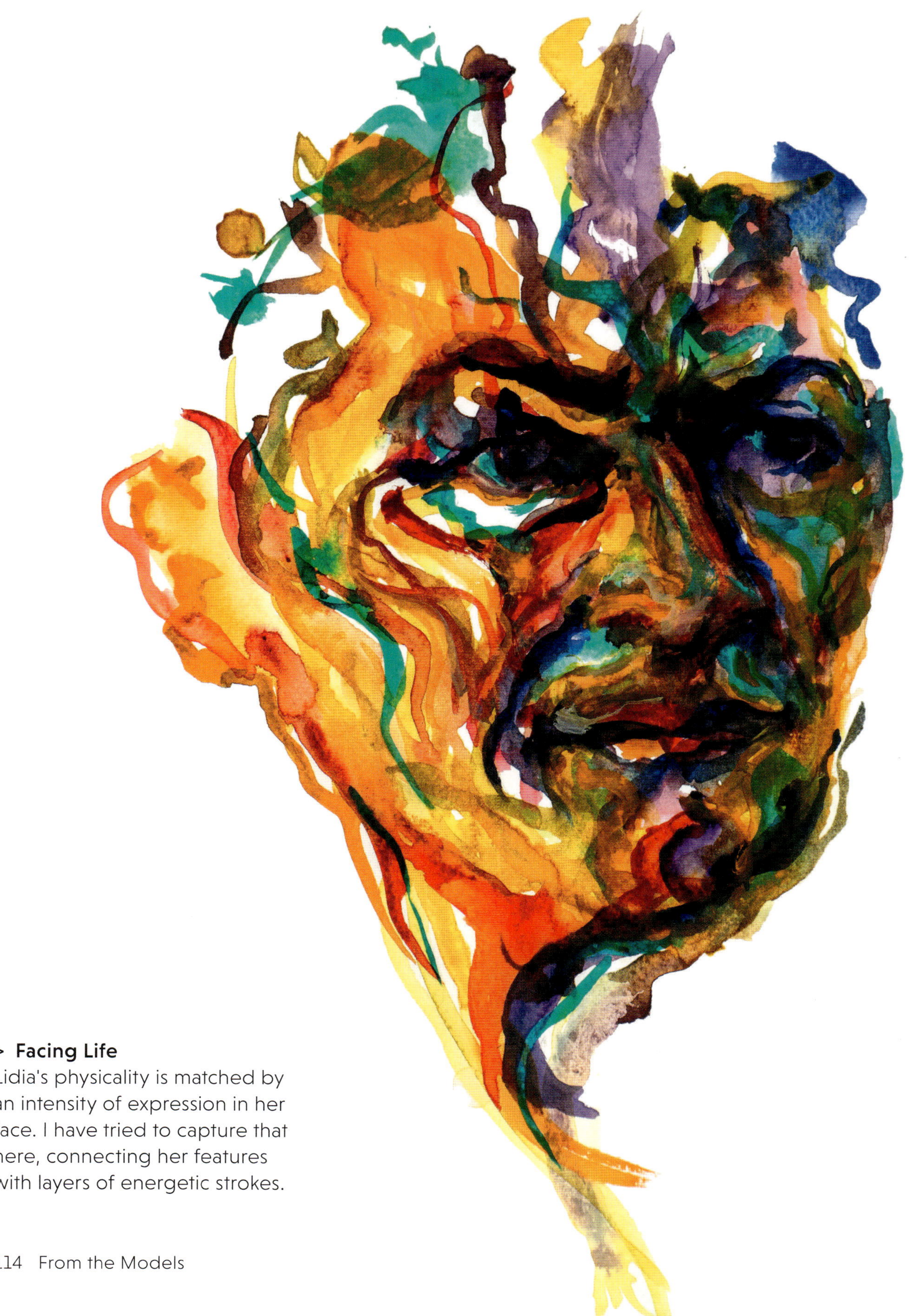

> Facing Life
Lidia's physicality is matched by an intensity of expression in her face. I have tried to capture that here, connecting her features with layers of energetic strokes.

Lidia

Lidia is an activist and fine artist who began life modelling in her native Italy and has also worked in the US and the UK. With a background in dance and physical theatre, life modelling started for her as a way to learn stillness. It has since developed into one of Lidia's primary vehicles for self-expression and creative endeavour.

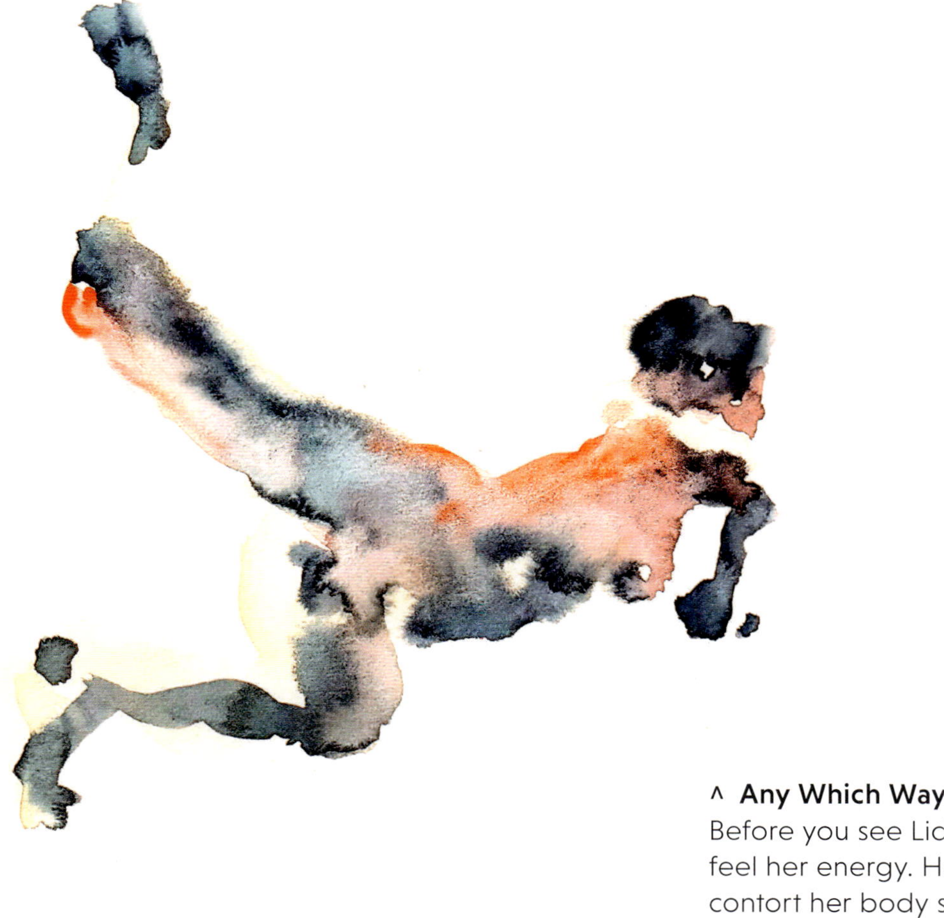

^ Any Which Way
Before you see Lidia, you can feel her energy. Her quick poses contort her body so that your painting may work just as well upside down.

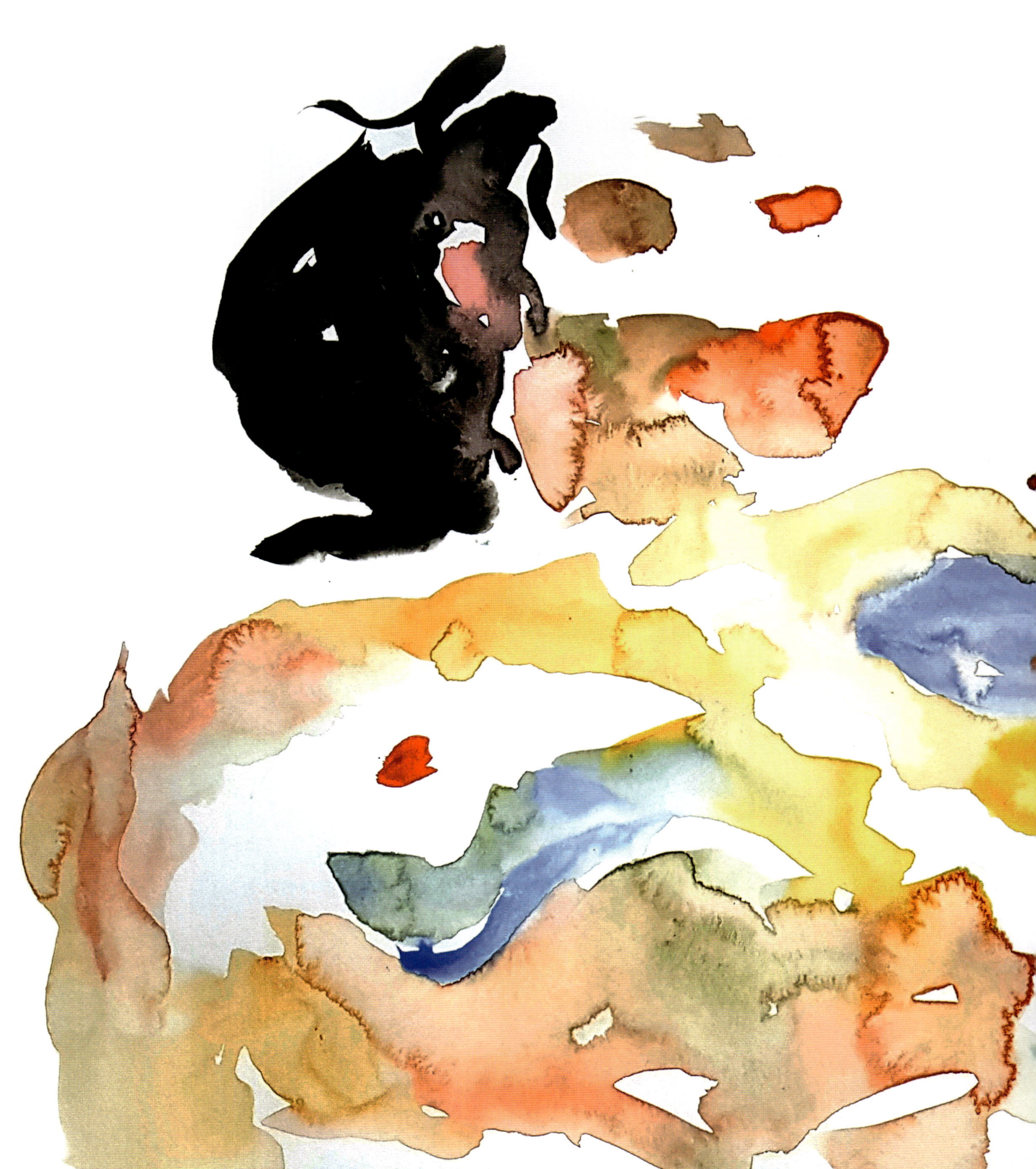

ENERGY

'Painting from life is an exchange of energy – a constructive energy. There is always something to learn from how you develop this energy together. Generally, I leave a class or a private sitting very enriched. I don't just need food for survival; I need something else. And what I have back when I model is this other sort of nourishment that gives me back energy and gives meaning to what I do and makes me feel part of a creation. And that is quite extraordinary.'

Lidia

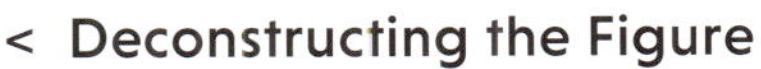

< Deconstructing the Figure

When Lidia poses, you really feel the contrast between external stillness and internal motion. During this reclining pose, her bodily container seemed secondary to the energy within it. I made a series of studies at speed. Of all of them, it was this one that seemed to respond most truthfully to her energy. The watercolour created its own flowing landscape, pooling into the rich colours of the shadows. It seemed right to leave as much of the paper as possible in order to deconstruct the surface of the flesh.

Kam

Kam left a job with the BBC, in his own words, to 'take back time for myself to do something more creative'. He began life modelling in 2018 at Figuration's Starkers Academy, a drop-in drawing experience featuring first-time life models. Now a full-time model, Kam has also become a champion of the life-modelling profession.

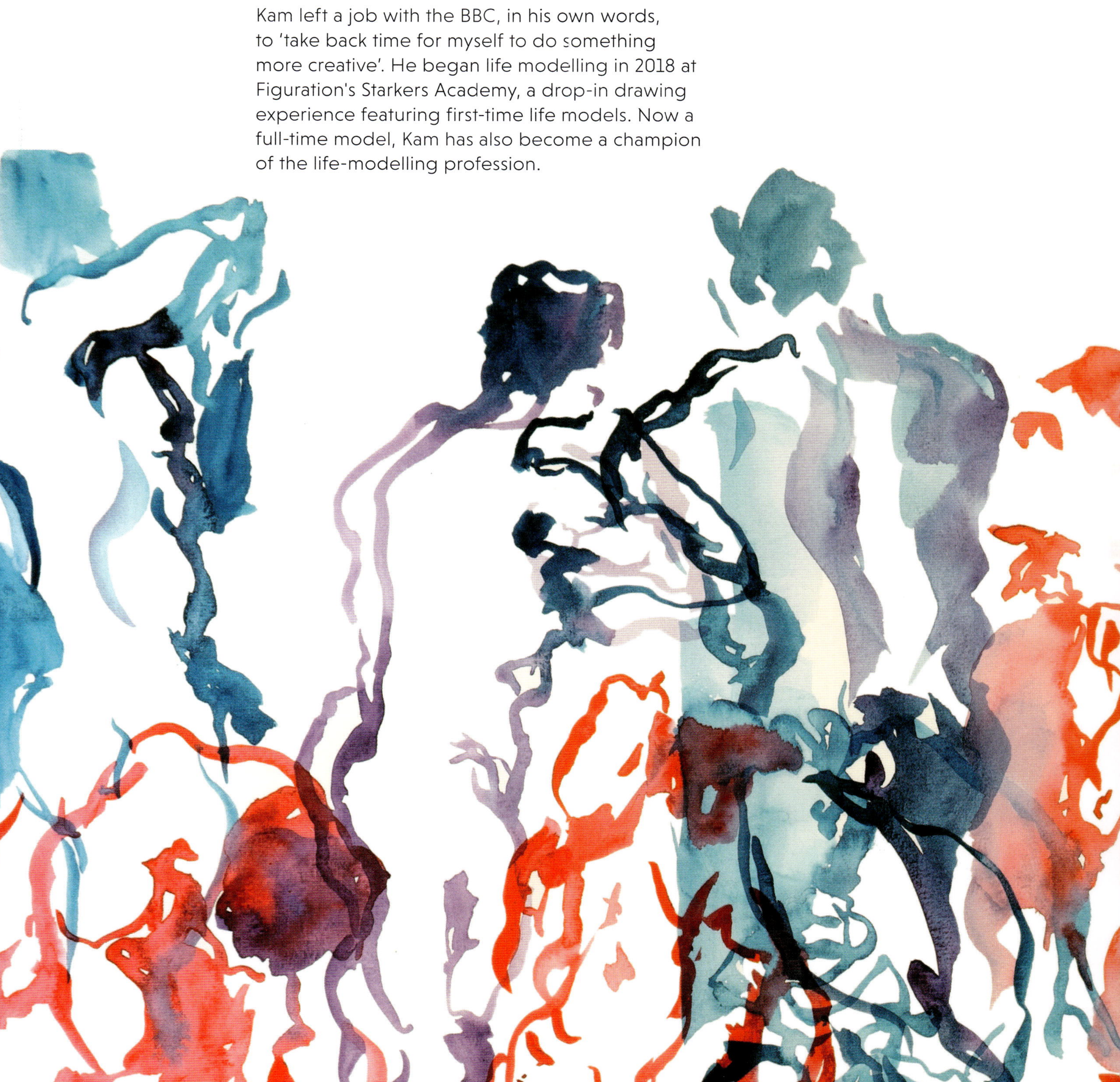

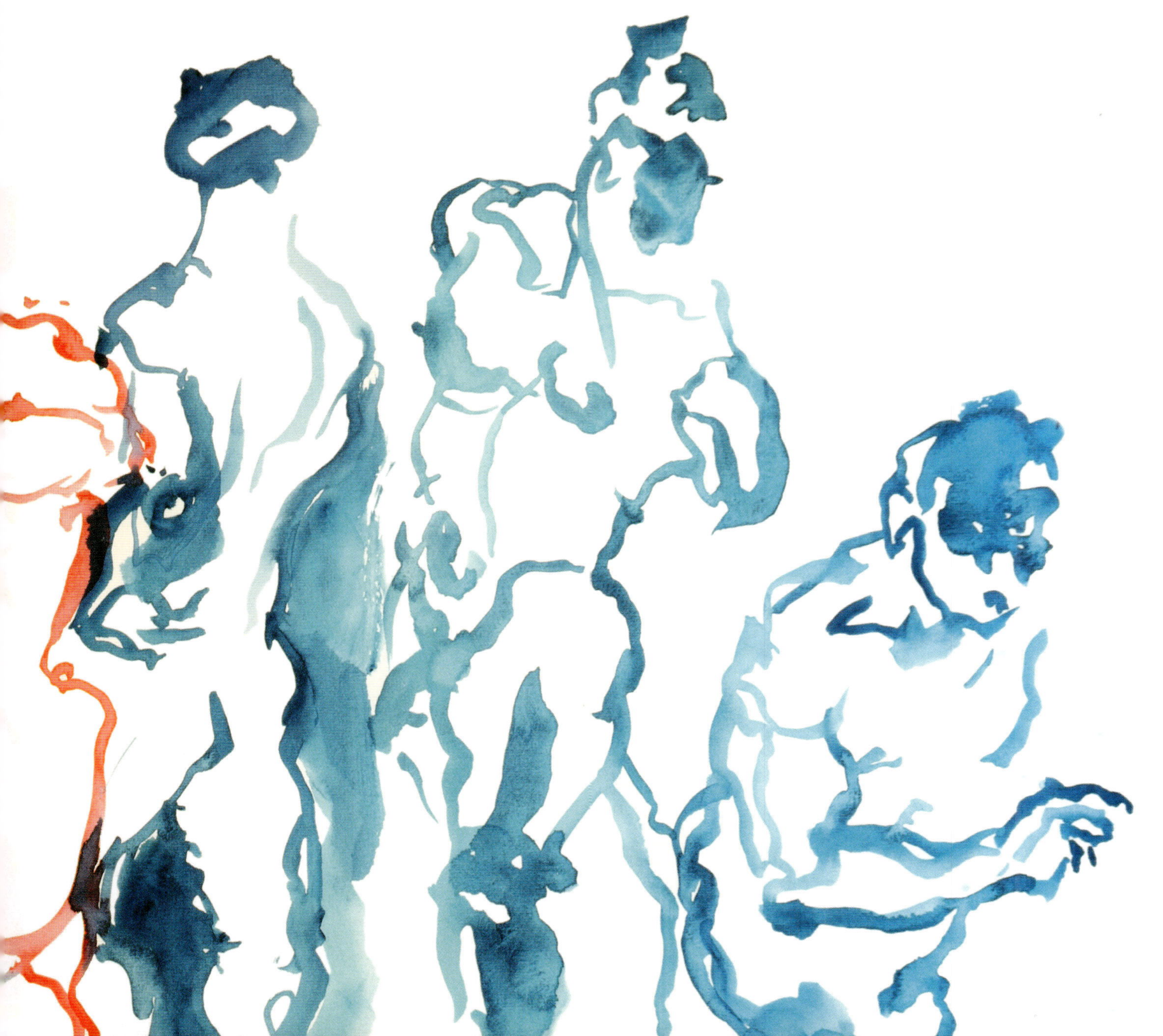

v   **Forever Dancing**
Kam's thorough knowledge of his body has enabled him to develop an extensive repertoire of poses. Each new series has an instinctive choreography that comes to life in a multi-layered composition.

EQUILIBRIUM

'There's a joy I get from being able to
embody a gesture. It's like I'm moving,
but I've chosen a particular position to
stop. There's an equilibrium, not just
in my centre of gravity but also in my
mind: that sweet spot where I'm relaxed
but there's activation as well. I feel the
gesture, the physicality of it. The stresses
and strains remind you what the pose is,
what the gesture of the pose is. This feeds
back information to help me keep the
pose and get it right. If there's a bit of pain
that goes with that, then so be it.'

Kam

Kam Contre-Jour >

Kam was posing for my painting group. From my
position he was against the bright light of the
window beyond, an effect known as contre-jour.
This created deep shadows that undulated across
his body as he carefully held his pose. The forward
thrust of his hips contrasted with the downward
turn of the head, suggesting a figure both
confident and contemplative. I instinctively chose
a bold, contrasting palette to play with the energy
contained within the strong silhouette of his body.

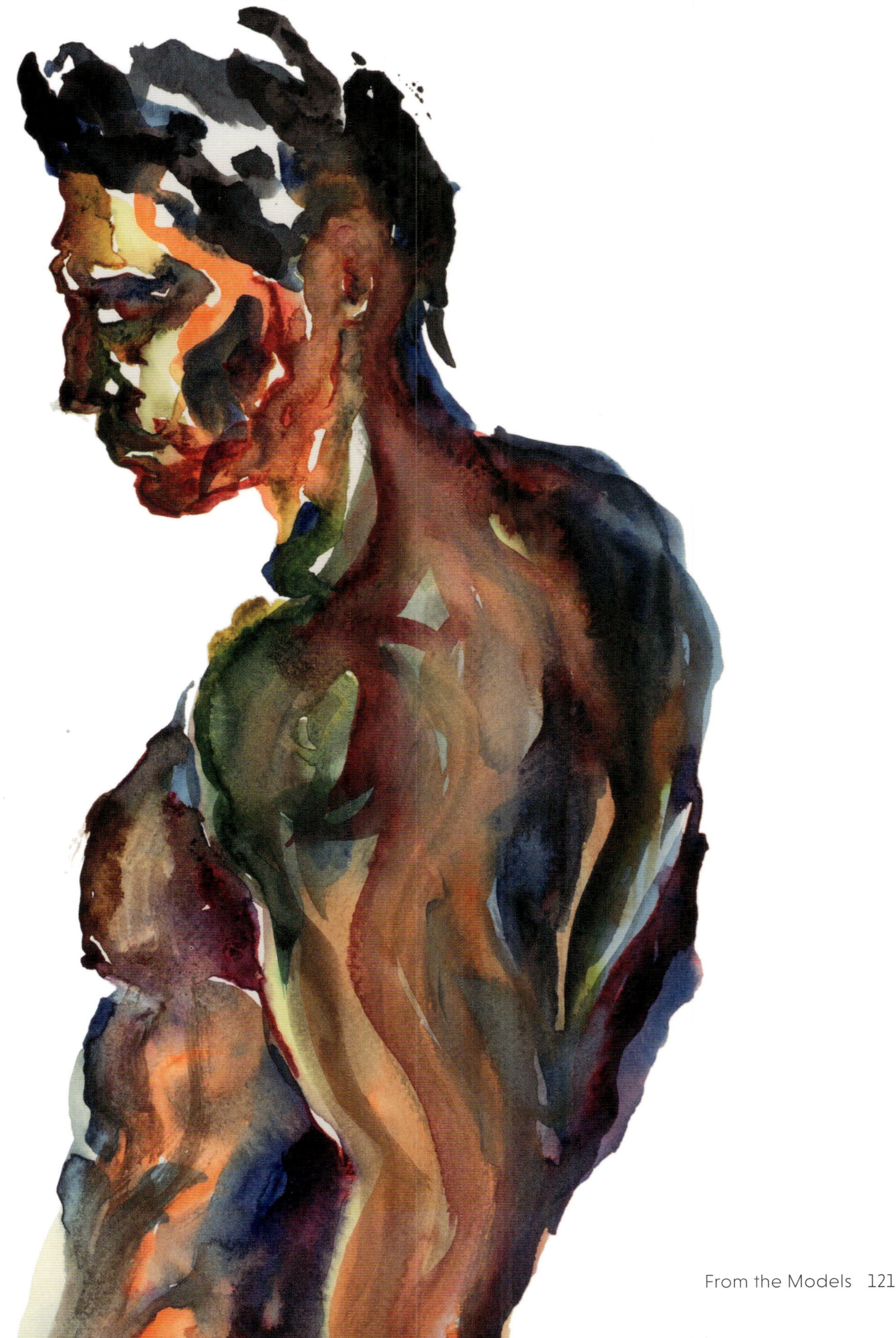

Leonora

Leonora is a professional artist's model who splits her time between the life room and one-to-one care support work. She is known for her flexibility (thanks to hypermobile joints) and strength, with life modelling for her being both that which pays the bills and the glue that fortifies her. Leonora uses the moniker 'Jiggle Chick' as a celebration of her plus-size body.

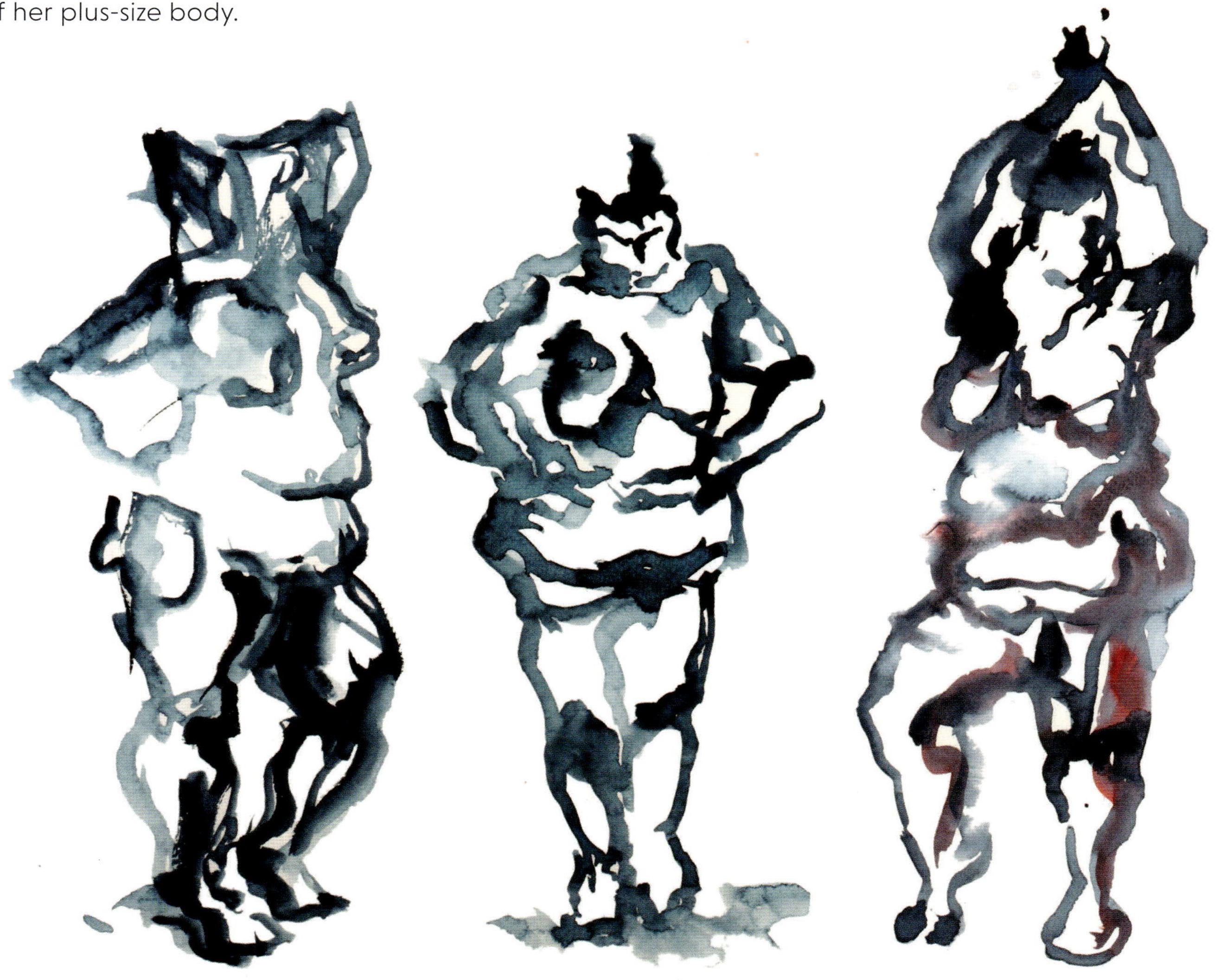

Agility and stamina are Leonora's hallmarks, along with a self-confessed stubbornness that says: 'No, you will not give in!'. This means she can hold any number of poses, from two- or five-minute quickies (like these) to 60-hour studies held over a number of days.

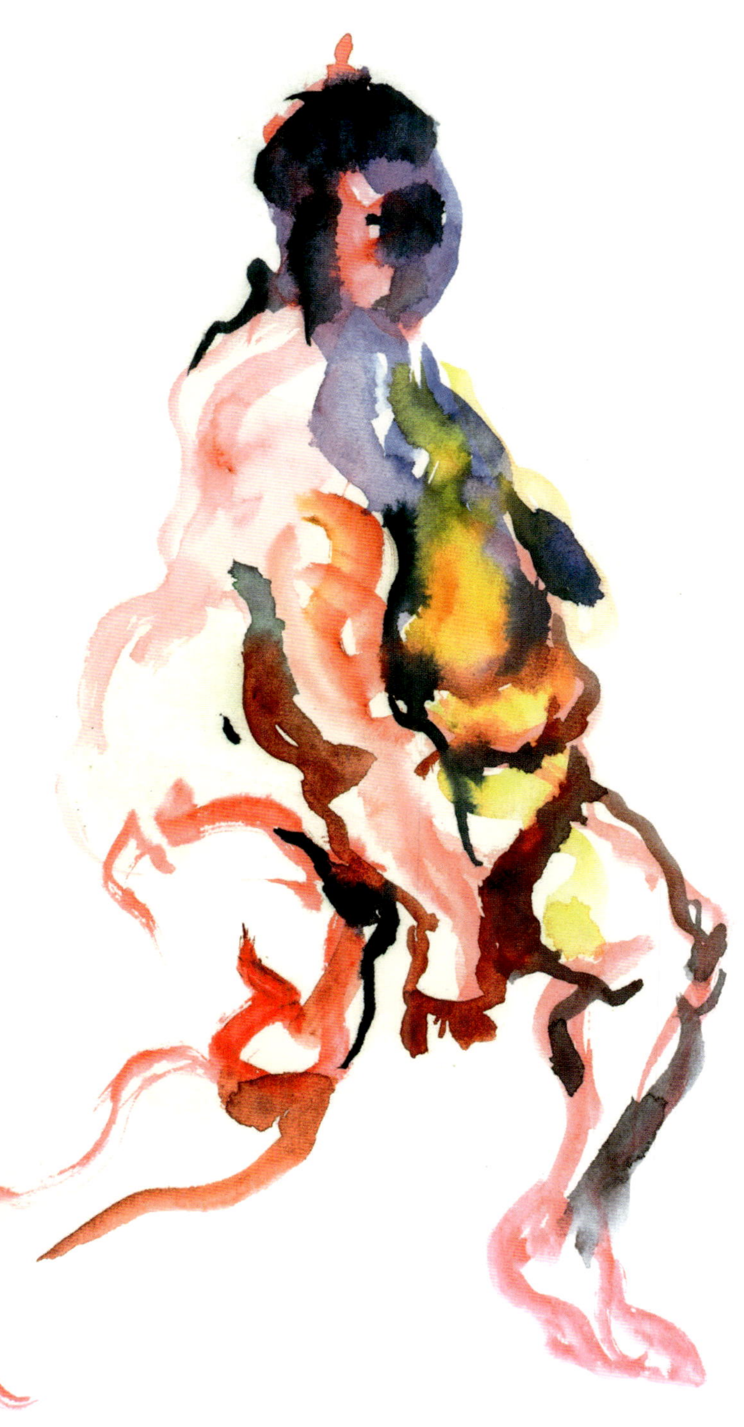

SIMPLICITY

'You need the simplicity of
a pose to provide the space
for the artist to add their
own complexity. If the tutor
is pushing you to do things
that are going to make you
uncomfortable and make the
pose overly complicated, it's a
too-many-cooks-spoil-the-broth
situation. It's a delicate
balance, but simplicity
is definitely better as a
launching platform.'

Leonora

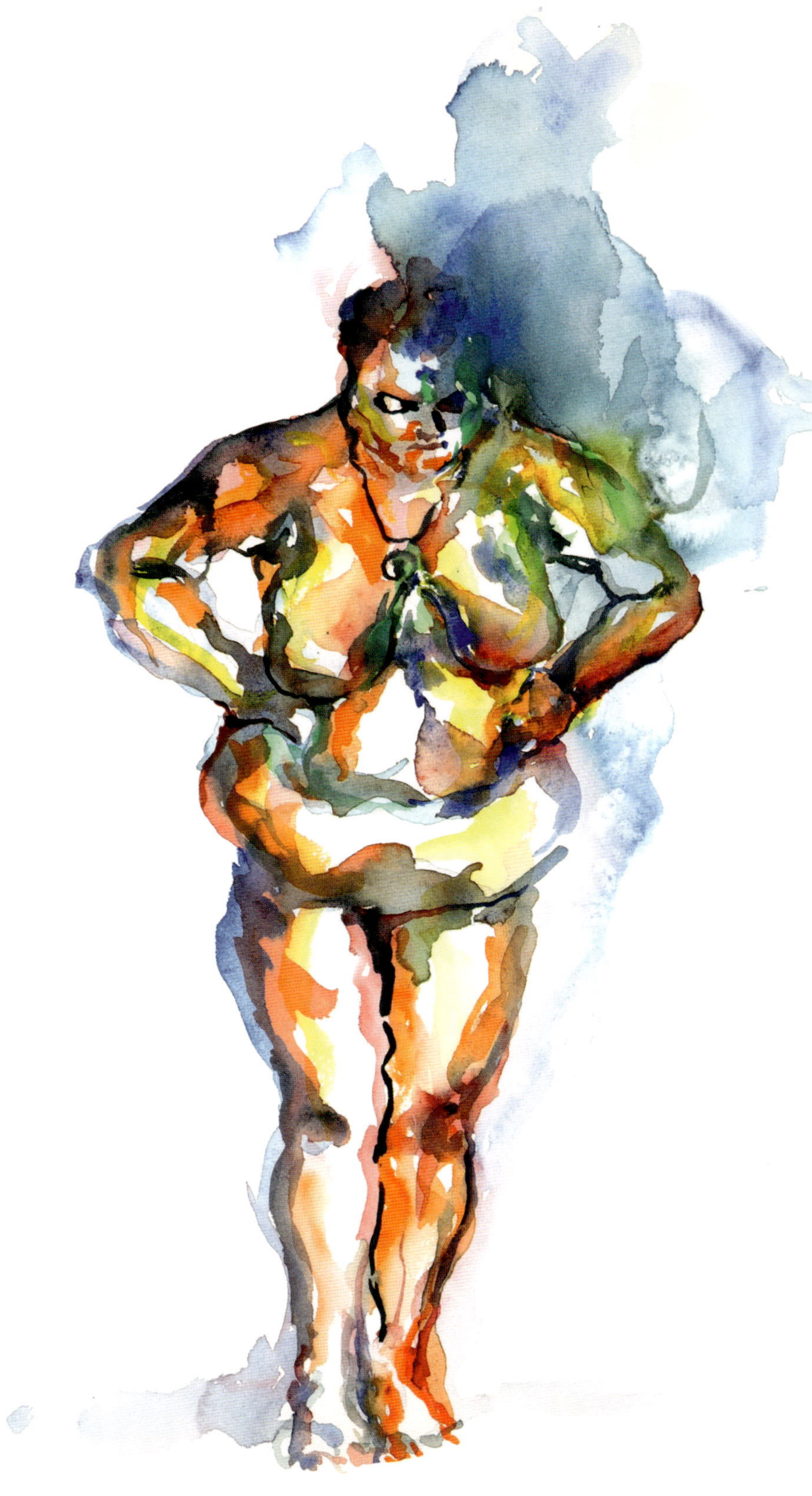

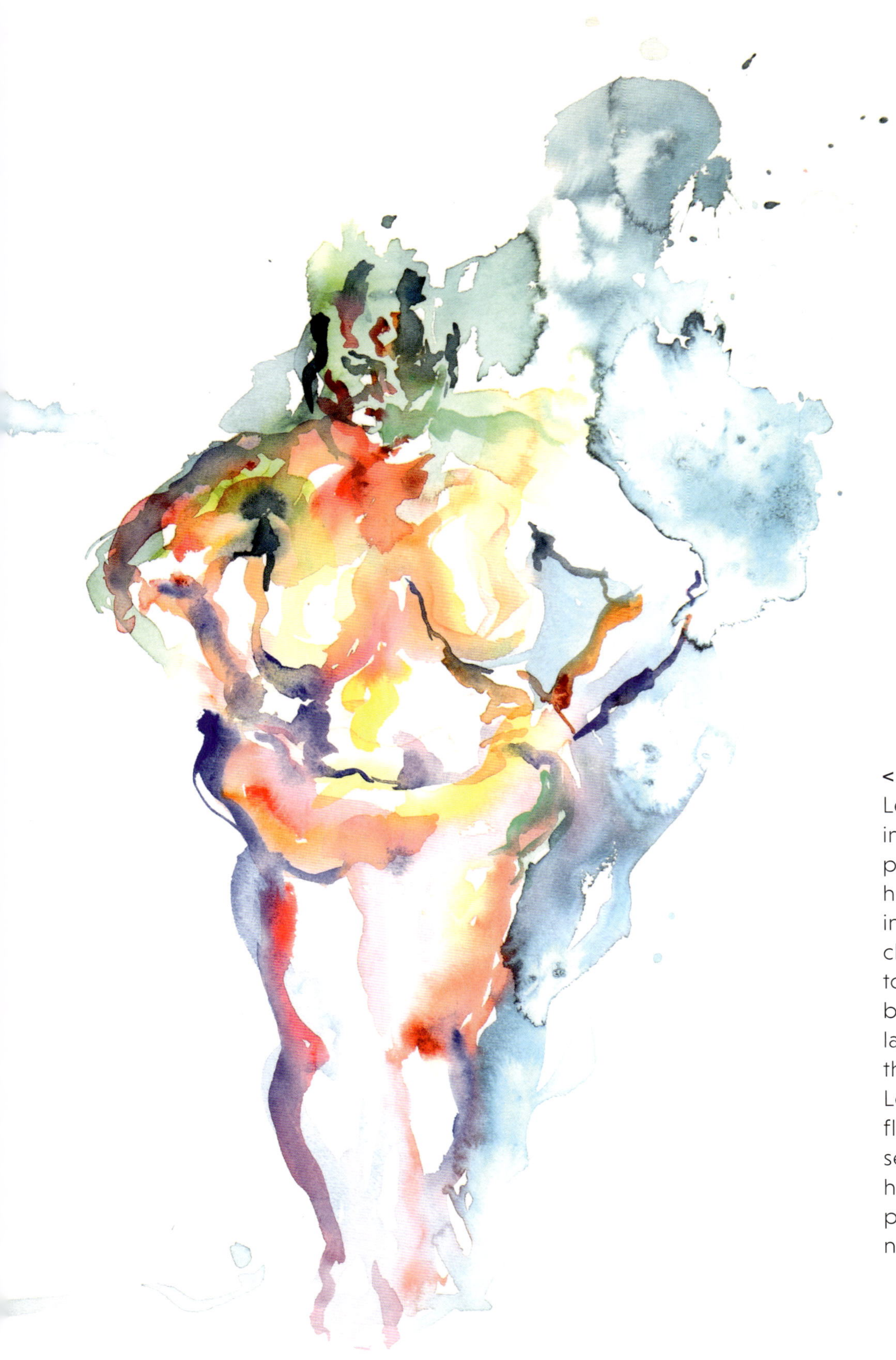

< Simply Standing

Leonora took up this pose initially as a two-minute gesture painting. The implied symmetry highlights the differences in the body as well as the change in light from one side to the other. I worked on both paintings at once on one large sheet of paper, finding the relationship between Leonora's solid flesh and the flat shadow behind her. For a seemingly simple pose, I could have made a whole series of paintings and found something new to say each time.

Index

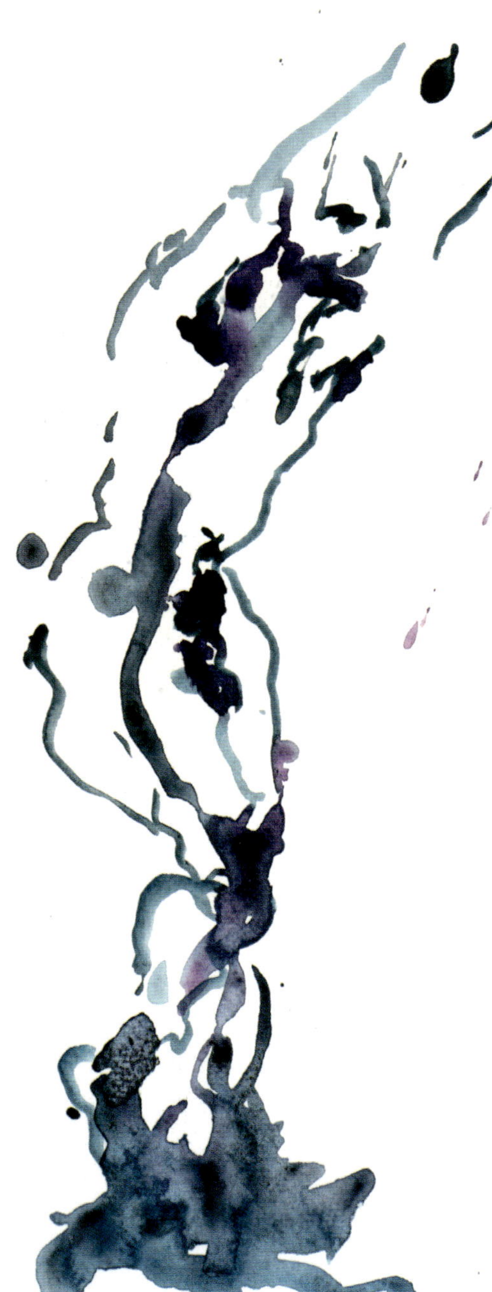

Acknowledgements

Sincere thanks to Pavilion for inviting me to write this book: to Tina Persaud for initiating and developing the idea, and to Kristy Richardson for guiding me through the publishing process. I am grateful to GreatArt for sponsoring my materials and supporting London's vibrant creative community.

About the Authors

Leo Crane and **Roy Joseph Butler** are co-founders of Figuration, a creative studio specializing in fine art and animation. They produce films, exhibitions, workshops and events in partnership with cultural and community spaces across the UK, including the V&A, British Library, Sotheby's Institute of Art and The Hepworth Wakefield. They have been featured in print, radio and TV, including the BBC's *Radio 2 Arts Show* and Sky's *Portrait Artist of the Year*. In 2020, they completed the acclaimed watercolour animation *Nude Triumphant*, which explores the painter–model relationship and was the catalyst for this book.